D1365215

Labor U.S.A.

LABOR U.S.A.

BY Lester Velie

HARPER & BROTHERS

PUBLISHERS H|B NEW YORK

To Frances,
who helped produce this book,
and Alan and Frankie

ACKNOWLEDGMENT

I am deeply indebted to De Witt Wallace,
editor of *The Reader's Digest,*
and to Kenneth W. Payne, Alfred S. Dashiell, Harry H. Harper, Jr.,
Hobart Lewis, and others of the *Reader's Digest* family
for support and encouragement in the difficult assignments
from which this book grew.

L. V.

Contents

CONTENTS

IV

Looking backward—and forward. How America's unions got that middle-class way, as seen through the lives of the unions' two fathers: Samuel Gompers and John L. Lewis.

V

The troubles the unions have seen.

VI

What the unions do, and things you didn't suspect they do.

VII

How can we return stolen unions to their members? And turn labor leaders into quasi-public servants? And what of the future?

The strongest bond of human sympathy
outside the family relation should be
one uniting all working . . . people.
Nor should this lead to a war on property.

ABRAHAM LINCOLN

To the Reader

This book stems from a journalistic treasure hunt in a fascinating field peopled by as diverse an array of saints and cynics, gifted men and dullards, martyrs, parasites, winners and losers as can be found in any area of human effort.

Some 17,500,000 men and women—one-third of the nation with their families—belong to unions and, collectively, can work miracles or disasters for themselves and the rest of us. They can stand up to giant corporations and win gains that have changed them from proletarians to a home-owning and a car-owning middle class. And they can, through their collective power, wreck the economy. For all the shortcomings of some of the unions, the Labor movement has become a necessary fixture of American industrial government—in which management represents the interests of stockholders, and unions represent the interests of wage earners.

I began to write about the men and women in the unions and their leaders through curiosity about some rascals who were using workers' medical and pension dollars to buy themselves yachts, trips abroad and mistresses. I stayed on for five years—to find a cause and an education.

The cause concerned the working people, inside the unions, who were being pushed around: Men like Teamster Ed McFarland, who hobbled back from the war on crutches and was told by his union boss that he'd have to hand over all of his discharge pay to make up for the back dues he didn't pay while he was fighting in the Pacific. And Willie Bennett, who exposed his local boss as a union thief—then was tried by the union thief and kicked out of the union and out of a job.

The education came in the search for answers that couldn't be found on library shelves but had to be dug out from people.

"What is a union leader?" Dave Dubinsky of the Garment Workers asked one day—just as Pontius Pilate might have asked, "What is truth?"

"I'm a union leader," Dubinsky reflected, "and Joe Fay [the convicted extortionist] was a union leader!"

A labor leader, I went on to learn, could be a superbly cultured human being with a vision—a figure like Philip Randolph of the Sleeping Car Porters, who used his union to help his Negro people; or he could be one who rose to power with gangster guns and conspired with employers to shortchange workers. A union leader could be a gallant woman like Min Matheson who defied the Eastern underworld to organize dress-shop locals in Pennsylvania; and it could be a William Presser, the Teamster boss—and jukebox czar—of the state of Ohio.

And what is a union? To businessman-unionist Dave Beck a union was a marketing co-operative to sell so many head of labor to employers at the highest market price. To other leaders, a union is a social force that wins higher Social Security payments for all Americans; an economic force that improves worker security in key industries. From the worm's eye view of a rank and filer, a union—to a garment worker—means "bread and roses"—bread for steady work and a just wage; roses for union painting classes at night and a union country club to spend one's summer vacations in. To a New York factory worker-member of some racket locals, a union is a trap that locks him into substandard wages.

Education brought surprises. I started by asking, "Why are some unions corrupt?" Soon, I was asking, "Who corrupts whom?" Employers, I sometimes found, were not the victims of corruption—but the corrupters who made soft ("sweetheart") deals with faithless union leaders to shortchange employees. This corruption was even institutionalized in a network of middlemen who brought employers and union leaders together.

Learning, in this field, takes strong legs and the will to travel—sometimes to the darkest places on our continent—the underworlds of our big cities. Why do gangsters infiltrate some unions? For reasons that may surprise you. The gangster who controls a union needs no gunmen to "enforce" or protect a racket territory. The union does it for him.

This education of mine, I've tried to distill—through portraits of people and problems—into a book that gives some of the sweep of tidal events that made our unions what they are today. And seeks to provide a guide to understanding the most significant, exciting—yet perplexing—domestic story of our time—the unfolding story of the men and women in our unions.

*   *   *

This story of Labor U.S.A. makes no attempt to be all-inclusive. It isn't a history—but through the lives of two great men, Sam Gompers and John L. Lewis, I have tried to tell how American unions grew and took their own special middle-class direction.

Perhaps some labor leaders—both good and bad—who might be in an encyclopedic book, are not included in this story. But I have tried in a series of human studies to portray those men who give Labor U.S.A. its special flavor. I've tried to give the reader a good look at what the unions do—their bread-and-butter job of negotiating wages and conditions as well as their extracurricular activities, such as their fight on the Kremlin abroad. I've explored, too, how far laws can go in regulating unions and union leaders.

Lastly, as the story comes to a close, I have looked ahead to what the unions face in the unfolding second industrial revolution, caused by automation, to picture both the hope and the terror that the new machines—which don't need men—bring to union leaders and union men.

L. V.

I

A visit to the House of Labor, divided, and a close-up
view of the Head of the House, George Meany.

> I guess you're wondering what a
> Bronx plumber is doing upstairs.
>
> GEORGE MEANY

CHAPTER 1

Six Days That Shook
the Union World

The time is December, 1957.

The place is Atlantic City, and the action takes place in the five-thousand-seat Convention Auditorium, on the boardwalk and in hotel rooms.

A Federation convention is the greatest union show on earth, and the supreme authority of the Labor movement. Every other year, the unions in the AFL-CIO perform as if under a big tent. In many rings, some open to view in the Convention Hall, others hidden in smoke-filled hotel rooms, the unions make laws, hold court and set the course which the Federation will follow.

All who come want something. Suspended union bosses come to fight for their union lives, treasuries and power; rank-and-file members come for help to redress wrongs. Union emissaries from overseas come to seek American union cash. These had sent convention currents swirling around Federation president George Meany as he struggled with the central problem of corruption.

Now, on the eve of the convention's key act—the vote to expel the Teamsters—Meany's hotel suite resembled a state governor's office in the final hours before an execution.

Communication lines were kept open between AFL-CIO president Meany and go-betweens for the condemned man, James R. Hoffa, president-elect of the Teamsters. On trial on federal wire-tapping charges ninety miles away in New York City, Hoffa was trying to get court permission to dash to Atlantic City for a last-minute plea—or surrender. Meany waited as the hours slipped by and midnight approached.

For Meany, as for Hoffa, it had been a difficult day.

In a sense, it was not Hoffa alone but all of Labor that was on trial. The corruption disclosures had so outraged public opinion that Congress threatened to strike back with anti-Labor laws.

Meany had to find a way out of Labor's dilemma.

"Are we going to turn the McClellan Committee into a permanent investigating committee? Or are we going to show we can police ourselves?"

But for unions to police themselves, it would require revolutionary changes in the unions' over-all government. As a Federation, the AFL-CIO had no power of its own except the power to expel; it was a union of unions—a loose confederation of union states. A strong, central union government with police powers would have to be fashioned to do the clean-up job. The Federation presidency would have to be changed, too. From being merely Labor's ambassador to the public, Meany would have to transform himself into Labor's chief executive.

In six fateful days of the AFL-CIO convention he put his rugged strength to the hardest labor known to man—the job of making other men accept change.

The expulsion of Hoffa and the Teamsters would be the test demonstration of a necessary change, that the Federation was now greater than any of its parts.

Hoffa was fighting desperately to stay in the Federation. To be in meant respectability: the AFL-CIO with its six ethical practice codes was now a shield and a cover. To be out was to be branded. When a Senate Committee exposed you, that hurt. But when your own people, the Labor movement, threw you out, you were a marked man—even if you headed a 1,600,000-man union.

Hoffa couldn't understand that the union world he had grown up in was no longer acceptable. Senate testimony showed that only a few years ago he could, with impunity, put his wife secretly on union payrolls, let his union enforce jukebox rackets, accept favors from employers, give charters to gangsters—and regard all this as strictly

4

his own union's affair. What he couldn't understand was that this was now the affair of all Labor—and the American public's affair too. Unions were now affected with the public interest and could no longer be permitted to hurt their own members or the public.

Hoffa could think of his troubles only in personal terms. "Somebody don't like us," he felt. Somebody like Walter Reuther of the Automobile Workers.

So Hoffa waged a contest of wills with Meany. He pressed secret negotiations, offered to step down for a caretaker successor that he would name. He even volunteered to submit to supervision by a watchdog committee of public men.

Meany steadfastly said no. A Federation vice-president put it this way: "We talk about corrupt influence. We don't spell it out. We don't want to spell it out. But we're drawing the line at the underworld." As an underworld associate in the Labor movement, Hoffa could not remain in the Federation, nor could anyone he named or dominated be accepted.

Now, in his hotel suite, Meany waited for word from the Teamsters. The telephone rang.

"We have Jimmy [Hoffa] on the phone," the voice on the line said. A car was ready, and Jimmy would hurry down from New York. Could Meany wait up for a predawn conference?

Meany glanced at his watch—10:40 P.M. It would be 3 A.M. before Hoffa could arrive.

"Why don't you get a commitment from him [Hoffa] and bring it to the convention?" Meany suggested.

"No," said the voice on the phone. "We can't try that, because he might repudiate it. We don't trust him."

Meany refused to wait up for Hoffa. The die was cast.

The wind that swept in from the ocean, spattering a chilling rain on the bent backs of the delegates, was no bleaker than their spirits as they trudged the boardwalk to the convention's second-day session.

A subdued lot, they had shown little stomach for the usual convention horseplay. They had gone to bed early the night before, and the hotel corridors were strangely still.

I picked up a conversation with the seventy-two-year-old ex-president of the Bakers, Herman Winter. He was a member of La-

5

bor's house of elders, the Executive Council, and his own union was under suspension.

"I've seen fifty-six years of the Labor movement," the aged man said gloomily, "and I'm glad I won't be around to see the next fifty-six."

At the Convention Hall entrance, a veteran labor reporter studied the delegates' faces.

"Have you ever seen such a scared and bewildered bunch?" he said.

The delegates had a right to be scared. Most unions can hurt the public—if they go on strike. But the Teamsters control the movement of goods and so can hurt other unions: those who voted against them, for instance.

Inside the hall, George Meany, limping heavily from an old heel injury, crossed the dais and signaled the opening of the debate.

An aged, lean and dour man arose: the $50,000-a-year secretary-treasurer of the Teamsters, John F. English.

He had achieved fleeting fame by refusing to O.K. some of Dave Beck's spending. When Beck was booted from the Executive Council, Meany replaced him with English—in the hope that English would clean up the Teamsters from the inside. The hope had turned into deep embarrassment. English, true enough, was anti-Beck. But he was also violently pro-Hoffa.

The aging English, proud and straight under the klieg lights on the convention floor, was a symbol of the Teamsters' resistance to change in a changing union world. He was spokesman for an era that was passing—the era of "union autonomy"—in which the union regarded itself as a private affair, such as an Elks Lodge. Like a mastodon caught in the ice, English struggled against forces that had trapped him, and that he didn't understand.

"I am nearing the end of my days," the old teamster began in the high-pitched twang of his native New England. With deep emotion that visibly shook his listeners, he pleaded for his union in the primitive terms that his hero, Jimmy Hoffa, might have employed.

First, there was the flick of the dragon's tail—the Teamsters' defiance.

"How many times in your lives," English asked, "if it hadn't been for the Teamsters, would you have lost strikes and maybe you would not be here?"

Then there was the bewilderment of the mastodon from the union ice age. Why, despite all their power and despite all they'd done for other unions, were the Teamsters now being punished?

"Some people don't like us, because we are a big organization, and they are afraid we are going to be overpowerful." English pointed a finger at the dais where "some people" like Walter Reuther of the Auto Workers and James Carey of the Electrical Workers—fire-eating foes of Hoffa—stared back, unperturbed.

There was the call on old friendships, and the demand for repayment of old debts.

"Don't forget, Mr. Meany, you never had a better friend than Dan Tobin [when he was head of the Teamsters] and you never had a better friend than the Teamsters. The Teamsters stood by you. What are you going to do for us?"

Finally, there was the plea for compassion.

"My friends, the penalty is too severe. It is too severe.

"We ask for one year. After giving you fifty years, giving you all our time and money, we ask for one year to clean up our house.

"If Dan Tobin and Big Bill Hutcheson were alive today," the old teamster finished, "this never would have happened. Oh, it makes my blood run cold. I never thought I would live to see this." (Tobin of the Teamsters and Hutcheson of the Carpenters, between them, had long dominated the old AF of L.)

A convention is usually a noisy affair, and the clattering of delegates' tongues can add up to a roar like that of a subway train. But as English spoke, the great hall with its two thousand-odd delegates and spectators was quiet.

On the floor, delegations from 144 unions leaned forward. These ranged from the Horse Shoers "International" with its 266 members and the Wire Weavers with 430, to the Automobile Workers and the Steelworkers with more than a million members each. In the gallery, several hundred rank and filers who had come at their own expense to pour tales of persecution by racketeers into official ears strained to catch every word. Some two hundred reporters, about as many as cover a championship fight, shifted in their ringside seats

7

near the dais. Television crews played their cameras and brilliant lights on the speaker and on the dais with its burden of dignitaries, as a reminder that the outside world was looking in.

The debate revealed deep misgivings about the Federation's emerging great power.

One of the most respected and democratic unions in the Federation, the Typographers,[1] fought the expulsion of the Teamsters. Every union had the right to order its own affairs, the Typographers' president, Woodruff Randolph, argued. Autonomy was the rock on which the Federation had been founded. Now it was being eroded. By dictating to the Teamsters, the Federation itself would become a dictatorship of "twenty-nine old men" (Meany's Executive Council).

One expulsion foe inadvertently revealed the tangled skein of Teamster interconnections. The president of the Upholsterers, Sal B. Hoffman, pleaded so eloquently for union liberty, and quoted so learnedly from such sources as the London *Times,* that this writer made a note to find out who had written his speech. The author turned out to be the lawyer for a business partner of Jimmy Hoffa. Written in Chicago, the speech for Hoffa was transmitted to the Upholsterers in Philadelphia for delivery at Atlantic City.

As the debate rolled on, it was clear that two men dominated the convention. One was the solid man visible on the dais, George Meany. The other wasn't even at the convention, but was on everyone's mind and tongue, the junior Senator from Arkansas and chairman of the Senate Rackets Committee,[2] John L. McClellan.

The judge and lord high executioner of the convention—Alex Rose of the Hatters Union—who had the job of turning down union appeals, then asking the convention to lop off union heads— summed it up:

"Labor cannot stand alone," union judge Rose said. "It must look outside itself. It must have the support of the middle class, of the white-collar workers and professional people. Or punishing laws will follow."

---

[1] International Typographical Union.

[2] Formally known as The Select Committee on Improper Activities in the Labor or Management Field.

Not one delegate rose from the convention floor to speak against the Teamsters. The powerful AFL-CIO vice-presidents on the dais remained silent, too. No one would bell the cat. Meany, pale and visibly moved, walked heavily to the dais lectern to do the job himself.

Two years before, when the AF of L had merged with the CIO, Meany had vowed in his inaugural address, "I will never surrender principle for expediency. . . . Decisions will be made without regard to how big or how little a union is. . . ."

Meany could still grant the Teamsters a face-saving year to clean up. The convention would support him with cheers. Instead, his gravelly voice punched out the plain, short, infighting sentences that gave no quarter and sought no compromise.

Meany reminded his audience that the Teamsters had made no effort to investigate their officers' "crimes against the Labor movement."

With angry sarcasm, he pictured the recent Teamster meeting at Miami Beach. "They went through a performance, and they read the Ethical Practices Committee Report in an atmosphere of hilarity. They had quite a nice time doing it."

One Teamster vice-president had been convicted of the worst crime in the union book—taking bribes from an employer to break a strike. He was still vice-president, Meany said.

"We have to free the membership from these men, from this dictatorship," Meany finished. "The secretary will call the roll. You vote yes or no."

The voting, like the debate, revealed the union leaders' agony. As the roll call droned on, David McDonald, the president of the Steelworkers, left the dais to visit the corner benches where a delegation of Teamsters was huddled. He shook hands with several as if asking their forgiveness for voting with Meany.

Ed Miller, president of the Hotel and Restaurant Workers, torn between voting against his friend Hoffa and voting respectably for the expulsion, had an upset stomach about it the day before. In a weak and shaken voice he voted no (against expulsion).

The vote was tallied. A two-thirds majority was needed to expel. The vote was five to one against the Teamsters. Meany had carried with him the old AF of L craft unions as well as the new reformist

9

CIO unions. One era had ended for the unions. Another had begun.

The vote on the Teamsters brought to the surface and dramatized the vast changes that had been seething since the AFL-CIO merger and the early corruption disclosures.

With the expulsion, Meany turned the ponderous, merged Labor movement around, changing its angle of vision from that of a self-centered introvert to that of an extrovert who looks outward and cares for the world's opinion. The government had intervened with the Wagner Act in 1935[3] to help the unions recruit millions of new members. By accepting this help and rocketing to great power, the unions could no longer claim they were voluntary associations, private clubs, and so exempt from outside regulation.

Meany shifted the balance of power from the great internationals to the Federation. No longer could the member unions dominate the Federation as the Teamsters and Carpenters once did. From now on the Federation would dominate them. The unions could no longer stretch the plea of autonomy to cover up evil.

When the late William Green dared speak out against labor crooks in 1929, Teamster Boss Dan Tobin took him aside.

"No more of that," said Tobin. There was no more of that.

This was because Tobin, as boss of the Teamsters, had a "power base," and Green, as Federation president, had none. A "base" in labor lingo is the membership power a union leader commands. Jim Hoffa, for instance, has a "base" of 1,600,000 members. Meany, technically, has no such power base. Actually—as the convention showed—he had the most powerful base of all—public opinion.

With this base he went on to hammer out new tools for coping with corruption. In the Teamster vote, the Federation showed it was master. No longer could any single union—nor any combination of unions—dominate the Federation and dictate to its president. In the case of another transgressor union, the Bakers, Meany went further.

James Cross, the president of the Bakers, dramatized this further change before the convention by appealing in person and with great emotion against the loss of his union-head.

"The Federation has ordered us to hold a convention and elect

---

[3] Replaced in 1947 by the Taft-Hartley Act.

new officers," Cross said. "But if the Federation doesn't like whom we elect, we'll be expelled. Let the members of my own union judge whether I should be president."

The plea failed. The convention voted to expel.

This vote showed Meany *could,* under certain conditions, dictate who could hold office in an International. He went on to demonstrate further that he could even put Federation "policemen" inside the once sacrosanct affiliated unions. These cops, known as "monitors," took corrupt unions in hand, called conventions, supervised elections. Six unions agreed to accept policemen named by Meany. Peter McGavin, Meany's troubleshooter, became a virtual caretaker of some of them.

Meany had sent the union world spinning along a new orbit. But new perils lay ahead.

Because of the power of the Teamsters there was grave danger of a destructive civil war among the unions. Meany was determined to avoid a struggle with the Teamsters over members. There were some who urged that Meany grant a charter for a new drivers' union—and make a fight to "liberate," i.e., woo away, the members of the old. That is what the old Congress of Industrial Organizations had done in its war against Communist-dominated unions. Meany said no. The Federation would not charter a competing truckers' union, at least not now. Meany hoped that the Teamsters could shed Hoffa and return intact to the AFL-CIO.

Still, if Hoffa surmounted his troubles in the courts,[4] there could be war as Hoffa raided the AFL-CIO unions' jurisidictions—and as the Federation fought to capture Teamster local members, union halls and treasuries.

The gravest peril lay in the possible further need for surgery. Only a year before, union presidents protested to this writer that corruption had tainted only a few unions. Now, many privately admitted the corruption had gone deep. Five Federation unions were expelled at the convention. Another was under suspension. In addition, the 800,000-man Carpenters Union, investigated by the AFL-CIO, was threatening to secede.

---

[4] At this writing Hoffa holds office only as "provisional president" under supervision of "monitors" appointed by U.S. District Judge F. Dickinson Letts of Washington, D.C.

11

Once, in a bitter fight inside the old AF of L, Sam Gompers, the Federation's founder, fought the expulsion of the Carpenters with a parable. An Eastern Caliph loved to lop off subjects' heads; when he ran out of heads, he chopped off his own. Would the Federation wind up by lopping off its own head?

Some Thoughts on Labor's Top Job

The job of leading America's unions is as big or as small as the man who holds it.

Actually, the Federation president—as head of a trade association of unions—has less power than the president of any member union. He can't even call a strike or negotiate a contract.

Yet Sam Gompers, as the AFL's first head, gave the unions idealistic direction, set the organizing pattern (skilled workers into craft unions) and ordained an anti-Socialist, and anti-Labor party line that the unions still follow.

After Gompers, William L. Green slept through twenty-eight years of a do-nothing administration—in which the unions shrank in numbers and influence and almost vanished.

Today a new flood of problems pours over the unions. Corruption is only one. Automation shrinks union membership by hundreds of thousands. This unleashes a bitter civil war as unions fight to organize the new skilled workers who are taking over the old assembly-line jobs.

The segregation struggle in the South bars unions from their chief recruiting area. For the unions fight segregation, and this makes them *persona non grata* in the South.

And, although employers stopped hiring spies and armed guards to fight unions several decades ago, a new war of containment emerges. Great corporations fight to cut unions down to size—both at the bargaining table and through political drives to win state laws that the unions say will hamstring them.

So the man who heads America's unions today has both a salvage job (the racketeering clean-up) and a building job. The unions must keep pace with a growing America, or they will dwindle in numbers and influence. Let's see what tools ex-plumber George Meany brings to these tasks.

12

CHAPTER 2

Plumber with
His Finger in the Dike

When George Meany, president of the AFL-CIO, was named a delegate to the United Nations in 1957, one of the first things he did on reaching the UN Headquarters on New York City's East River was to head for the building's subbasement.

There, in the maintenance men's locker room, Meany shook hands all around with electricians, plumbers, carpenters, and said, "I guess you're wondering what a Bronx plumber is doing upstairs instead of down here?"

The question as to what (and how) ex-plumber George Meany is "doing upstairs" has been asked with increasing wonder in and out of the unions ever since Meany moved "upstairs" to the AF of L presidency in 1952—and immediately exploded with massive energy all over the union map. The wonder didn't arise because of Meany's humble origin; most every labor leader begins modestly, is self-taught and self-made. It was because there was little in Meany's past on which to predict a brilliant or crusading future. He was already fifty-six when he took over the leadership of the AF of L, an age when men have dreamed their dreams and leave the making and shaking of new worlds to younger men. Meany, besides, had evolved from that section of the Labor movement—the building trades unions—where corruption was extensive. And, although honest himself, Meany—on the face of it—had been the typical New York labor politician, saying nothing and doing nothing about the corruption that sent key union bosses, including a friend, to jail.

LABOR U.S.A.

For fourteen years, George Meany—as secretary-treasurer of the old AF of L—was frustrated by President William L. Green—who, the older he got, the more he delighted in keeping responsibility from the younger man. Only the leaders at the Federation summit could see occasional flashes of the leadership that was to emerge later.

Many veteran observers, sizing up Meany, were dubious.

"Why doesn't Meany denounce union racketeers?" one writer asked nine years before Meany became AFL president. "If some people hope that he is just biding his time waiting to be president before undertaking to delouse the Federation's unions, they're going to be disappointed," the writer predicted.[1]

If there was any union idealism in George Meany, it lay locked inside him, behind the casual grammar and West Side New Yorkese in which he expressed himself. To observers, he was the perfect embodiment of the AFL bureaucrat, who would go along with the Federation's essential philosophy: what the bosses of the constituent unions did was their own business.

Yet, in five turbulent years, Meany made history. He united the AF of L and CIO, so creating a merged Federation of 144 unions with 15,500,000 members. He created the image of a moral union movement. He turned the unions into a major unofficial force that fights Communism on a world-wide front.

When Anastas Mikoyan, the Russian deputy premier, visited here early in 1959, he asked to see the American "union trade center"— the AFL-CIO headquarters. Arrived at the new $4,000,000 structure, a stone's throw from the White House, Mikoyan pressed his nose like a little boy against the cold glass of a lobby door and peered inside. This was as close as he, or any other Soviet official, could get to the AFL-CIO. None has yet been invited in. To George Meany, Soviet unions are not bona fide labor organizations, but instruments of the Communist party.

Meany is the human hinge on which virtually every recent crucial event in the Labor movement has turned and must continue to turn. These have not only involved the fight on corruption. Although merged, the craft unions of the old AF of L, and the industrial unions of the old CIO are locked in a subterranean struggle for empire—

[1] "The Honest Plumber" by Merlyn Pitzele, ex-labor editor of *Business Week,* in the *Saturday Evening Post,* November 20, 1943.

14

who shall organize whom—that threatens the very life of the Federation. It's Meany's Solomon-like job to make and keep the peace.

Sam Gompers founded the unions; John L. Lewis mushroomed them from a minority to a major force in American life. George Meany fights to preserve them and give them a sense of responsibility to society.

The tools Gompers used were a scholar's intellect and a diplomat's wiles. John L. Lewis had the grand manner of the leader who stirs the multitudes. George Meany, providentially for today's union movement, has the strength to make the lonely decisions.

Mr. Labor

When George Meany lowers his 230-pound bulk into the president's chair at the great oval table around which the AFL-CIO's Executive Council meets, he—more than any other of the leaders—looks the part of a laboring man.

Jacob S. Potofsky of the Amalgamated Clothing Workers—sensitive-faced, handsomely bearded and fond of walking canes and homburg hats—could easily pass for a professor of medicine. David McDonald of the Steelworkers with his wavy platinum hair, finely chiseled nose with flaring nostrils, looks an aging matinee idol. George M. Harrison, conservatively tailored and self-assured, is a picture of the big business executive (which is not far wrong, for his union pays him $61,700 yearly for his businesslike services).

But there is no mistaking the onetime journeyman plumber in massive George Meany. The great neck that's too big for the biggest standard-sized collar; the large bald head; the snub-nosed Irish face with the mouth turned down belligerently, from which a ten-cent cigar protrudes; the great, meaty hands. Put them all together, and they spell Mr. Labor.

Meany looks like a rock and is a rock. He is incapable of, and indifferent to, subtleties. For him, it is all truth, and to hell with the consequences.

Once in Washington, French officials wined and dined Meany while plying him with sweetly reasonable arguments that the French colonial policy in North Africa was good for the natives.

"Any questions, Monsieur Meany?" his hosts asked when the

15

brandy was being served. "Only one," said "Monsieur" Meany in his gravelly New York accent. "When are you going to stop kicking the Algerians around?"

Much has been made of Meany's bluntness. It is a clue to inner resources and a fierce independence which may even border on contempt of what others think. Even if one of the others happens to be the President of the United States.

When labor leaders called on President Harry Truman during the Korean War to protest the minor role they had been given in the mobilization agencies, the President promised that he would do something about it.

Both the late William Green as president of the AF of L, and the late Philip Murray, as head of the CIO, said that was good enough for them. Then Meany spoke up from in back of the room.

"That doesn't take care of it, Mr. President," he said. "The trouble is there's not enough responsibility in the agencies themselves—they're run by businessmen."

Somewhere along the way, Meany acquired the feeling that the best one you could rely on is yourself. So he has played the role of loner. This breaks every rule of politics, including labor politics, where a man has to develop friends, a coterie, a following on his way up. Instead, Meany told off the men who had his future in their hands. He is one of the few men who stood up to the formidable John L. Lewis. The picture of these two massive-faced, bulldog men glaring at each other was a memorable one, but it was Lewis who retreated.

Lewis had proposed that labor leaders refuse to sign the Taft-Hartley non-Communist affidavit and so defy and defeat the Act. None dared take him on, until Meany rose. He began by accusing Lewis of palship with "stinking America haters who love Moscow." Said Meany, "I'm prepared to sign a non-Communist affidavit. I'm prepared to sign an affidavit that I was never a comrade of the comrades." Lewis (a lifelong Republican) never forgave Meany.

Meany, when secretary-treasurer, so antagonized Boss Dan Tobin of the Teamsters that Tobin, riled, sought to make George Harrison of the Railway Clerks president—rather than Meany. Harrison refused to go along, and so Meany made it anyway.

Today, as head of the Federation, Meany is still the loner. An aide has said, "George doesn't build power. He is a power himself."

16

Another president might build a personal political machine and have a corps of press agents to build him up. Meany has no personal machine, no bloc of unions on which he can rely during a showdown in the Executive Council. And no press agents.

Having no personal machine, Meany doesn't count noses on an issue in advance of a Council meeting. He lays the biggest problems on the table without advance warning—and bulls through his point of view.

Much of the credit the unions today enjoy for fighting the racketeers stems from Meany's blunt, black and white, no compromise decisions.

When Meany threw the gangster-infiltrated Longshoremen's Union out of the old AF of L, an aide brought Meany a message from Tony Anastasia, boss of the Brooklyn dockers, and brother of the late Albert Anastasia, onetime head of Murder, Inc.

"Let me and my local come back into the AF of L," said Tony, "and I'll drive out the gangsters in the rest of the union."

"O.K.," said Meany. "We'll let Tony Anastasia's local back in. But he can't come with it." Tony's local—and Tony—stayed out.

But the bluntness which helps save the good name of the Labor movement is hard on the men around Meany.

Although union men talk of "solidarity" and call each other "brother," there's a curious lack of manners among the labor leaders, and little or no compassion for each other. Under the forthright Meany, Executive Council meetings often leave bruised feelings and sometimes come close to leaving bruised heads.

During the early days of the merger, there was a good deal of rancor between George Meany and Walter Reuther because of problems raised by the merger. Once, Meany—who can be brutal—startled Labor's elders by shouting at Reuther, "I don't trust you."

Reuther was so shaken by this that he considered resigning his AFL-CIO vice-presidency, but friends talked him out of it.

Another time, Meany and big Joe Curran of the Maritime Union indulged in a cold and unsmiling exchange of insults in which Meany shouted "Liar" at Curran.

"If you were fifteen years younger," the ham-fisted Curran stormed, "I'd climb over this table and beat the hell out of you."

"It's a lucky thing he didn't get over that table," one Council member observed. "Meany would have been there first."

Troubled Elders

As tensions grow inside the Executive Council over the agonizing problem of automation unemployment, Meany's qualities of bluntness and inflexibility—fine for an uncompromising fight on corruption—tend to become a liability and to stir further explosions.

When Meany failed to arrive for the first day of the Executive Council meeting at Puerto Rico in early 1959, Walter Reuther won initial support for a pet project: a march on Washington to dramatize unemployment.

George Harrison bitterly opposed the scheme as a leftist tactic. Bested by Reuther, he took his troubles to Bill Schnitzler, the AFL-CIO's secretary treasurer. Schnitzler, ex-head of the Bakers Union, is a jolly man, more given to making peace than to stirring up storms. But he had his own personal gripe against Reuther and the CIO faction. That morning—with Meany absent—Jim Carey and Walter Reuther had sought to take the seats customarily occupied at Executive Council meetings by Bill Schnitzler and George Meany. To Schnitzler, it was as if the CIO faction was symbolically taking over the Federation—while Meany was still president.

George Harrison, too, like Schnitzler, is an equable man—and has often conciliated warring Federation factions. Now peacemakers Schnitzler and Harrison hastened to the airport to meet Meany as he flew in from Washington and to stir him up with tales of the morning's doings.

Strained feelings exploded with a bang at the next day's Executive Council meeting.

"You little bastard," Meany shouted at one vice president. "I've leaned over backwards to be fair!" Then Meany turned to Reuther, and the two men went at it hammer and tongs over Reuther's March on Washington plan. Here Meany won, and the scheme was modified.

Because of the Meany flare-ups, two AFL-CIO vice presidents have resigned key committee posts. One is the mild-mannered Jacob Potofsky, the other, Jim Carey—who seems to steam up Meany the most.

Philip Taft, the distinguished labor historian, has compared the solid Meany to a fullback who is good for five yards with every plunge. But to Meany's critics, the time had passed for bowling over opposition. In the face of the new unemployment problem, imagination and vision were needed.

Meany's aggressiveness and inflexibility get him into trouble as an administrator, too.

As president of the AFL-CIO, Meany is somewhat of an employer himself, bossing a staff of seven hundred economists, editors, clerical workers and others. These include some one hundred union organizers who help unions affiliated with the Federation. When these organizers wanted to form their own union and bargain with the boss, i.e., George Meany, the Federation president reacted like some of the employers he'd often excoriated. Meany argued that his organizers were "part of management" and shouldn't have a union. He was accused of discriminating against ringleaders and was dragged reluctantly before the National Labor Relations Board where a pro-union vote by his employees forced him to accept and bargain in good faith with a union.

To his rugged qualities Meany adds a muscular mind of surprising intellectual power—surprising because of the casual grammar in which ideas are sometimes couched. In the midst of a skilled exposition of a foreign problem, for instance, Meany will say, "I'll tell you what he done."

Meany owns a flypaper memory which seems incapable of letting go a name, a time, a fact. "When I got my plumber's apprentice papers on January 17, 1917," Meany will reminisce in the most matter-of-fact way. This gift Meany has used to store his mind with a scholar's knowledge of union history. Meany is, in fact, one of the best read men in Labor. He likes to reveal that he's read every speech Sam Gompers, the founder of the AF of L, ever made, which means thousands of speeches.

With the passion of a Ph.D. researcher, Meany has made his way through the massive archives of the Federation, absorbing in punishing detail the published discussion of problems now forgotten, by labor elders long dead. The facts that Meany has mined he uses effectively in a type of speech-making that is strictly his own. Meany's talks consist of incisive, jabbing sentences and are free of any flourish or oratorical side.

When Meany was negotiating the AFL merger with the CIO, Walter Reuther made a long, opening statement of principles that

19

modore Hotel, to care for his widowed mother and seven brothers and sisters. But, sad to say, he was the sort of union member he today deplores. During his first two years in the union, Meany went to no meetings. When he did take an interest in the local, fellow dues payers recognized in "Mike Meany's boy" the leadership qualities they had seen in the father, and elected George business agent. So, at twenty-eight, Meany put away his Stillson wrench and pipe fittings and took up the trade he was to follow the rest of his life: that of union civil servant or labor politician.

Meany's own local, as he revealed with his usual unsparing candor later,[2] "was a closed union, closed in the fact that it didn't take in any new members. It would supply plumbers "only to our own contractors"—who, in turn, belonged to a closed employers' association that barred other contractors from work.

"We even went so far," Meany said, "that we wouldn't take clearance [transfer cards] . . . and so shut out union members of our own craft from other cities."

"I am not bragging about it. I am not proud of it," said Meany. "That was what we did thirty-five or forty years ago."

Deals in which the union polices and protects the employers' monopoly over contracts in the area (by withholding labor from outsiders) usually mean graft for the union official. And, while there was never a hint of scandal about George Meany, the fact remains that he was part of, and remained discreetly silent about, a system that invited corruption and exploded, from time to time, in sensational scandals.

The notorious Pier Carpenter boss, Robert P. Brindell, went to prison for extortion the year before George Meany became a Plumbers' business agent in 1922. "Brindellism" became a generic term for widespread building trades corruption. Later, the equally notorious Joe Fay of the Operating Engineers, whose members drive heavy earth-moving equipment, went to Sing Sing Prison in a $400,000 extortion that rocked the country.

In the middle thirties, when Meany had advanced to the presidency of the State Federation of Labor, he played golf with Fay and later said that Fay was "a nice guy to be with—except when he got

[2] In a speech to the Building and Construction Trades Department of the AFL-CIO, at Atlantic City, December, 1957.

drunk." Yet Fay had other important friends besides Meany. One Fay buddy was the New Jersey gangster boss, Longy Zwillman. In fact, in his day, Fay was the underworld's back door to the unions. When a mild anti-racketeering resolution was introduced at the AF of L convention of 1940, Fay caught up later with the busybody who introduced it—David Dubinsky of the Garment Workers—and knocked him down.

The blow became page-one news. Yet Meany raised no protest, sent no solacing word to Dubinsky—which caused Dubinsky more anguish than the beating, for he stayed away from the next year's AF of L convention in protest. And when Joe Fay went to jail, George Meany went to visit him.

The labor boss who dominated the New York City scene when Meany was coming up the labor politics ladder in the thirties was Joe Ryan, president of the International Longshoremen's Association, who left the Labor movement in disgrace later. Ryan, in 1934, was head of the powerful New York City Central Labor Trades Council, and so had the delegate strength to influence state federation conventions. For that reason, Meany critics such as John L. Lewis like to assert with satisfaction that "Joe Ryan made George Meany president of the New York Federation of Labor."

These are the bare facts of Meany's early rise. If left to stand by themselves, they could provide a dramatic contrast between an early, discreetly silent Meany and the reformer he later turned out to be.

But, as always in life, the picture is a mixed one.

For instance:

Young Meany's Plumbers' local was no better in its dealings with employers than it should be. But, internally, it was a clean and democratic union. When Meany came to Wednesday night meetings, the union hall chairs would be lined with mimeographed sheets giving the local's monthly expenditures for paper towels, drinking cups, stamps, officials' wages and expenses. There were yearly elections, and candidates lined up before the ballot boxes where the voting dues payers could look them over and question them—and where, I suppose, the office seeker could keep an eye on the voting.

Concerning his friendship with Joe Fay, George Meany once was asked, "Is it valid to compare your visit to Joe Fay in prison with Harry Truman's controversial trip to Kansas City for Boss Tom

23

Pendergast's funeral?"

"No, it isn't," Meany shot back. "Truman owed his early rise to Pendergast. I owed nothing to Joe Fay."

As for his relations with Joe Ryan of the Longshoremen, soon after he (Meany) became president of the New York State Federation, he tangled with Ryan over the mayoralty election in New York City and forced Ryan to quit his post as head of the New York City Central Trades Council. If Meany had any obligations to Joe Ryan, he didn't show it.

Ryan, as a supporter of the old, corrupt Tammany Hall political machine, had backed its Democratic candidate for Mayor. Meany worked for the election of the reform candidate Fiorello La Guardia —so breaking with the old-line labor leaders.

At Albany, as a State Labor Federation official, Meany worked with and came under the influence of the New Deal liberals who had been swept into power by the Roosevelt landslides of 1932 and 1936. An important part of Meany's job was that of lobbyist. He established a record of 141 bills passed. Meany's friendship with the then Governor, Herbert H. Lehman, helped. So did his skill in marshaling facts and driving them home before legislative committees.

An old friend summed up Meany's New York career.

"Sure, he came from the building trades. That was his world, and he spoke for it. But he also lived and worked in the liberal New York climate. He had a ringside seat at the pioneering work of such progressive unions as the Garment Workers and Amalgamated Clothing Workers, with their co-operative housing and medical plans.

"George doesn't show he's absorbing anything," his friend went on. "So, in some ways, he was like Franklin Roosevelt, who didn't shine as a Governor.

"Meany didn't show much as head of the State Federation. But once he got to be president of the AF of L, and had responsibility— then you saw you had before you a man!"

George Meany became the third president of the American Federation of Labor in late 1952. William Green, his predecessor, had clung to the presidency until his death at age eighty-four; he had sat

24

like a mountain on all notions for change, and the House of Labor was in disrepair. Meany, as new head of the House, had several urgent tasks. Racketeering termites had gotten into the foundations. More urgent still was the need to end the twenty-year war with a rival House, the CIO.

To end this civil war meant negotiating with Walter Reuther, who had just been elected president of the CIO. Meany and Reuther had sized each other up for the first time at a labor dinner back in 1949. Fellow labor leaders, observing them, began to make book as to who would emerge as top man on the labor totem pole.

The two men were different in temperament and in union background. Yet when they met in 1953 to talk merger, there was a bond between them. They needed each other. Reuther had only a shaky hold on the CIO, and there were threats of secession by big member unions. Meany could wait and pick up the pieces into the AF of L, or he could make an honorable peace. Meany chose a merger of equals.

Into the new Federation's constitution were written some new ground rules which member unions had to observe. These bore the fancy title of Ethical Practice Codes, but some of the language bore Meany's blunt stamp: "No person should hold or retain office in the AFL-CIO or in any of the affiliated unions who is commonly known as a crook or racketeer."

To cleanse the unions, Meany had to purge his own mind of the union beliefs of a lifetime. Meany had grown up with the belief that a union is a voluntary organization like a lodge or a church. It was bred into his bones, too, that the Federation had no right to reach into and interfere with the internal affairs of its member unions.

Meany had to change the beliefs of his colleagues on the Executive Council, too. Many of these were aging men, well over sixty— a time of life when men aren't eager for change. Harry Bates of the Bricklayers was seventy-five. David Dubinsky of the Garment Workers was sixty-seven. George Harrison was sixty-three. Others, younger, might not take kindly to change either. Maurice Hutcheson, president of the 800,000-man Carpenters, had inherited his union and a million-dollar fortune from his father, the late Big Bill Hutcheson, and was soon to be indicted in a land scandal.

Yet Meany won two crucial tests involving revolutionary change.

First, Meany proposed that Union officers who took refuge in the Fifth Amendment—to conceal possible union skulduggery—should be booted from their jobs. This was a radical invasion by the Federation of member union self-rule. Yet all except one Council member voted with Meany. The nay, prophetically, came from Dave Beck, the Teamster boss. When Beck pleaded the Fifth Amendment before a Senate Committee soon after, Meany promptly called a special Council meeting and ousted him as AFL-CIO vice-president.

Several months later Meany asked the Council to suspend the Teamsters—as a prelude to their expulsion at the coming convention.

It was a bitter ordeal for Meany and for the Council members.

Cutting away the then 1,500,000-member union—which paid $1,000,000 of taxes into the AFL-CIO yearly—meant putting asunder the union empire Meany himself had joined together. The Council members, fearing union civil war, sought a face-saving device that would keep the Teamsters in. Al Hayes, president of the Machinists and head of the Ethical Practices Committee, checked up with his own officials and found them two to one against suspension.

On the eve of the meeting, Meany could be sure of only one vote to suspend. His own. But the Council backed him.

George Meany's cleansing operation—by an odd twist of history—has come none too soon. The unions are entering a period of wrenching change in which they'll need every resource of public good will. A new industrial revolution threatens to shrink the unions' size and influence, unless George Meany and other leaders find a way out.

Early in 1959, as the recession began to wane, it became clear that despite booming production hundreds of thousands of laid-off workers would never get their jobs back again.

Goods were being produced with less human effort. Electronic brains, directing mechanical muscles—automation—were taking the place of the unskilled wage earner.

26

He was being replaced in part by engineers, technicians, computer clerks—white-collar technical and professional workers.

The character of the work force was changing. To labor leaders, this historic shift is a nightmare. For fully 85 per cent of the 17,500,000-odd members of unions are blue-collar wage earners.

Every year, some 700,000 persons pour into the country's work force. To maintain their relative position of influence, the unions have to recruit new members just to stand still.

That is why "organize the unorganized" has been the key slogan of the unions. Until now the organizing was done chiefly among unskilled workers. Now it must be done among workers who have resisted unionism—among white-collar and professional employees.

The picture of plumber Meany with his finger in the dike—holding back a sea of union troubles—is not an exaggerated one.

II

Two views of America's (and the world's) most powerful
union—the Teamsters. From the top down:
Jim Hoffa and Co. From the bottom up: the dues payers.

Everybody fears the Teamster . . . because there's
no successful strike . . . that a union doesn't have to
see the Teamster to help them win the strike.

JAMES R. HOFFA

Well, and what are you going to do about it?

TAMMANY BOSS RICHARD CROKER, 1894

CHAPTER 3

Jimmy Hoffa:
Dead End Kid with a Plus

The Teamsters Union—more formally, the International Brotherhood of Teamsters, Chauffeurs, Warehousemen and Helpers of America—is Big Brother to all the unions. Not only is it the biggest —some 1,600,000 strong at the last count—but, with its power over deliveries, the Teamsters can make or break the organizing drives and strikes of other unions. Some, like the Laundry Workers, depend on the Teamsters for their very lives.

In fact, the Teamsters Union is a labor federation all by itself, a vast catch-all whose constitution claims virtually everything that some other union hasn't nailed down, and much that it has.[1]

Today, only one-third of the Teamsters are drivers. The man who wrestles crates in a warehouse is a teamster, and so is the girl who works in a mattress factory. Brewery workers wear Teamster union buttons, and so do girls who pound typewriters. So are dairy farmers and dairy workers. Store clerks? Gas station attendants? Jukebox repairmen? They may be Teamsters too.

---

[1] An excerpt: "This organization has jurisdiction over all teamsters, chauffeurs, warehousemen and helpers; . . . all classes of dairy employes; brewery and soft drink workers; workers . . . in ice cream plants; all other workers employed in manufacturing, sales and distribution of food, milk, dairy and other products; all cannery workers; *and other workers where the security of the bargaining position of the above . . . requires the organization of such other workers.*" (Emphasis mine.)

The man who heads the Teamster empire is one of the Labor movement's biggest wheels. Indeed, the hand that rules the Teamsters can rock the nation. This hand is the hand of James Riddle Hoffa. The brains, as we shall see, are the brains of two other fellows.

For three weeks, during the summer of 1958, Senators bombarded Jim Hoffa with questions as to why he didn't get rid of the criminals in his union. But it seemed to me as I watched Hoffa that the Senators couldn't establish communication with him. The Senators and Hoffa were men from two different worlds.

"Have you checked up on business agent Joe Mug who took bribes from employers?" a Senator would demand.

"Yes, I've checked up on him," Hoffa would reply.

"What did you find out?"

"I found out he didn't do it."

"How did you find this out?"

"I asked Joe, and he denied it."

Was Hoffa a supercynic? Or did he have the scale of values and moral outlook of the underworld?

I have sometimes felt in following the career of a Frank Costello or an Albert Anastasia that these were atavistic throwbacks to an earlier tooth-and-claw time when men had not yet developed—inside their heads—the governor over their actions that is known today as conscience.

Could this explain Hoffa, too?

It is hard for Hoffa to understand, for instance, that a man's actions may spring from other motives than the desire to make a quick buck.

For years, Hoffa referred to Walter Reuther and his dedicated Auto Workers across town in Detroit as "them squares from Milwaukee Avenue."

"Jimmy thinks every man has a price," a friend has said of him. And Hoffa's closest brush with disaster stemmed from a McClellan Committee investigator's charge that Hoffa had hired him to pry out Committee secrets. (Hoffa, tried, was acquitted.)

There is, finally, within Hoffa the seeming underworld solidarity with those who are in trouble with the cops. A lamister (fugitive), an ex-convict emerging from jail, and even the fellow caught red-handed and serving time—can expect union money and union jobs from Hoffa, it was testified before the McClellan Committee.[2]

"Hoffa will always be in trouble," one observer summed it up. "Not in jail necessarily, nor even under indictment—just in trouble. This is a man at war in his heart with orthodox society. He was probably a cop-hater as a kid, and he has not changed; but the cop image has changed for him. Today it is the Senate, the courts, the press, the whole sprawling, occasionally majestic apparatus of the social order."[3]

Hoffa is, in other words, Labor's Dead End Kid.

But a Dead End Kid plus inner authority, plus an outsized drive for power and great creative organizing talent. These he has used to help make the Teamsters the big and brawny union it is today, and the teamster one of America's highest paid unionists. So, if Hoffa is a man at war with society, he's also a man divided against himself: part legitimate trade unionist—part condoner and supporter of labor racketeers. This contradiction, packaged within one human wrapper, makes for just about the most complex and fascinating character in Labor. And not the least of Hoffa's fascinating facets is that, for his top aides, tough guy Hoffa has surrounded himself with a coterie of once-radical intellectuals.

Face to face, Hoffa looks so boyish that everyone calls him "Jimmy." This is because of his size, a chunky five feet five inches, his disarmingly direct manner of speech and his muscular face which becomes animated and young with talk. But the face that can be engaging—as when Jimmy grins—can become glacier-cold and hard as when Hoffa is pushed into a corner by questions. And the open blue eyes can harden into icy cold, shiny little marbles.

Hoffa's strength emerges at once.

---

2 Teamster treasuries controlled by Hoffa poured out $625,700 in legal fees to defend criminal suits and for other purposes, according to the McClellan Committee.

3 Eric Sevareid in a broadcast over CBS radio.

Although Hoffa is usually the smallest figure in a room, he's likely to be the biggest man in it.

At an employer-Teamster conference for settling workers' grievances, I once heard the employers and the drivers state their case. Then all heads would turn expectantly to Hoffa.

"This is my decision," he'd say with finality. And, as he put it, "That's it, brother!"

When I first interviewed Hoffa in Chicago in 1955, Harold Gibbons, now his top aide, sat in. Gibbons is a Teamster power in his own right in St. Louis and is used to giving orders. Yet his demeanor toward Jimmy—who comes to his shoulder—was that of a respectful junior clerk to the senior partner of the firm.

With the inner authority goes toughness.

As a tough kid, it was testified before a Congressional Committee, Hoffa lashed a rival union man across the back with chains. As a tough guy, Hoffa was still at it not long ago, fighting it out with his fists in a street brawl that followed contract negotiations in the South.

The fist has played an important role in Hoffa's union life.

It was used, first, as a means of survival when Hoffa was a young organizer in Detroit—and had to cope with thugs hired by anti-union employers.

"Our cars were bombed out," he has said. "Somebody broke into our office and destroyed our furniture. There was only one way to survive—fight back. And we used to slug it out in the streets."

Later, the fist was used for survival of a different sort.

"Why do you keep hoodlums on the union payroll?" Pulitzer prize winning reporter Clark Mollenhoff asked Hoffa, referring to a local in Tennessee.

"To kick those hillbillies around and to keep them in line," Hoffa replied. (Questioned on this by Robert Kennedy, counsel for the McClellan Committee, Hoffa would neither affirm nor deny the statement.)

When the International Association of Retail Clerks discovered that its Detroit local was dominated by Hoffa,[4] and sent an aide to the Teamster headquarters building to retrieve the records, Hoffa pointed to a hulking aide in a corner.

---

[4] Hoffa had organized the local and turned it over to a nephew to run.

"See that guy? He'd just as soon shoot you as look at you," Hoffa said, according to the Retail Clerks' aide. Hoffa denied this.

Being tough, to Hoffa, also means feats of endurance of body—and mind—that lesser men could only marvel at. This Dead End Kid is no loafer.

Once, after an all-day grilling before the McClellan Committee that would have wilted another man, Hoffa flew from Washington to West Virginia for an evening meeting with a local there. That done, Hoffa boarded a plane for Detroit, arriving close to midnight to preside over a cheering rally of his home local. He then returned to Washington, winding up at 4 A.M., a working day that had started as usual at seven the morning before.

"He just ain't human," one critic cried.

As for toughness of mind and seeming nervelessness, here is what Hoffa endured, and survived, in a nine-month period that began in late 1957. He was tried twice on criminal charges and acquitted. He was haled before the Executive Council of the AFL-CIO, and was told that his union would be booted from the Federation if he, a corrupt influence, remained a power in it. (I saw Hoffa emerge from this meeting, grim-faced but hurling a defiant "no comment" at the pack of reporters that closed in on him—symbolic of a hostile world closing in for the kill.)

"How much can a man take without breaking?" an observer asked.

A good deal apparently, if that man is Hoffa. For soon after, he battled his way with equal defiance through three weeks of McClellan Committee grilling. Unperturbed, and unrested, Hoffa launched a whirlwind barnstorming campaign around the country to mend his union political fences.

Hoffa, the hard-working Dead End Kid, doesn't drink or smoke, being as abstemious as Walter Reuther in this regard. He eats modestly, concentrating on a virtually all-meat diet, and stays clear of rich desserts. He rounds out his meal with tea.

For all his dabblings in business, Hoffa doesn't seem to have accumulated many goods, nor does he care to make a splash. His clothes are store bought, and in summer he's likely to be seen in a sleeveless shirt open at the neck, in ill-cut slacks and cheap white cotton socks. Where Hoffa's predecessor, Dave Beck, lived in a

35

$150,000 mansion with swimming pool and private movie projection room, Hoffa still lives in a modest brick house for which he paid $6,800 in 1939.

Beck traveled in his own private plane and junketed often abroad. The only recreation that Hoffa takes from his murderous early morning to midnight workday are two fishing and hunting trips yearly with his teen-age son, Jim, Jr. For the Dead End Kid is also a model, even sentimental family man. He spends weekends with his family which includes, besides his wife, Josephine, and son Jim, his daughter Barbara Ann. Hoffa's daughter is majoring in psychology at Albion College and—such are life's little ironies—hopes some day to go into social work.

Empire Builder

A friend of Hoffa's refers to him as Napoleon, noting with mock seriousness that Jimmy looks like the "Little Corporal," has his oversized drive for power and even has a wife by the name of Josephine.

Hoffa is, in fact, an empire builder of considerable proportions. The Teamsters, when Hoffa was getting started in the early thirties, had only 5 per cent of the members they boast today (75,000 in 1932 as against 1,600,000 in 1958). The union embraced drivers and helpers almost exclusively. The word "warehouseman" had not even been added to the union's name. The Teamster Brotherhood consisted of isolated locals that bargained their own contracts and paid little mind to the then president, Dan Tobin.

In a quarter century, the Teamsters Union not only mushroomed in size, but changed its character and assumed a unique power. Federal laws helped spur the Teamsters' growth. But for much in the Teamsters' reconstruction, Hoffa must be regarded as a chief architect.

Run, Jimmy, Run!

Jim Hoffa began his hard journey through life on a sentimental day—Valentine's Day, 1913. The place was Brazil, Indiana, a drab mining town and last stop of Jim's father John, a coal driller. John Hoffa had followed his trade through Kentucky and Illinois, had

36

brought four kids into the world—then died when Jimmy was seven, leaving the brood to his widow to feed and shelter as best she could.

Hoffa's official biography has this to say:[5] "Jimmy, running barefoot, strung clam lines in the river for food, stole green apples, and shot rabbits."

Jimmy has been running ever since.

Brought to Detroit at twelve, young Hoffa left school at the seventh grade to help make ends meet—and at eighteen struck his first blow for the workingman.

His job, at thirty-two cents an hour, was to unload produce from freight cars during a night shift that began at 4:30 P.M. In between cars, young Hoffa and his friends sat out the night hours—without pay.

"We got tired being kicked around," he said later. And he organized his first union by signing up the men around him—so winning better conditions from the boss, a chain store.

Hoffa's feat so impressed union men that he was soon entrusted with a Teamster charter.

The man who controls a Teamster local is a power in Labor and in the community. For in Hoffa's own words, "Everybody fears the Teamster, and he fears him because there is no successful strike vote that a union doesn't have to come and see the Teamster business agent to help them win the strike."

The syntax may be casual, but Hoffa's words embrace a truth and a secret to power.

Soon, at nineteen, Hoffa reached for a higher rung, the leadership of the Joint Detroit Teamster Council, which in those days controlled the town's three Teamster locals.

Hoffa got only four of the twenty Council delegates' votes. But he made himself president anyway. "I just went in and took over," he later boasted. Inside the Teamsters, there was a more plausible explanation. The chunky, fist-swinging kid had support behind him which even the hard-bitten teamsters in the Joint Council had to respect.

I once asked Hoffa about reports by Detroit union men that he had taken over the Council with the help of hoodlum muscle.

---

[5] *The Name Is Hoffa,* published in 1956 in connection with a testimonial dinner to Hoffa.

37

"They did the same thing to me then that you're doing now," Hoffa shot back.

"What am I doing now?" I asked.

"You're trying to put me in the mob."

Mob, or no mob, Hoffa knows a good idea when he sees one. Back in 1933, Hoffa watched with great interest as a union idea fought for its life. The idea, improved and expanded by Hoffa and Beck, was to change the Teamsters.

The idea belonged to a band of men who controlled Teamster Local 574 in Minneapolis, Minnesota. In the midst of a depression which had reduced union membership by 50 per cent, and had the unions gasping for their lives, the brothers Vincent, Grant and Miles Dunne, and Farrell Dobbs had a vision.

The Teamsters, they felt, were destined to dominate the labor scene as trucks replaced railroads in handling freight. The dreamers already held the crucial control of truck terminals and the unloading in Minneapolis. By insisting that Minneapolis union men would not unload incoming trucks unless teamsters were driving them, they forced truck owners outside Minneapolis to recognize and deal with the Teamsters. These newly organized union drivers could then organize other terminals—and this "leapfrogging" process could go on and on, to the greater power and glory of the Teamsters.

The Minneapolis Teamsters did something else that was new. They recruited into the union workers who weren't drivers. They signed up workers in warehouses.

Jimmy Hoffa, then in his twenties, watched, fascinated, from Detroit as the Minneapolis group expanded its domain far beyond Minneapolis.

The Dead End Kid perceived that the Teamsters there had fashioned an economic fist against which few employers could stand up. Inside this fist were the wheels that move goods and the warehouses that shelter them.

Hoffa put it this way, "If you can't take it in or out [because the Teamsters control the trucks], and if you have no place to put it [because the Teamsters control the warehouses], what are you going to do with it?"

Rather than find out, employers usually signed up.

Hoffa pushed out beyond Detroit. He organized a statewide

Teamster Conference, the first of its kind. This turned the isolated Teamster locals of Michigan into a powerful mutual-assistance network. Hoffa went on to form a loose association of Teamster locals in twelve states.

Out in the Far West, another rising star in the Teamsters, Dave Beck, was also extending his influence in the Teamsters by forming a regional organization which he called the Western Conference of Teamsters. But Hoffa went one step further and so topped Beck. He invented the regional or area-wide agreement. Even under the ambitious Beck, the Teamsters bargained, at most, on a city-wide basis. Now Hoffa negotiated revolutionary single contracts embracing employers and drivers in as many as twenty-three states.

By the mid-1950's, no matter how you looked at it, Jimmy Hoffa had run far.

He could swing enough weight to elect Dave Beck president of the Teamsters and himself a vice-president. He became head of the newly formed Central Conference of Teamsters—and master of 650,000 dues payers.

Hoffa was also a big man outside his union. Around him clustered a growing group of satellite unions, mostly tainted. George Meany could be the head of all organized labor, but when leaders of the Hotel and Restaurant Workers, or Laundry Workers, or Bakery or Distillery Workers, needed organizing or strike help, they called Jimmy Hoffa. Gangsters who needed union charters to set up in labor racketeering called Hoffa too. He became the underworld's back door to the unions—the powerful "Man to See" who could pick up the phone and order some union to do a favor for a friend— or lose Jimmy's all-important friendship.

Hoffa became a political power in Michigan. At a meeting of the state's Democratic Committee, Hoffa's lawyer and business partner, George Fitzgerald, became the National Committeeman from Michigan, with power over patronage dispensed in the state by Harry Truman's administration.[6] Hoffa ran his own man for Lieutenant Governor. Although he lost here, he contributed generously to campaigns and helped elect judges. And just as a Congressional investigation was beginning to question him where it hurt, it ended.

---

[6] For a fuller account of Hoffa, the politician, see Chapter 5: "Why They Hate Walter Reuther."

Representative Wint Smith (Republican) of Kansas said, "Pressure came from so high that I can't even discuss it."

Then, at the height of his unique power, Hoffa was plunged into a struggle for survival.

Like a man who has incurred a debt, Hoffa was presented with a bill at a time it was most embarrassing for him to pay it. The debt was exposure. And the collectors were the journalists and the Congressional investigators who began to lift some rocks under which a curious breed of union life proliferated.

The McClellan Committee itemized 82 charges against Hoffa—ranging from acceptance of favors from employers to the harboring of criminals, and the protection of rackets and use of terror against members.

Under fire, Dave Beck and other offenders quit their unions. But not Hoffa. Not only did he survive, but he went on to greater power still.

Why?

The answer lies partly in Hoffa's own tough hide. It lies also in one of the strangest rescue expeditions in labor annals. To the aid of tough guy Hoffa, in his time of need, came two intellectuals from the other side of the union movement's tracks. One was a once-dedicated Socialist who is still involved in liberal causes, Harold J. Gibbons. The other was Eddie Cheyfitz, who had been a Communist in his youth. As idealists, both had entered the union movement to change the world. They had the organizing and propaganda skills acquired in early leftist union days. They had ideas. And they had the understanding into men's strengths and weaknesses that they acquired as practitioners of the class struggle. All these they put at the service of Hoffa to help pull him through.

Two Eggheads in Yoke for Hoffa

Since Hoffa's story now becomes entwined with Harold Gibbons and Eddie Cheyfitz—and since they exert influence at the summit of the country's biggest union—let's take a moment to get a closer look at them.

Gibbons is a rangy, handsome man in his mid-forties with the thoughtful face and disciplined speech of an English professor. When the McClellan Committee questioned Gibbons about violence in St. Louis—where Gibbons is Teamster boss—his press agent handed out a mimeographed biography to reporters.

Gibbons is a "student of economics and history and the Labor movement," said the handout, and a thinker who had lectured at five universities, including Harvard.

The twenty-third child of a Pennsylvania coal miner, Gibbons came up from that part of the union movement which Hoffa most despised, the CIO part that produced Walter Reuther. A protégé of Chicago Socialists, Gibbons was the vice-president of the American Federation of Teachers at twenty-five, then gravitated to Sidney Hillman's Amalgamated Clothing Workers. At thirty-one he came to St. Louis, where he started with a clerks' union and wound up as head of a Teamster local under circumstances that caused Bob Kennedy of the McClellan Committee to describe Gibbons as buying his way into the Teamsters.

When the St. Louis underworld blocked Gibbons' further rise in the city-wide Joint Council of Teamsters, he took a trip to Detroit. There, he met and talked with Jimmy Hoffa.

"Hoffa made a few phone calls," a friend explained later. Whom Hoffa called and what he said are not precisely known. The gist, however, was that anyone who tangled with Gibbons would have "trouble with Hoffa." Gibbons returned to St. Louis and was soon master of all the Teamsters there.

The Hoffa-Gibbons acquaintanceship ripened. Hoffa had the shirttails on which a clinging Gibbons could ride to great Teamster power. Gibbons had the brain and propaganda savvy that could help Hoffa cope with the chain reaction of crises exploding about his ears.

So close did the two become that, during the day, Hoffa and Gibbons are continually in each other's adjoining offices in the marble Teamster headquarters in Washington. At night they share a suite of rooms in the Woodner Hotel. Wherever Hoffa goes, in his constant travels, Gibbons is sure to go. With Hoffa, Gibbons shares all the decisions.

"Together," a friend said of Hoffa and Gibbons, "they are the International."

This is perhaps an oversimplification. For it leaves out the third man in a fateful triangle—Edward T. Cheyfitz.

41

Eddie Cheyfitz was a brilliant mathematics major at the University of Michigan, a member of the Young Communist League, made a pilgrimage to Moscow, then returned to become a boy-wonder union leader (like Hoffa and Gibbons). He became disenchanted with Communism in his twenties, and later left union work altogether and took up the trade of counseling employers on how to deal with unions. Later, he picked up a law degree to help him with his work.

Today, Eddie Cheyfitz is an open-faced man in his early forties, with arresting red hair, an equally arresting flow of talk and tumbling ideas—and a little-understood, behind-the-scenes trade. He is, as one prominent labor lawyer described it, a "channel." When employers' and unions' bargaining negotiations falter, Eddie is the channel through which confidential compromise proposals can be passed.

Being a successful "channel" requires wide acquaintance among labor leaders—which Eddie Cheyfitz has—and access to the Teamsters, which means Hoffa. This is how Cheyfitz came to the Teamsters:

As a onetime advisor to Eric Johnston of the Motion Picture Association, Cheyfitz was asked one day for a solution to a problem. Dave Beck, newly elected president of the Teamsters in 1952, was going to Europe and unashamedly had asked the movie industry to send along some cameramen with him to record his trip.

"Just give him the cameras, and let him take his own pictures," suggested ideaman Cheyfitz. Then Cheyfitz tipped the story to columnist Victor Riesel, who had a column's worth of fun with it. When Dave Beck protested this bit of *lèse-majesté*, Cheyfitz had another idea. He called Riesel, with further material, and now another column appeared, less damaging.

This palship with newspapermen so impressed Beck that he invited Cheyfitz to come with him and be his press agent. This Cheyfitz did, managing to hold on to his employer clients as well. As Beck's good boy, Cheyfitz inevitably met Hoffa, who—impressed with Eddie's fast talk and fast thinking—took to having dinner with Cheyfitz when he came to Washington. Cheyfitz became the man to see for reporters who wanted stories from Hoffa—and for labor men who wanted favors. From Dave Beck's sinking

42

ship, Ed Cheyfitz leaped easily to Jimmy Hoffa's bandwagon.

Hercules once had the strong man's job of cleaning out the Augean stables. Gibbons and Cheyfitz were confronted with a similarly Herculean (and redolent) task: the job of cleaning up the Teamsters and repairing Jimmy's reputation.

The surest way would have been surgery. If Hoffa would submit to cutting away the hoodlums, he'd be cleansed.

But the anti-hoodlum surgery that might cure the Teamsters could be the death of Hoffa. He couldn't or wouldn't get rid of the hoodlums.

So Harold Gibbons turned instead to press-agent gimmicks. He engineered a 2,500-guest testimonial dinner for Jimmy at the Michigan Fair Grounds Coliseum. The guests came by the carload.

As a crowning piece of cynicism, the dinner had as a chairman a Chicago department store owner who had fought unions all his life.

Everything about the dinner was big. Even the menu proclaimed "Jumbo shrimp, Colossal green olives, Mammoth ripe olives."

And there was at each table—to set matters straight about Hoffa—an authorized pamphlet biography: *The Name Is Hoffa.*

Not long after this, "the name Hoffa" appeared on a U.S. indictment charging bribery. The FBI arrested Hoffa, charging he had Senate committee documents on him. Now Hoffa needed more than respectability. He needed to stay out of jail. So to his rescue came Eddie Cheyfitz.

Shortly before his arrest, Hoffa had been a guest at a most curious dinner. Eddie Cheyfitz was the proud host in his own home. And he could indeed be proud, for he had as his other guest Washington's lion of the moment, Bob Kennedy, counsel for the McClellan Committee.

Only in America, as Harry Golden might have put it, could there have been such contrast in guests. On one side of the table was Kennedy, just thirty-one, but looking no more than twenty-five—multimillionaire's son and product of Harvard University. Facing him was Jimmy Hoffa, also boyish at forty-four, cynical product of Detroit's streets. The two men sized each other up. Inside Hoffa's head, so he thought, was locked a secret, the secret that—so a later indictment charged—he had hired a Kennedy

43

staff member to find out what the McClellan Committee had on Hoffa.

But the man Hoffa hired had told all to the FBI and to Kennedy. So in Bob Kennedy's head, at that very moment, raced the thought that Hoffa would soon be arrested on bribery charges.

When this came about soon after, dinner host Cheyfitz swung into action. First he procured for Hoffa the gifted Washington lawyer, Edward Bennett Williams, a courtroom strategist and spellbinder in the grand tradition of a Clarence Darrow. Cheyfitz knew Williams at Georgetown University—and had set up law offices with him.

Hoffa was tried before a jury of eight Negroes and four whites. One spectator at the trial was ex-heavyweight Joe Louis. The Negro ex-champion followed the proceedings with conspicuous interest, and during the breathers in the trial would—just as conspicuously— chat with Hoffa. Joe Louis' Washington food and lodgings, it was testified before the McClellan Committee later, were provided by the Teamsters. Also, ads appeared in the Negro press telling of Hoffa's battles for Negro rights.

Hoffa's aides denied that they had anything to do with Joe Louis' presence in the courtroom, or with the ads in the Negro press. In any case, Hoffa was acquitted.

Soon after, Ed Cheyfitz, Harold Gibbons and Jim Hoffa sat down to ponder a momentous decision. Beck—disgraced and discredited—was on his way out as Teamster president. Now, Gibbons and Cheyfitz urged Hoffa not to abandon his aim of becoming Teamster president.

Hoffa hesitated. He had already had more than his share of attention from investigators and prosecutors. The additional heat he'd attract by seeking one of the biggest jobs in American life could dwarf anything that had gone before. Could Hoffa stand the microscopic study to which his past—and present—would be subjected?

On the other hand, if Hoffa didn't gain the presidency, and some other man did, wouldn't that man have to clean Hoffa out of the Teamsters under pressure of the AFL-CIO?

Gibbons and Cheyfitz urged Hoffa to run.

It is a fascinating speculation as to whether Hoffa held another confab on this question with other less respectable advisors. Gangsters in Detroit, Chicago and elsewhere who needed Teamster power to maintain their jukebox rackets and other business monopolies could wonder, too, whether Hoffa's election as president would attract unwelcome heat. Or whether Hoffa, as president, would assure protection against busybodies who might try to cleanse the union.

Whether Hoffa discussed these matters with underworld friends is not known.

Gibbons flew out to Chicago to organize a meeting "to get the views of Jimmy's friends on the best course for the union to follow." The best course, of course, was for Jimmy to run for president. This Hoffa did in late '57. Thanks to Gibbons' savvy in organizing Hoffa's campaign, Hoffa dominated the proceedings and was elected president.

Cheyfitz saved Hoffa again when outraged rank and filers went to court and blocked Hoffa from taking office. This time Cheyfitz came up with a compromise. If the rank and filers would agree to let Hoffa take office, provisionally, he in turn would agree to submit to the supervision of a board of monitors.[7]

So Hoffa became provisional president—a qualified office he still holds as this is written.

Cheyfitz and Gibbons are still trying to make Hoffa acceptable —but an old problem persists that even their resourceful eggheads can't solve.

One day Ed Cheyfitz was holding forth before Gibbons and several others—in Hoffa's Woodner Hotel suite in Washington— about the need of making at least a token clean-up.

If only one ex-criminal were to be kicked out of the Teamsters in each of a dozen key cities, it would do wonders for Hoffa's name, Cheyfitz was saying.

At this point, Hoffa entered the room, listened until he got the drift of Cheyfitz' discourse, then broke into a violent tantrum.

_____
[7] This historic deal in which a great union submitted voluntarily to virtual court receivership—and its consequences for Hoffa—are described more fully in Chapter 4: "The Teamsters from the Bottom Up."

"Who do you think you are, firing guys out of the Teamsters?" Hoffa raged. It was clear that Hoffa could not or would not take on the underworld.

Since Hoffa can only stop being controversial by ridding himself of underworld influence, his tantrum meant that he couldn't stop being controversial and stay alive.

The "If" in Hoffa's Future

What's going to happen to Hoffa? Of all the questions about labor leaders, this is the one that is most asked.

As this is written, Hoffa is riding high. Neither exposure by McClellan Committee, nor expulsion by the AFL-CIO has slowed the Teamsters' onward rush to greater membership and increased power. The ouster, ironically, may have helped the Teamsters. Hoffa has used the million dollars that the union once paid yearly to the AFL-CIO as per capita taxes to finance aggressive recruiting drives—and in 1958 picked up 135,000 new members.

While automation reduces factory work forces and shrinks the membership of such unions as the Auto Workers—and others— Hoffa sits astride a service industry union that will benefit from the greater wealth that the new automatic machines will bring. In addition to his jurisdiction over the movement and storage of goods, Hoffa is busily organizing stores, farms, small factories.

If nothing interferes, Hoffa will be the first union leader to command a union of 2,000,000 men.

But that is a big "if."

For, hanging over Hoffa, is the threat that the AFL-CIO may charter a rival Teamster union to "liberate," i.e., raid Hoffa's members.

George Meany and his advisors have played a wait-and-see game with Hoffa. They hope, in time, to win back the Teamsters intact, and have been waiting to see whether there will be further prosecutions against Hoffa—that could remove him from the scene. If not, after a suitable interval, the AFL-CIO could charter a new Teamster union. It is believed that some one hundred locals—one of every eight in the Teamsters—are ready to secede. This could mean a new union of 250,000 members, a launching platform for an all-out raiding war on Hoffa's Teamsters.

When the CIO expelled eleven Communist-led unions in 1950, it chartered rival unions and ultimately destroyed all but three of the red-led expelled affiliates. The same kind of struggle could be expected again. It would mean civil war—and last for years as rival unions fought for members, local treasuries, and welfare funds.

Whether Hoffa could survive this, only time could tell.

CHAPTER 4

The Teamsters
from the Bottom Up

The story of a union is told too often through its leaders. To understand the Teamsters and the exciting struggle, from within, to break the grip of hoodlums in the union—the story must be told from the bottom up: through the rank-and-file members.

When his local is cleanly run, the teamster's rewards are the envy of all other union men. He earns from $2.25 to $3.17 an hour—and with steady work can earn from $4,000 to $8,000 yearly. Many teamsters get three weeks' vacation with pay as well as a half dozen or more paid holidays, including, in some locals, a paid day off on a teamster's birthday.

But in many locals run by cronies of James R. Hoffa, the union takes on a Through-the-Looking-Glass quality. Instead of serving the men, the union is reversed perversely to suppress him. Here black is white as union officers, at bargaining time, fight *against* their own men; where men are punished for serving their country in war, where eagerness to serve a union is regarded as treason against the union and where talented members who might improve the local's government are hounded out as troublemakers.

Consider Ed McFarland, whose Teamster local punished him for fighting for his country.

Ed McFarland is a long-legged fellow of forty-four with the big, strong hands that are needed to dominate a twenty-wheel, sixty-ton cement-mix truck. As an infantry corporal in the South Pacific campaigns he lay ill for seventeen months in an army hospital with a jungle rot that numbed his legs. When he returned on crutches and hobbled to the office of his New York Teamster local, to offer four dollars monthly dues and regain his union card, the union's boss shook his head.

"Sorry, bud, you'll have to pay back dues for all them four years you was away," the man said.

McFarland argued with the local's boss, Johnny O'Rourke, the Hoffa lieutenant who heads all of New York City's Teamsters (as president of Joint Council 16) and is a vice-president in the International.

O'Rourke, whose cadaverous frame and sunken eyes belie the iron will with which he has kept the members in their place, shook his head.

"You didn't take out a withdrawal card," (indicating inactive status) O'Rourke said. "We had a meetin' while you was away and decided them without a withdrawal card would have to pay up."

"How could I know there'd be any more meetings for me?" Ed McFarland asked bitterly.

Ed had to dig down into his pocket and hand over his entire muster-out pay—a hundred dollars—virtually all the cash he had.

In the curious union world of Hoffa's man, Johnny O'Rourke, a member can be punished, too, for trying to get more for the worker.

This brings us to Andy Boggia, a 230-pound, five-foot-five rock of a man who looks like one of the trucks he wheels—and is a born leader.

Andy earns $3.12 an hour and, thanks to fourteen years of seniority, gets steady work that brings him some $6,800 a year. A union welfare fund takes care of sickness in his family (he has two boys, ten and six, who will be pro-rank-and-file labor lawyers some day,

48

Andy says). Andy will get a small pension when he is too old to work. To win the pay and benefits, Andy had to fight his own leader. He also took a cruel slugging that almost blinded him.

A combat veteran like Ed McFarland, Andy decided in 1953 that the time had come to fight the conspiracy between union bosses and employers that deprived him of the sort of living that other union men were making.

Sand and gravel truck drivers in O'Rourke's local earned a half dollar less per hour than other union men who did the same work. Nor did the local's welfare benefits come up to those of other unions.

Contract negotiations had always been a strictly secret affair between O'Rourke and some of the employers. Members were never consulted about the terms. The contract—once drawn—was a classified top secret too. The members complained that O'Rourke had "lost it," or that only a few copies had been printed and none were available.

Andy Boggia led a revolt, and its story runs like that of an uprising by a Fidel Castro against a Batista. First, he met secretly in a basement, in the dark of night, with a handful of trusted rank and filers. It was an innocent and legitimate caucus to plan strategy for the next meeting. Yet to have met openly would have meant expulsion on the charge of "dual" unionism (forming a rival union).

From the secret meeting came a simple demand—that rank and filers be named to the negotiating committee—and the strategy to force it on O'Rourke; a big turnout of angry dues payers and trusted members scattered about the union hall to protect Boggia and others from being roughed up.

Taken aback by the uproarious demand for the election of a rank-and-file negotiating committee, O'Rourke first stormed against the radical idea, then compromised with a proposal.

"Let's do it democratic," he suggested. "Let's nominate the men for the committee, then put 'em all in a hat and pull out the names."

With O'Rourke's henchmen shouting out nominations, there were soon some fifty names in the hat. But, miraculously, when the names were pulled out, the second was that of Andy Boggia, and the fourth that of Ed McFarland.

Boggia, speaking for the members, demanded a raise in pay and benefits to bring wages up to those in other unions.

49

When the employers and his own officers resisted, Boggia organized a strike.

Now Boggia was put to the test as a leader, a man and as the head of a family.

First came a telephone call.

"If it's money you want," a hard voice said, "you can have $3,000. Just get the men back to work."

Next, "a darkish fellow in natty clothes" sought out Boggia. "He pushed his unbuttoned coat aside so as to display his hardware, a gun strapped under his shoulder," Boggia said later.

"Don't push your luck," said the man with the hardware.

When the strike continued, telephone calls came to Andy's wife, then pregnant with the Boggias' second boy.

It was the tearful voice of a woman, demanding to know where Andy was.

"I'm going to have a baby," the voice sobbed. "Andy is the father, and he's got to take care of me."

Andy returned that night to find his wife in a state of near collapse. The telephone number the troubled lady had left turned out to be a "wrong number."

Several nights later, Andy and two fellow strikers were set upon by seven huskies. Andy, no weakling, knocked one hoodlum down.

"Then I looked up into the glare of the street lamp and saw something flashing at me and I ducked," Andy recalls. A hoodlum jabbed the jagged end of a broken bottle at Boggia's eyes, and, as Boggia fell away, the glass ripped the tip of his nose and shredded his upper lip. The blood-soaked Andy spent the night in the hospital. Then, sewn together again, he returned to see the rank-and-file strike-revolt go to arbitration and win many of the men's demands. The men had won despite their officers. During nine weeks of the strike, the local paid no strike benefits; O'Rourke didn't even call a meeting to rally the men.

A look at the Teamsters from the bottom up has other surprises. Let's move across the Hudson River to the New Jersey domain of John Conlin—where a teamster who wants to serve his union can be banished from the local and from a job.

Conlin, now seventy-eight, has bossed Local 560 in Hoboken for forty-five years—most of them without elections. Here, in 1955, a

50

twenty-eight-year-old, three-hundred-pound driver, "Tiny" Sladow, urged his friends to show up at the next meeting to nominate a rank-and-file slate.

Tiny was called into the aging Conlin's office.

"You didn't get a transfer from your old local," the union boss told Tiny, who had dropped out of another local to go to college for two years. "Got to give up your card until you straighten out with them," the union boss said. But his old local wouldn't let Tiny straighten out. It refused to take Tiny's two full years of back dues. So, trapped between two Teamster locals, Tiny lost his union card and got no more work from the union hiring hall.

Over in Perth Amboy, a stone's throw from Hoboken, where Tiny was cut down to size, another potential leader, towheaded, wiry John Wilczynski, studied up on the bylaws, printed pamphlets and got some eight hundred dues payers out to a meeting. Here, for the first time in anybody's memory, a slate was named to oppose the incumbents.

Soon after, the rank-and-file nominees were hauled before the local's president and his lawyer.

"What you got against the union?" the union boss demanded.

"Nothing," said John Wilczynski and his running mates. "We just want to help run it." The local's boss told them they were disqualified. They had failed to pay dues promptly on each first of the month for two full years.[1] The nominees were then asked to sign a paper disqualifying themselves from running. They were ineligible, anyway, they were told. So, in their ignorance, the men signed.

In the strange unionism of the Teamsters, it is a crime to uncover a crime against the union. Such a busybody is likely to be punished —by the man who committed the crime.

Willie Bennett, a slight, 36-year-old, 127-pounder with six mouths to feed, discovered that the man who was running his local (390 at Miami) had been tried by a Buffalo, New York, local for treasury looting. The union convicted him, suspended him from membership for ten years, and fined him $50,000 (which he didn't pay).

---

[1] This standard dodge with which rank and filers are kept from running is described in Chapter 18.

The union boodler then went south where a regional Teamster official put him in charge of the funds and fortunes of the members of Local 390 at Miami. There, rank and filer Willie Bennett rose in meeting one day, and exposed the union thief. The members rioted and chased the thief from the rostrum. But he had the last word. He and his henchmen tried Willie Bennett for conduct unbecoming a union member, and threw him out of the union.

We'll return to Willie Bennett in a moment. But first, let's leap kitty-corner across the continent from Miami to Anchorage, Alaska.

Mike Cserepes, father of four boys and two girls, "four of them in school—and am trying to buy my own home"—wrote this to me: "I have lived in Alaska for fourteen years, and I am proud to vote on the issue of Statehood. At the same time I think I should be able to vote in my own union also."

First, Mike lost his job as union business agent because, along with 150 other members, he put his name to petitions asking the International to free them from a ten-year-old trustee-dictatorship. The petitions were sent back to the trustee against whom they had been aimed, making the signers fair game for the dictator's wrath. Next, Mike and sixteen other dues payers sent a telegram to the Teamsters' Miami Beach convention, charging that their local's delegate had been illegally picked. The delegate got seated anyway—to vote for Hoffa—but Mike Cserepes was tried by the men he had accused, and suspended from the union.

Mike's plight in Alaska at this point was the same as that of Willie Bennett at Miami, Florida—of Tiny Sladow at Hoboken, New Jersey, and many rank and filers elsewhere. For seeking an honest union shake, they had been expelled and couldn't make a living.

Here, their stories would have ended, except for a miracle the rank and filers themselves wrought. Mike Cserepes has regained his union card and is back at work. So is Willie Bennett—and help is on the way for Tiny Sladow and others. Mike Cserepes and Willie Bennett got their cards and jobs back because, for the first time in Teamster history, there was an effective outside friend to appeal to. This friend is the Board of Monitors, named by a federal court to supervise the Teamsters.

The monitors came into being because thirteen rank and filers gambled their futures on an unequal fight against the Teamsters International—and won.

In the summer of 1957, Jim Hoffa was making preparations to get himself elected president. It was later testified before the Mc-Clellan Committee that Hoffa and his henchmen were snatching the presidency from under the noses of the members by dealing themselves convention delegates through bogus elections or by appointments that violated the Teamster constitution.

How could the ordinary teamster—without money or union organization—stop the Hoffa juggernaut or hope to win a legal fight with a foe who could hire the best lawyers a $35,000,000 union treasury could buy?

On what grounds could they wage battle?

Rank and filers Andy Boggia and Ed McFarland, whom we've already met, sought out a lawyer who had electrified Teamster dues payers a few months back by reversing the rigged election with which a Hoffa man, backed by the underworld, had won the leadership of New York City's Teamsters. The lawyer was Godfrey Schmidt, a wiry, fifty-six-year-old scholar of the law who teaches at Fordham University—and behind whose high forehead lay a simple legal theory for the case of the dues payers vs. James R. Hoffa, *et al.*: the union constitution is a contract between union and members. Officers who violate the union constitution breach a contract and can be held to account in a civil court.

But who would stand up in open court as plaintiff against the Teamster boss and his criminal understrappers? What teamster, with kids to support, would give evidence against the hooligans in his local?

Here entered a Rabelaisian fellow six feet big, with massive belly to match, with massive appetites, a lurid past and a richly obscene wrath against "them four-letter-word fink bastids"—the Teamster hierarchy. John Patrick Kennedy is so implausible, he is an original. Although he was once a union strong-arm man who organized employers from the top down and bears a half-closed, battered eye as a memento of his earlier days, he later battled leaders in his milk drivers' local and was thrown out for his pains. He spent an eighteen months term for assault and robbery seventeen years ago. But, re-

53

habilitated, he now enjoys the confidence of many honest men. Innocent of formal education, Kennedy has a flair for languages and can curse and converse as easily in Yiddish and Italian as in his own English—which can be bawdy and ungrammatical or precise and disciplined, depending on whom he talks to.

Pat Kennedy recruited a committee of thirteen rank and filers, including Andy Boggia and Ed McFarland and other rebels. Although another man became the Committee's chairman, Pat Kennedy—in the background because of his past—became the Committee's unofficial leader and spokesman. Kennedy set up communications with rank and filers throughout the country and Canada. He raised money, dug up witnesses and became a one-man grand jury repository of information on Teamster skulduggery.

First target of lawyer Godfrey Schmidt, teamster-without-portfolio Pat Kennedy and "the Thirteen" was to prove that the Teamster convention scheduled for October, 1957, was being rigged. Lawyer Schmidt drew up an affidavit form, attesting that delegates had been fraudulently named. Kennedy shipped hundreds of these to rank-and-file volunteers who stationed themselves at key truck terminals across the continent and soon had statements from some four hundred drivers in locals all over the country that they had had no chance to vote for delegates.

Lawyer Schmidt took the affidavits before U.S. District Judge F. Dickinson Letts at Washington, D.C., and won a historic injunction ordering the Teamsters to stay their election.

Although the injunction was promptly set aside by higher federal courts, the decision gave "the Thirteen" an engraved judicial invitation to return to court again if, *after* the Teamster election, they could prove that the convention had been fixed.

When Hoffa was elected president, "the Thirteen" were back in court, and, by a comic opera turn of events, the Teamster convention itself at Miami Beach supplied evidence of fraud.

The key to the Teamster presidential election was the Hoffa-controlled Credentials Committee which passed on the seating of convention delegates. Alerted by the rebel rank and filers, McClellan Committee investigators descended on the plush Eden Roc Hotel in search of the Credential Committee's minutes.

"They've been accidentally burned," the investigators were told.

"A maid threw them into the incinerator."

At the scene of the crime, a hotel employee pointed to the "incinerator" chute where the papers had been consigned. But the knaves had been fools, for it wasn't an incinerator chute; it led to the hotel laundry. In the bowels of the hotel, intact, were the incriminating credentials minutes. They revealed that at least 561 delegates had been seated improperly.

So casual was the selection of delegates that, as one Teamster boss explained, "If we follow the constitution on the legality of delegates, we can't hold a convention." This was true. Testimony before the McClellan Committee confirmed that more than half of the delegates had no right to be there.

Judge Letts issued a new injunction ordering Teamster president-elect Hoffa *not* to take office, and *not* to draw any pay for the job—until a new suit by rank and filers, challenging the election, could be tried.

The ensuing four-week trial went so badly against Hoffa that his lawyers offered a compromise plan to end it.

Agree to let Hoffa take office, they said, and Hoffa will agree to let the court name a three-man board of monitors to supervise the reform of the Teamsters.

For a great union to put its neck under a court-imposed monitor yoke was something new in union annals. Besides, Hoffa could have dragged out the rebels' suit in the higher courts for years—and so worn them out.

Why then did Hoffa seek a compromise? For two reasons. First, he was still, under court injunction, only the president-elect, while Dave Beck continued in office. Delaying the suit would only keep Beck in and Hoffa out. Second, to the cynical Hoffa, agreements are only as good as the men who execute them. His lawyers could protect him against the selection of overzealous monitors. He would take office and take his chances.

In the first six months of the settlement it seemed that Hoffa and the lawyers, alone, got anything from it. Three lawyers for the rank and filers asked the court for $300,000 in fees and were awarded $210,000. Hoffa assumed office, nominally as provisional president under the thumb of a federal court, but actually in full and undisputed command of the Teamsters. Untrammeled and unprodded,

55

Hoffa permitted thugs to continue their suppression of the rank and file as usual. Many of the rank and filers who had dared give testimony against Hoffa at the suit were cruelly booted from or otherwise discriminated against by the locals. Hoffa, riding high, announced a grand scheme to unify the country's transport—with himself in the driver's seat. Reporters started to write pieces about the fall and rise of Jimmy Hoffa.

Then there befell one of those curious twists of fortune that change the course of history. The chairman of the three-man board of monitors quit, and the court named a soft-spoken labor lawyer and former law professor by the name of Martin O'Donoghue.

As conceived by Hoffa's aides, the Monitor Board had a Teamster spokesman, a public representative and a spokesman for the rank and file. Nat Wells, a Teamster lawyer from Dallas, Texas, was the Teamsters' watchdog on the board. Godfrey Schmidt—whom Hoffa had tried to keep out—represented the rank and filers. Now, when Judge Letts suggested O'Donoghue as public representative and chairman, Hoffa was delighted. O'Donoghue had represented Teamster groups in Washington, and defended the Teamsters early in the rank-and-file suit.

But there were things about O'Donoghue that Hoffa and his lawyers didn't know.

"I love the law," monitor O'Donoghue told this writer. "And without law there can be no justice." For twenty-six years, O'Donoghue had represented the Plumbers, a meticulously honest union that had sent one plumber, Martin Durkin, to the cabinet as Secretary of Labor under President Eisenhower, and another, George Meany, to head the AFL-CIO. With Meany wielding a broom in the AFL-CIO, and with Plumbers' lawyer O'Donoghue heading the Teamster Monitor Board, the Plumbers Union was destined to exert influence on Labor far beyond its modest size and strength.

O'Donoghue called his fellow monitors, Godfrey Schmidt and Nat Wells, to the headquarters of the Teamsters in Washington, D.C. For a few moments the men silently sized each other up. Then O'Donoghue—as chairman—turned to Schmidt.

"Godfrey," he said, "what do you think of the Philadelphia situation and Raymond Cohen?" (As boss of the Philadelphia Teamsters,

Cohen had just pleaded the Fifth Amendment 97 times in answer to McClellan Committee questions about $491,000 of union funds.)

"I think it's outrageous," Schmidt answered with feeling. "That man should be removed."

Nat Wells, for the Teamsters, defended Ray Cohen.

"I agree with Godfrey," O'Donoghue said quietly. "I move we order Hoffa to investigate his local."

It was O'Donoghue's first indication as to how he interpreted his duties as monitor. With Schmidt, he would now form a majority that could order a clean-up. Schmidt, a volatile man, repressed a whoop of joy. O'Donoghue, as chairman, and Schmidt, as his supporter, went happily to work.

First thing O'Donoghue did was to move his monitor's office out of the Teamsters' headquarters and into his own law office. It was a declaration of independence and a declaration of war.

Next, O'Donoghue combined with Schmidt to stop elections that, under the guise of restoring 109 trusteed locals to their members, were perpetuating the old pro-Hoffa leadership. Because rank-and-filers were largely being disqualified, the monitors decided to look into election methods.

Procedure is this: A majority vote among the monitors results in an "order of recommendation" to Hoffa. If he balks, the monitors can ask Judge Letts to act.

When O'Donoghue, on behalf of the monitors, challenged the right of a key Hoffa man to hold a regional office, Hoffa staged a bellowing, raging tantrum.

Hoffa's closest union advisor, Teamster vice-president Harold Gibbons, had been elected head of the St. Louis Teamsters under circumstances that caused his opponent to charge fraud before the McClellan Committee. When Hoffa and his rubber-stamp executive board quietly O.K.'d the Gibbons election—against O'Donoghue's orders—the monitor hastened to the Teamsters' headquarters.

From his physical height of six feet and his moral height O'Donoghue looked down on the stocky Hoffa and gently demanded that Hoffa turn over the Gibbons file and prepare a new Gibbons hearing.

At interference from this unexpected quarter, Hoffa exploded.

"If you want to be the four-letter-word president of this union, take this four-letter-word office," Hoffa raged.

But the quiet man before him merely waited for the tirade to end. Then he said, "If you don't hand over the Gibbons file, the court will order you to do it."

As ordered by the monitors, Hoffa also agreed to the resignation of a henchman in New York and to an ouster trial for a power in a Philadelphia local. But when O'Donoghue ordered reforms at headquarters, Hoffa began to stall.

O'Donoghue found that Teamsters International headquarters kept no lists of local members. The local bosses alone knew how many members they had. They could thus cheat on per capita taxes paid to the International, and they could steal elections, such as Hoffa's, by sending more delegates to conventions than they were entitled to. O'Donoghue also found that most of the Teamsters' 890-odd locals had no bylaws to limit local bosses' powers. Backed by a professional survey, O'Donoghue ordered the Teamsters to maintain accurate membership records and to introduce new election rules. Hoffa did not defy these moves, but he argued and pleaded against them, playing for time.

Gradually, the monitorship, which Hoffa had originally regarded as just a public relations gimmick to enable him to take office, began to look more and more like a closing steel trap.

When O'Donoghue ordered an ouster trial for Hoffa's lifelong friend and business partner, Owen Brennan, Hoffa didn't attempt outright defiance. One of his lawyers made a personal plea instead. Putting aside legal arguments he urged O'Donoghue to "do this for me. . . ." O'Donoghue, unmoved, asked a federal court to speed the ouster action against Hoffa's friend.

When monitor Godfrey Schmidt helped rank and filers draw up 263 charges against Hoffa himself, and prepared to confront him with an ouster trial, Hoffa knew he was in grave trouble. He saw that if he did not get rid of the monitors they would get rid of him.

The chief author of his plight, Hoffa felt, was Godfrey Schmidt, who had brought the original suit of the Thirteen against him and who had so drawn the consent decree that it was now closing like a noose around his neck. So Hoffa withheld Schmidt's monitor fees and expenses in an effort to starve out the lawyer who had given up his practice to work at his monitorship. He even attempted to get the court to oust monitor Schmidt on the ground that he had conflicting private interests.

When none of these moves succeeded, Hoffa tried an end run by ordering a quickie national convention. Since the clean-up had not as yet destroyed his political machine, he felt sure of re-election. And if he were re-elected, he would be free of the monitors.

But here, too, the monitors opposed him. When Schmidt and O'Donoghue stood firm against holding the election, Hoffa made a dramatic move to win them over. He ordered his rubber-stamp executive board to fly to Washington for a night meeting and invited monitors O'Donoghue and Schmidt to attend.

That night, in the lavish board room in Teamster headquarters, Hoffa, flanked by four lawyers, alternately pleaded and bullied as the monitors defended their action. Why, he asked plaintively, did the monitors want to block an election?

"Because you are under charges," O'Donoghue answered. "And Vice-President O'Rourke over there is under charges. And so is Vice-President Brennan, over there." A new convention, run by the men who had rigged the previous one, would be a mockery.

When Hoffa and his chief lawyer, Edward Bennett Williams, failed to move O'Donoghue and Schmidt with four and a half hours of argument, the monitors left. Then Hoffa's board defied the monitors by voting a special convention for February. The next day the monitors went into court and obtained an order to block it. Judge Letts subsequently said that the monitors had broad powers to clean up the union.

So the artful Hoffa, invulnerable to legal attacks in the past, is now caught in a double squeeze. From above, by the monitors. From below, by restive members who, as the news filters back that the monitors are behind them, are beginning to stand up and fight back in their local union meetings.

I made my way, uninvited, into a meeting of New York Local 282, bossed by Johnny O'Rourke, a major Hoffa ally. Some eight hundred drivers overflowed the hall and crowded the doorways. "O'Rourke won't dare show his face," a rank and filer had said—and O'Rourke didn't. A sweating vice-president was on the rostrum instead, coping as best he could with the turbulently aggressive members.

The rank and filers' leader, Andy Boggia, stood like a rock on the floor, directing the prearranged strategy with which the members were storming officer resistance to win a key victory: the right to elect shop stewards—the men who police each contract on the job and so can protect the members—or sell them out.

Members had asked the monitors and the Teamsters International to oust O'Rourke, alleging collusion with employers. Now at the meeting, it was clear, from the members' confident defiance, that Johnny O'Rourke was holding office on borrowed time. And, thanks to the monitors, so were other Hoffa allies around the country. The reform tide, churned up by the rank and filers themselves, was rolling in. Mr. Hoffa, who stands five feet five inches in his stocking feet, had got himself into some very deep water.

III

Why they behave like union leaders.
Some portraits light and gray.

The [union] leader is not of the elite of money
or of prestige . . . but of the elite of
power . . . he accumulates power, and he exerts it over
the union man and over property.

C. WRIGHT MILLS, *The New Men of Power*

CHAPTER 5

Why They Hate
Walter Reuther

There are some men who are always on center stage no matter what is happening. In labor it's Walter Reuther. When the sit-down strikes broke in the late 1930's, it was Walter who was found sitting in a key General Motors plant. When the underworld sought to eliminate a labor leader, it was Walter Reuther whom the gangsters shot and almost got.[1] When the Republicans wanted a labor bogey-man with which to scare the voters in the fall of 1958, it was Walter they elected.

And now that the unions are facing their biggest crisis as machines without men wipe out the jobs of unskilled workers, whose union is in the forefront of the struggle to survive? It's Walter P. Reuther's United Automobile, Aircraft & Agricultural Implement Workers of America.

Walter Reuther is the key figure in Labor today. George Meany may wield greater influence in the labor movement; Jim Hoffa may wield greater union power. But Reuther heads the crucible union—the laboratory union in which the impact of automation will be tested. How Reuther and his Auto Workers come through this ordeal of industrial change will largely determine how the rest of the labor movement comes through.

The streets of Detroit with their burden of 300,000 idle auto

---

[1] For more on this, see Chapter 11, "Journey to the Underworld."

workers who will never return to the assembly lines—because ma-chines have replaced men, or plants have moved away—dramatize Reuther's problem.

His UAW, once 1,500,000 strong, had shrunk to some 1,000,000 dues payers by 1959. Should customers take to the coming small cars—and be content with a standardized model that remains un-changed for several years—Reuther's union could shrink much more. For then, as an auto executive told me, machinery could conceivably be developed to assemble a car automatically.

Reuther must recruit replacements from the white-collar-class office workers, technicians, engineers—or face the world with a diminished power base.

Lessened power would hurt Reuther where he lives. For no other labor leader so regards his union power base as a launching pad for explosive ideas both at the bargaining table and away from it.

Reuther has cultivated power all his life. He has a surer sense of power and more skill in manipulating it than any other leader. He doesn't want this power in the sordid sense—to line his pockets. McClellan Committee accountants, combing the UAW (at the na-tional headquarters level) found the union belligerently honest. Reuther wants power as a lever for reform. For he is a reformer of almost Messianic intensity. He wants to save the country. He wants to save the labor movement—to give it an ideology, a social mis-sion, a final goal. "No one should be in the labor movement unless he's tied to a cause," Reuther told me.

So Reuther plays up to the liberals and outrages the conservatives.

Not that Reuther today is a Socialist. The ideological heir of a Socialist grandfather and father, who regarded their socialism as "practicing Christianity," Reuther, briefly a Socialist himself, today abjures government ownership. "I'd rather bargain with Gen-eral Motors than with the government," he says. "General Motors has no army."

But the faith in social engineering is still there. And so, until quite recently, were the words—if not the deeds—of the radical leader. "The peoples of the world want neither Stalin nor Standard Oil," he orated to a European trade union conference in 1949. At which a delegate quipped: "I'll settle for Standard Oil."

Today Walter Reuther is more conservative in his public utter-

64

ances. Yet he is forever a cause in articulate and whirring human form—looking for a place to light.

Or, to put it another way, Walter Reuther is forever a man on a beachhead, storming some industrial or political rampart with his mighty Auto Workers at his back.

Being Walter Reuther, he's a man of many beachheads.

As Walter Reuther, labor leader, he was the first to win paid vacations and pensions for industrial workers in the mass industries —plus what now comes mighty close to being a guaranteed annual wage.

As Walter Reuther, politician, he has been the first to use his union manpower to build a county political machine—so powerful that it has helped to revive the Democratic party of his home state, Michigan.

As Walter Reuther, public figure and idea man, he argues before Congressional Committees for laws to police corporation prices. He has plans for saving India, for solving inflation, for abolishing unemployment—and for a hundred-billion-dollar scheme to make the planet prosperous—and non-Communist.

With all this, Walter Reuther has created a public image of himself that is only part union leader. He is one of the few labor leaders who has captured the public imagination.

Being out front, he stirs bitter feelings.

Few men can arouse hate enough, and be great enough to become known as "That Man." Franklin D. Roosevelt was one. John L. Lewis was another. Today, it's Walter Reuther.

A Day with Walter Reuther

First thing Reuther opens his eyes on in the morning is a view from a picture window of a tumbling stream and a pond. Both the room and the view tell of a man who's improving his world—even in his spare time. For both the room and the pond were built by Reuther.

When police advised him to take security measures after gangsters almost shot his left arm away in an attempt to kill him in 1948, Reuther bought a small house and four acres of land outside Detroit, for which he paid $10,000. When doctors advised him to exercise his injured arm and hand, he took to cabinetmaking, and as a one-time skilled toolmaker was soon filling his house with floor-to-ceiling bookcases, with tables and hi-fi cabinets. But, being Reuther, he went on to build whole rooms as well, getting assists from friends as needed. So the house that started out modestly with living room, kitchen and one bedroom grew into a rambling glass and redwood structure with two additional bedrooms, a sun porch and TV room —all carpentered by Reuther. And on the grounds, with the help of friends, he dug his pond.

As Reuther begins his day, he is likely to have three or four dogs yipping at his heels—among them a canine of indeterminate origin which Reuther's teen-age daughter, Linda, brought home and dubbed "Soapy," because on the dog's chest is a mark reminiscent of the bow ties worn by "Soapy" Williams, the Governor of Michigan.

Linda is away at boarding school and Reuther shares the dogs, and the home, with his wife May, a former schoolteacher, and with their daughter Lisa.

An abstemious man who neither drinks nor smokes, Reuther makes no vice of food either, taking a breakfast of toast, tea and fruit. Later he'll nibble on some fruit or a hamburger at his desk for lunch, dictating or conferring at the same time. So, in effect, he has but one full meal a day.

When the notoriety concerning Dave Beck's high living and $150,000 mansion made all labor leaders self-conscious about the way they live, Reuther invited reporters to visit his home—to scotch rumors that he lived on a luxurious estate. The reporters explored Reuther's "do-it-yourself" home, made small talk with a surprisingly relaxed and warm Reuther, gobbled May Reuther's cooking—and were asked only one thing in return. Would they keep a closely guarded secret—the location of Reuther's place? Would they say, merely, that it is thirty-five miles northwest of Detroit?

To get to his car for the hour drive to his Detroit office, Reuther must cross a small bridge across the trout stream that makes an island of his home. "I'm the only union leader who lives behind a moat," he quips.

A path soon brings Reuther to another bridge, and another small island, and from there across a wide expanse of lawn to a small security house at the gate of a ten-foot-high steel fence. Two German shepherd dogs who roam the grounds at night frolic around Reuther as he greets the armed guard at the gate and enters his car.

For a year after the assassination attempt, Reuther was driven to work in an armored limousine at the suggestion of Secret Service experts, who pointed out that the most likely place for another ambush might be Reuther's daily traveled route to his office. But Reuther balked at the idea of a labor leader riding in a limousine even to protect his life and gave up the armored car for the medium-priced autos his union rents for its staff.

Reuther's discomfort in the limousine underlies a rejection of conspicuous consumption so stern as to border on the fanatic. Although Reuther's old salary of $18,000 was but a fraction of the $50,000 and more paid to other union presidents, he stoutly resisted an increase until his vice-presidents complained his wage was holding down theirs. He then consented glumly to a $4,000-a-year boost to $22,000.

Reuther made a public show of his distaste for the AFL-CIO Executive Council's habit of holding its winter meetings at plush Miami Beach, Florida. He'd fly down there in a cut-rate overnight airplane coach flight. He would squeeze his own orange juice for breakfast in his hotel room—then for dinner would take May Reuther and the kids several blocks down the street to a cafeteria that featured a $1.70 special.

This conspicuous underconsumption didn't increase Reuther's popularity with fellow unionists. And when Reuther's constant beefing against meeting at Miami Beach precipitated a full-dress heated Executive Council debate, even Reuther's old friend, David Dubinsky, took after him. Even a laborer's leader is worthy of his hire, Dubinsky remonstrated. But Reuther, ever effective, had his way. (P.S. Reuther or no Reuther, Labor's foxy elders took their 1959 winter meeting to sunny San Juan, Puerto Rico.)

67

Reuther drives to his office with one of three bodyguards. These unsmiling young men are quietly on hand, nearby, wherever Reuther happens to be. If you call on Reuther at his hotel room, a guard will probably open the door. If you walk down the street with Reuther, one or two of the young men will walk along behind. Even when Reuther is locked in secret bargaining sessions with auto executives, a guard is outside—usually playing poker with the waiting reporters, his gun tucked handily inside his pants belt.

As Reuther's car enters the driveway to the United Auto Workers' headquarters on the Detroit River in Detroit, Reuther might muse on the mutability of things. His UAW, which began by meeting secretly in a basement, is now housed in a striking three-story tile and glass structure—with a penthouse for executives' meetings. Called Solidarity House, it rests on land that once was Edsel Ford's estate. In fact, the UAW now uses as a health center the graystone mansion in which Edsel Ford was born.

Reuther enters this businesslike headquarters that houses five hundred executives, technicians and clerical workers who provide the manifold services a giant union gives to its members.

Like a big corporation, the UAW has legal, auditing and purchasing departments, community and public relations staffs. But Reuther's union has departments that corporations—and many other unions—don't have. There is the political action department that turns members into voters and party workers. And, as you might expect of a union run by Reuther, there is a "special projects" office—a kind of "forward planning" department headed by a "brain" who could be called a vice-president in charge of thinking.[2]

Reuther's paneled office, the size of a large living room, has a wall-to-wall picture window, just as his bedroom has. Through it, from behind the oversized conference table-desk of his own design, Reuther can look out on a majestic oak on the lawn that once was Edsel Ford's, and beyond that to the Detroit River and Canada.[3]

Close up, Reuther, now past fifty, has the look and bounce of a

---

[2] Nat Weinberg, the respected economist who holds this post, is no elected vice-president, but a staff man with the title "Director of Special Projects."

[3] Ford family real estate has an odd way of turning up in union hands. In New York City David Dubinsky of the Garment Workers occupies the office once used by Edsel Ford.

man in his vigorous thirties. That is because time has neither thinned nor dulled the vivid thatch of hair that won Reuther his nickname, "the redhead." His slight, trim figure (he's about five feet seven inches tall) shows no sign of middle-age spread. And his fine-featured face lights up with youthful excitement when Reuther talks —which is a good deal of the time.

I saw Reuther soon after he had endured some thirty-eight hours of almost continuous bargaining with the Ford Motor Company. Yet, with only a few hours of sleep, his hazel eyes sparkled, and, when he was carried away by some point he was making, he'd tuck one foot under him in his chair, like a boy. Reuther's fresh and youthful appearance is furthered by a meticulous neatness, a heritage of orderliness bequeathed by his Teutonic parents.

Reuther may be as "controversial" as John L. Lewis was, but cartoonists won't have the holiday with him that they did with Lewis' brooding face and bulldog dewlaps. For how can you caricature the perpetual clean-cut all-American boy who didn't miss a Sunday school session in seven years?

For two decades now, Reuther has been called a "young labor leader," and you have a feeling as you watch him that he'll still be called a "youthful union leader" when he's sixty.

Reuther's press aide, Frank Winn, had said, "Walter can give you an hour."

But Walter, launched on talk, forgets his own time strictures. Talk is the vice-free Walter Reuther's one great indulgence, his meat and drink. "Ask Walter what time it is," a friend quipped, "and he'll tell you how to put together a watch."

Although Reuther is a stimulating conversationalist and effective platform performer ("What an amazing, stimulating fellow he is," India's Nehru said of him), his enthusiasm sometimes leads him into punishing verbosity. When he was elected president of the old CIO in 1952, he rewarded his brother delegates with two hours of lofty rhetoric that almost put them to sleep. Neither time nor place can deter Reuther. Although it was 3 A.M., and his own negotiators as well as those of Ford were heavy-lidded and emotionally spent as the end of the 1958 contract negotiations approached, Reuther launched on an hour's sermon concerning, "bargaining attitudes."

"I reached them philosophically," Reuther reported happily later.

69

It may have been a coincidence, but right after Reuther's predawn philosophizing the negotiators took a five-hour respite.

Reuther's answers to questions are studded with phrases which, in another man, might seem self-conscious. "The human family without a cause deteriorates," he'll say. Or: "Are the new frontiers more TV sets for people? Or should people have a sense of self-fulfillment?"

Yet Reuther gets these off with such eagerness and warmth that there is nothing ponderous about them. And in his office are reminders to visitors that the talk about causes is more than just words. In the bookshelf behind him are plaques and medals. One honors Reuther's successful fight to open up job opportunities for Negroes. Imbedded in a bookend, of his own make, is a tear-gas shell that was fired into the auto plant which Reuther commanded and held during the sitdown strikes.

Reuther's desk also reminds the visitor that Reuther—who deals with some of the world's biggest managements—is a manager of considerable proportions himself. A panel of six push buttons connects him with four executive assistants and two elected subordinates. The latter, elected with Reuther at the union's biennial conventions, are part of the union hierarchy whom rank and filers half fondly, and half suspiciously call "porkchoppers"—union payrollers. In the brawling UAW, the politicking has been so turbulent that few of the union's early porkchoppers have survived in office.

One exception, besides Reuther, is the union's jolly, round-faced secretary-treasurer, Emil Mazey. A onetime Hungarian fiddler, Mazey achieved UAW immortality when he was thrown bodily from a plant he was trying to organize—and, picking himself off his back, shouted, "I'll be back, you sons of bitches. I'll be back and organize this plant."

Mazey not only kept his word but had the shrewd sense to tie his union fortunes to those of Reuther—then only a factional leader.

The UAW may be the "world's most democratic union," as its own literature says, but Reuther has achieved such political mastery over it that he has been able to pick his likely successor, the man with whom Reuther and Mazey share Solidarity House's executive suite. This is the thoughtful and bespectacled Leonard Woodcock. Educated in England, Woodcock for years was Reuther's executive

70

assistant, a non-elective staff job. Then, with Reuther's support, he ran for local office and quickly rose to be vice-president in charge of the General Motors Department—the No. 2 spot in the union.

As an executive, Reuther is an "involver." A cautious and calculating man—despite his glibness—he involves his subordinates in talk fests that test ideas and plans. Before Reuther took the stand to answer McClellan Committee questions concerning the UAW's three-year strike against Kohler of Kohler (Wisconsin), Reuther's executive assistant, Jack Conway, spent hours digesting prior Committee testimony. Reuther, briefed with this material, then spent three hours testing ideas and notions on Conway—who has done graduate work in sociology at two universities—and on his Washington lawyer, Joseph Rauh, who specializes in civil rights cases, and his press man, Frank Winn.

The intellectual candlepower available to Reuther—through staff technicians and elected subordinates—is regarded by union men as among the brightest in Labor.

Concerning Walter Reuther, Politician

Walter Reuther was catapulted into practical politics because of a strange problem of coexistence. He shared the same home base, Detroit, with another great labor power—James R. Hoffa. The inevitable clash took the form of a subterranean struggle which turned the UAW into a county political boss, reshaped the politics of a state—and made Walter Reuther an important political figure.

"Candidates for office in this town can't win unless they have the endorsement of the Auto Workers," a Detroit judge told me.

"They'd get down on their knees and kiss Walter Reuther's feet on the steps of the City Hall to get it," the judge said.

This is because Walter Reuther and the Auto Workers have built in Wayne County—which embraces Detroit and suburbs—a political machine at which a professional politician might marvel. A political war between Reuther (and allies) and Hoffa brought it about.

In 1948, Hoffa, contributing Teamster funds, made a power grab for the Democratic party machinery of the state, then in such disrepair that Michigan was virtually a one-party, Republican state. First, Hoffa captured the state Democratic Committee at a stormy

71

meeting. Hoffa's lawyer and partner in deals later probed by the Senate was named national Democratic committeeman for the state. This was George Fitzgerald. The coup gave Hoffa a voice over federal patronage in Michigan, then valuable because the Democrats were in power in Washington. Another Hoffa lawyer took over as state chairman of the Democratic party.

At this point, Walter Reuther and allies counterattacked. The key to the control of Democratic party machinery in Michigan is the Detroit area—Wayne County. For from it come some 40 per cent of the delegates to the state Democratic convention.

Until now, Hoffa had grabbed for political power by manipulating at the top—by making deals that gave him a national committeeman and state chairman. But now, in 1950, he tried to build power at the bottom by going after the precinct delegates, who could make Hoffa the Democratic boss of the state.

It takes a petition with twenty signatures to put a delegate's name on the primary ballot. As filed by Hoffa's cronies, these were interesting for their informality.

"We noticed an astonishing number of petitions filed," a Hoffa critic said later. "Some one thousand out of twenty-three hundred petitions were fraudulent in the wildest way," Neil Staebler, the state Democratic chairman, told me. "On many petitions, all twenty signatures were in the same handwriting. Even the notary's signature was in the same hand, indicating that one penman had done it all."

Other petitions, it turned out, had been produced by a method known as the "round robin." Groups of Hoffa admirers had sat sociably around a table, signing fictitious names to the petitions, round-robin fashion, in varying handwritings.

Reuther rallied his Auto Workers to enter precinct politics and run for office as delegates. Hoffa was routed, yielding the Democratic party machinery of Wayne County to Reuther and the UAW.

Today, Walter Reuther—ever the man on a beachhead—has harnessed his UAW to a unique political operation that may have considerable significance to the future of American politics. By working strictly within the traditional two-party system, Reuther and his members have fashioned a miniature labor government on a local, county-wide scale that stands as a pilot plant operation for other labor leaders to copy.

72

It's true that conditions in Wayne County are unique. For in the area are concentrated some 350,000 members of a disciplined, aggressive union, the UAW. With their wives, these UAW members account for 60 per cent of Wayne County's registered voters. In the county, too, are the union headquarters and officers who can influence these voters.

Walter Reuther probably works harder than any other labor leader at the job of involving members in union work and union decisions—and in selling his point of view to them. Since relatively few members go to meetings, this takes a lot of doing. But Reuther is a pioneer here too.

"Even if a man doesn't want to come to meetings to listen, you can chase him with your point of view," a Reuther aide said.

The chasing is done with radio programs tailored for the auto workers and beamed at them twice daily as they drive to work for the early shift at 6 A.M. or for the afternoon shift at 3 P.M. A Sunday television program catches the auto worker, relaxed in his home.

The "chaser" is a gifted onetime Rhodes scholar by the name of Guy Nunn. Auto executives say of Guy Nunn and his broadcasts that he is "forever fighting the class struggle." And the Justice Department accused the Auto Workers of violating the Corrupt Practices Act by giving television time to favored political candidates and so making a disguised political contribution contrary to law. The union argued successfully before a jury that the television program was nothing more than a means of keeping in touch with union members. In any case, the Auto Workers spend some $400,000 yearly in communicating with the members and letting them have the union's view as to where their interests lie.

Naturally, the broadcasts play an important part in shaping members' political thinking. The second step is to get the members to the polls, and this is done through the citizenship and political action department—headed by a full-time director, Walter Reuther's younger brother, Roy.

How all this works out in the practical business of winning elections was spelled out by the UAW's own paper, *Solidarity*, soon after labor support helped sweep Mennen (Soapy) Williams into his sixth term as Governor, and sweep out Republican Senator Charles Potter.

"Here It Is, GOP; Democracy Is our Secret Weapon," a two-page,

73

center-spread headline proclaimed.

"In nearly half the states," an introduction read, "Republicans ran hard against 'labor bosses' in general and most especially against Walter Reuther. According to the GOP propaganda, these 'labor bosses' dictated the choice of candidates and herded the members behind them. Most UAW members know better; and those who know best are the hundreds, perhaps thousands of rank and filers who have devoted countless hours to the hard, indispensable routine of politics—without pay. . . ."

The article revealed that candidates seeking the coveted Wayne County labor endorsement must undergo a grilling by a precinct committee of union members, then fill out a searching questionnaire, probing personal as well as political matters.

Once the candidate is endorsed, an army of UAW members will ring doorbells for him, pass out literature, set up shop committees to register workers and on Election Day bring these workers to the polls—and serve as poll watchers.

For all the political power the Auto Workers wield in and around Detroit, Reuther keeps discreetly in the background, and control of the state Democratic machinery is in the hands of two other men. One is Michigan's Governor, Soapy Williams. The other is a well-to-do retired businessman, turned political pro, whom the Republican Detroit *Free Press* has described as "The Democrats' Miracle Man." This is the state Democratic chairman, Neil Staebler, who is credited with restoring two-party government to a state that once was so overwhelmingly Republican that, in 1925–26, there wasn't one Democrat in the state's 144-member legislature. Staebler, of course, works closely with the Auto Workers.

I asked Democratic State Chairman Staebler about Walter Reuther's role in state politics.

"Reuther gets labor active. That's his importance," Staebler said. "Since the Auto Workers muster about one-third of the state convention delegates, they have a veto power over candidates," Staebler added. "But Reuther, himself, doesn't get involved in choosing candidates."

In Detroit, you inevitably hear that "Walter [Reuther] has Soapy [Williams] in his pocket."

Concerning this, Staebler said, "If Williams and Reuther had an argument, Williams would win. If Labor tried to capture the Democratic party in this state," he went on, "they would wind up holding only themselves captive. For they'd lose public support."

On examination, Walter Reuther emerges as somewhat less than the putative czar of the national Democratic party—and of Congress —that the full-page political ads proclaimed him in the fall of 1958. In Reuther's own Michigan, for instance, eleven of the eighteen Congressional contests went to Republicans. Reuther himself, according to Democratic Chairman Neil Staebler, hasn't had occasion to see or talk to Soapy Williams since the Democratic national convention of 1956. But when lobbyists for the Auto Workers come up to the state capital at Lansing—according to one GOP observer—they both see and talk to Soapy. In fact, they sometimes do their lobbying right in the Governor's office—by bringing lawmakers to Soapy and discussing legislative problems in front of him.

What Walter Wants

Where Reuther is going and how he is going to get there is a speculation on which friends and enemies lavish considerable energy, ingenuity and heat.

Since people look for big things from Reuther, he is asked from time to time whether he has ambitions to be President of the United States. This he denies.

I once heard two reporters speculate approvingly about the sort of job "Walter could do as Secretary of State." Others, notably office seekers, have insisted that Reuther wants to grab Congress and rule a Socialist America.

One good way to find out what Reuther wants is to see what he has already won—and what he has tried to get but couldn't.

Back in 1946, Reuther rushed in where other labor leaders feared to tread. He asked the auto companies to raise wages but hold down auto prices, so making a bargaining issue out of a management prerogative. Reuther was still concerning himself with prices twelve years later, this time in Washington. As a witness before Senator Estes Kefauver's Anti-Trust Monopoly Subcommittee, early in 1958, Reuther unveiled a new "Reuther plan," a proposal for a

75

Public Review Board to watch over the prices of the big corporations.[4]

What Walter wanted here—government and union restraints on price setting—Walter didn't get—at least not yet.[5]

But other things he got, and he got them first. One Reuther aim was to have industry share with government the responsibility of caring for idle or aged workers. Here is how he achieved it.

First, in 1949, Reuther asked employers to grant pensions to factory workers, an historic innovation. When these were granted, Reuther then set out to increase old-age pensions for factory workers all over America. Social Security pension payments averaged thirty-two dollars monthly in 1949, and Labor's efforts to lobby increases had been blocked by business opposition.

Reuther gave business opponents an alternative. We want hundred-dollar monthly pensions, he indicated. Either we get the additional sixty-eight dollars from the government—to which you contribute half by law—or we'll use our economic power to get all of the sixty-eight dollars from you. Business opposition to the higher Social Security pension payments promptly vanished, and Congress soon increased them.

"The UAW did a job for the American people," Reuther said later.

Reuther wanted to protect his auto workers against layoffs and asked for a guaranteed annual wage. The Ford Company, fearful of having to accept an unworkable scheme, set a secret task force to work and surprised Reuther with a counterproposal, in which Ford would supplement the state unemployment insurance payments to idle workers. The plan, now prevalent in the auto and other industries, gives an idle worker up to 65 per cent of his regular pay for as long as thirty-nine weeks, three-fourths of a year.

General Motors, too, came through with historic voluntary benefits. One is an escalator clause which automatically raises auto workers' pay when living costs rise. Another is an automatic 2½

---

[4] Reuther proposed that corporations that dominate 20 per cent of any one market be made to justify proposed price increases in public hearings before a review board which, however, could have no veto power over price decisions.

[5] Senator Estes Kefauver announced in December, 1958, that he would seek legislation along the lines Walter Reuther suggested.

per cent yearly pay increase—to let the auto worker share in the continuing increase of productivity due to more efficient machinery.

When Reuther wants something he has no right to bargain for—like lower auto prices—he tends to strain relations with those around him.

"Is the UAW fighting the fight of the whole world?" A G.M. executive once demanded when Reuther was arguing at the bargaining table against higher auto prices.

"Why don't you get down to your size?" the executive went on. "And get down to the type of job you're supposed to be doing as a trade union leader and talk about money you'd like to have for your people—and let the labor statesmanship go to hell for a while?"

It's true that top auto executives regard Reuther as a leader who holds a disciplined work force together and so gives stability to the industry. It's true, too, there have been eras of good feeling. Charles E. Wilson when president of General Motors once told Reuther, "I have great respect for you and your leadership."

But, today, Reuther's relations with the industry are a mixture of grudging togetherness and hostile coexistence.

Executives can't forget Reuther's early Socialism or his trip as a youth to the Soviet Union, where he worked as a tool and die maker. They distrust his aims.

"Sure, he hasn't got his hand in the union till, as some leaders have," one executive said. "But he's got his hand in your kid's mind."

The industry's resentment also reflects Reuther's sizable dimensions as an antagonist—and his success in winning what he goes after.

"Why do they hate Walter Reuther?" I asked a Reuther admirer, his Washington lawyer.

"Because he's so effective," the friend said happily.

I asked the same question of a Detroit auto executive.

"Because he's so damned effective," the critic answered gloomily.

Criticism from within the industry—and from without—doesn't deter Reuther. He even has a Reuther plan for licking his wounds. Once a year, he gets together with Mrs. Eleanor Roosevelt, a close friend. Each gets out a clipping of the strongest thing that critics have said. Reuther may read aloud from a full-page political ad:

"This is an emergency—immediate and dangerous. Walter Reuther is already within reach of controlling your Congress." Mrs. Roosevelt will match this. "They talk it out," a Reuther aide said, "and each feels better."

So fortified, Walter Reuther goes on storming new beachheads.

The 1958 negotiations with Ford were barely over when Reuther was gathering his braintrusters around him in his office. The new contract, just negotiated, would run for three years. But Reuther was already setting his intellectual task force to work on the Reuther plan or plans that would explode over Detroit in 1961.

Within the labor movement, among his own peers, there are mixed feelings about Walter Reuther.

The old-line building trades leaders who came into the Federation from the old AF of L mistrust Reuther's social unionism. Besides, the scars of the old fights between the CIO industrial unionism and the AF of L craft unionism have not yet healed; new rows are breaking out—as to who should organize whom.

Although Reuther is just another one of the twenty-six vice presidents of the AFL-CIO he's recognized informally as the chief vice president, because he was president of the old CIO. Inside the Council, he acts like the first vice president. He's the most articulate to begin with. But he's also the most assertive and the most demanding.

"Let's look at it," he'll say. "Let me give you my opinion. Let's study it." Most of the other vice presidents are too lazy to indulge in this intellectual labor, but they resent Reuther anyway.

As for Meany and Reuther, there is a certain edginess about their relations.

Although many in the AFL-CIO grumble about Reuther, some of the wiser heads believe he's the man most likely to inherit George Meany's mantle.

"What's your hurry, you SOB," a fellow vice president, older in years and experience, asked Reuther. "Why are you so impatient? George Meany isn't a spring chicken any more. And you have something none of us have—and that's youth."

In the older man's judgment, there was no other heir except Reuther.

Perhaps. But the second industrial revolution confronts Reuther and his union with problems of crisis proportions. If Reuther comes up with creative solutions, there will be no way to defeat "That Man."

CHAPTER 6

The Man Who
Lives with a Ghost

David J. McDonald, president of the 1,000,000-member United Steelworkers of America, is a man whose doom it is to live with a ghost. The ghost is that of the late Philip Murray who was the Steelworkers' founder, first president—and much else besides. Phil Murray died in 1952, but no Steelworkers convention opens without its moment of prayer for the departed Phil; few speeches to a rally of Steelworkers may omit their respects to Murray. In fact, no day in the private or labor life of McDonald may pass without the inevitable comparisons with his great predecessor.

Since Murray is one of the saints of the Labor movement, no one can come off well in the comparison. To the steel workers, McDonald is a remote and aloof figure whom they rarely see in the flesh but more often in their newspapers, where he appears as an elegantly togged-out man who is indistinguishable from the company executive with whom he's posing.

What the steel worker remembers of Murray is the image of a humble, homespun man who spoke his men's language and had the fatherly answers to the steel workers' problems. The steel worker—when he thinks of it—doesn't like the change. In fact, the rank-and-file millhands feel so strongly about it that, in addition to living with a ghost, McDonald has had to live with a revolt. Murray was the

79

founding father. McDonald, his successor, had only to be the steward who preserves a going concern. On the face of it he has been a good steward. McDonald has won pay boosts that make the steel workers among the highest paid industrial workers in America.

For all that, a volcano of rank-and-file unrest boiled over in a fantastic election campaign in 1957 in which an obscure millhand ran against President McDonald and—in the face of McDonald's well-heeled campaign—gathered one of every three votes.

The heads of most unions have matters so well in hand that usually there is no opposition to them. To be opposed, then, as McDonald was, is bad enough. To be opposed by an unknown mill-hand is worse. To lose big locals to this unknown is to lose face with fellow labor leaders.

The USA, one of the three unions that can boast a million members or more,[1] is entitled to an important voice in the counsels of Labor. So McDonald is a vice-president of the AFL-CIO Executive Council and a member of its more select steering or executive committee. But McDonald's is a quiet voice.

To understand McDonald, it is necessary to digress, briefly, to Phil Murray.

The Steelworkers' executive suite on the twelfth floor of downtown Pittsburgh's Commonwealth Building differs little from the quietly plush diggings with which the big wheels of business surround themselves, say, on New York's Madison Avenue.

The floors are carpeted wall to wall; the furnishings, of mahogany, are in solid good taste. The walls, of course, are pine-paneled.

Here, the corner office, with cross ventilation and a double view, was occupied until his death by Phil Murray, then head of the union and the CIO, too. As any organization man knows, the corner office is the symbol of the arrived man—to be occupied, by hierarchic right, by the chief, the boss. Yet, symbolically, Dave McDonald, although president, abjures the corner office where Phil Murray once ruled. He continues to occupy the office he had as

---

[1] The Teamsters had 1,600,000 in 1959; the United Auto Workers, 1,000,000.

secretary-treasurer. Phil's office remains empty, a shrine to the great man.

To this corner office Phil Murray would come daily by streetcar from his modest six-room brick house in suburban Brookline nearby.

The streetcar ride typified the man who was once described as having a constitutional aversion to side.

Murray, although absolute master of his union, seldom summoned understrappers to his office; he got up and went to them. A humble man, he never forgot his origins, that of a coal digger. Nor did he, as he himself put it, "ever have any doubt what I wanted to do with my life,"—i.e., organize unions.

Murray became one of the mighty of the land, visited the White House, sat down to negotiate with the rugged individuals of the steel industry. To these he became, in time, a respected equal, and to some, like Benjamin F. Fairless, ex-chairman of the board of Big Steel, a friend. Yet, to relax, he would visit his kinfolk in the Pennsylvania coal towns from which he sprang. He remained a sentimental miner with a Scotch burr in his speech and could work on a man's emotions, shedding a tear himself if it served the occasion's purpose.

Murray reduced union negotiations with management to simple terms. "What do we want for our people?" he'd say. "Pictures on the wall, carpets on the floor and music in the home."

Although Murray did as much as any man to change the American worker "proletariat" to a contented middle class, he clung with fierce devotion to his early working family origins. He rejected the trappings of the well-to-do managerial class. He never owned a dinner jacket and would rent and wear one only on those occasions when he was honored by his own Catholic Church.

To the steel worker, Murray was Phil, the kindly father. He had a genuine affection for people. He was, as the steel and mine workers said, "one of us." He had the common touch.

Hamlet

Unlike Murray, who "never had a doubt in my mind about what I wanted to do," McDonald had grave doubts. McDonald, with one of the longest careers in the Labor movement—some thirty years—doesn't seem to be *of* the Labor movement.

81

In his late fifties, McDonald is a well-preserved, theatrically handsome man. His nose is finely chiseled, with flaring nostrils; his eyes are a deep blue and his hair a sparkling platinum gray, so meticulously parted and brushed as to give the impression that McDonald spent a good deal of time on it that morning.

The theatrical air is deepened by McDonald's ever-present pipe and his studied garb. The pipe McDonald uses as a prop, in the way a British officer uses a swagger stick. The clothes are usually the kind of custom-tailored, three-buttoned casual slack suits dispensed by the conservative but style-setting firm of Brooks Brothers on New York's Madison Avenue. This is for the role of businesslike unionist. For other roles there are other ensembles.

So, at conferences of labor leaders in Miami Beach, other union men may affect the informal air of the working class they stemmed from. But not McDonald. When others doffed their coats, rolled up their sleeves and opened their shirts at the neck during an outing on an aircraft carrier off Miami Beach, McDonald was conspicuously the last word in resort elegance. Over his wavy platinum hair was a jaunty cap of motley color. Beneath a tailored Harris tweed jacket was a cardigan sweater of the finest cashmere. The razor-edged slacks fell over fawn-colored sport shoes. McDonald had dressed for the occasion with the care of a stage figure who is always aware of his audience.

McDonald is, in fact, a labor leader who has always wanted to play Hamlet. He once studied for the theater and has a drama certificate from the Carnegie Institute of Technology to prove it. With McDonald, to be or not to be a professional union man rested on pure chance. McDonald was a male stenographer in his twenties when, at a chance street meeting with a friend, he heard there was a secretary's job open with a man by the name of Philip Murray. Who's Philip Murray, McDonald wanted to know. When young McDonald found out (Murray was then a vice-president of the United Mine Workers), and learned further that the salary would be three times that of his current earnings, he brushed up on his shorthand, applied for the job and got it.

He remained Murray's secretary, disciple and union housekeeper for more than thirteen years with a ringside view of great organizing drives of the late thirties. Yet for years he flirted with other careers.

He studied accounting nights at Duquesne University. Later he studied drama at Carnegie Tech. He took a Hollywood screen test and toyed with a proposition to become an assistant movie director. However, when the Steelworkers Organizing Committee was founded, Murray became president and McDonald secretary-treasurer. Then McDonald gave up the theater and the screen, but he never gave up being an actor.

Man of Steel

As president of the Steelworkers, McDonald is not content simply to administer a union of a million men. He plays a part. He is a man of steel. His authorized biography, written two years after McDonald assumed office, is actually entitled *Man of Steel*. The book, now mercifully suppressed by McDonald's own aides—and hard to come by—manfully struggles in the rhetoric of the Horatio Alger classics to portray the elegant McDonald as the son of exploited toilers who became the workers' dedicated Messiah.

"Instead of Three Bears and Goldilocks," the official biography states, "Mother McDonald told her children exciting and suspenseful stories of how their father had to sneak off to the woods for union meetings."

The matchless Dave, according to this biography, stood at the top of his class. "If he didn't make a grade of 98 in any subject, it irked him, and he would plug away until reaching that mark." But, lest the reader think that young David was a greasy grind and so unfit to lead the steel workers, the biography hastens to add: "Every afternoon, Dave would race home to get the games organized. His talent for organizing took root in these games."

The men who formed Murray's inner circle in the early steel-organizing days will tell you that McDonald's role in the Steelworkers Organizing Committee was little more than that of an office manager and keeper of the financial records. His official biography unashamedly casts him in a more heroic role.

"He [McDonald] smoothed off the rough edges of 'Big Steel,' completed the organization of 'Little Steel' [the book relates], and handled the contract negotiating conferences with Bethlehem, Republic, Youngstown and Inland Steel companies.

83

"It was a sizable assignment, accomplished with finesse. *Perhaps it was the actor, rising to a great role*."

"An actor rising to a great role" must speak like one when he addresses the people he leads.

McDonald's public utterances are reminiscent of the man on the balcony, talking to a cheering, crowded square.

"Today we number 1,224,000 men of steel," he will orate, then go on with something like: "I have gone into Central and South America, Canada and Europe to bring American industrial democracy to the troubled peoples of those troubled lands."

Famed for his tortured and turgid rhetoric, McDonald doesn't talk about Negroes, for instance; he talks about "members of minority groups bearing proudly the cross of darker skins." Naturally, the 250,000-odd Negroes in the USA, the thousands of Hungarians, Poles, Irish and other plain folk who make up the vast melting pot that is the Steelworkers Union have little idea of what McDonald is talking about. He probably has less communication with the members he leads than any union president in America.

Man of Silk

When McDonald married his first wife, the daughter of a socially prominent lawyer, it was in 1937, in the midst of the CIO drive to organize the bitterly resisting Little Steel companies. Steel workers were on strike, ragged and hungry. The picture of McDonald playing the bridegroom in a brilliant society wedding so angered some of them that there were threats of picketing the affair.

When McDonald's bride was pictured in Pittsburgh's society pages decked out in riding togs at a fashionable suburb, Phil Murray could barely control himself. "He ranted and raved about McDonald," an eyewitness recalls.

Later, as president, McDonald moved into a fine suburban home, the sort of home a United States Steel vice-president might live in. But, although he lived well, McDonald was not accepted by the social elite of Pittsburgh. The executives with whom he negotiated across the bargaining table were cordial, but the bid to the fashionable Duquesne Club on which McDonald had set his heart never came.

84

McDonald next set his cap for the University Club. Here a college degree was required. No college graduate, McDonald—a prominent Catholic—sought to obtain an honorary degree from some Catholic school. But here a personal problem intervened. McDonald had been divorced from his society wife, but could not obtain a Vatican divorce. McDonald had married a second time—his secretary. The McDonalds, devout Catholics both, go to Mass regularly, but are barred from the sacraments or confession. It is a matter, friends say, that weighs heavily on McDonald, who was born into a devout Irish family and educated in Catholic parochial schools. As one close associate of McDonald put it, "They [Dave and Rosemary McDonald] live together always in fear of the Good Lord upstairs."

Unable to make the higher reaches of Pittsburgh society, McDonald does the next best thing. He is seen in café society—where a man is welcome if he is a "celebrity," can hold his gibsons and pay for his *pâté de foie gras* and *filets mignons*.

In this café society milieu and elsewhere, union leader McDonald leads a life that is self-indulgent, or, as one observer put it, "Legal—but decadent."

He is chauffeured in limousines, is known and obsequiously "mistered" by headwaiters at "Club 21" in New York. At Miami Beach, for an AFL-CIO Executive Council meeting, he stayed at a $122-a-day suite in the most currently fashionable hotel—the Americana. With him in a fifty-dollar room nearby was a detective companion he had brought with him from Pittsburgh.

Denied the exclusive company of a swank Pittsburgh club, McDonald has sought companionship of a less respectable sort, consorting with a figure later excoriated before the McClellan Committee. Although the man was appealing a conviction and jail sentence for being a fence for stolen goods, McDonald was seen with him at labor meetings, and he attended a dinner in honor of McDonald.

During the last years of Phil Murray's life, there was doubt that Dave McDonald, by then the secretary-treasurer of the United Steelworkers, would succeed Murray as president.

Once when Murray lay seriously ill, McDonald hastily wired

other steel union leaders to stand by in case of Murray's death. Murray, recovering, administered a cruel tongue lashing to McDonald, winding up with, "I'm running this union, and I don't need an office boy to tell me how to do it."

Yet, like other strong leaders before him, Murray made no provision for the succession. Like other strong leaders, too, Murray so ruled that no strong second man could emerge. Able and respected leaders like Vice-President Clinton Golden fell away. McDonald, meanwhile—as the man in charge of records and money—made those contacts with staff employees in the field that served him well politically. When Murray died, there was scattered opposition to McDonald, but he had the votes on the executive board to win the presidency.

Murray had been president both of the Steelworkers and of the then CIO. His vacated leadership of the CIO fell to the president of the United Automobile Workers, Walter Reuther.

To live with the ghost of Phil Murray was bad enough, but to live in the shadow of Reuther was intolerable to McDonald's vanity. After all, McDonald headed a union as big and powerful as that of Reuther's Auto Workers. McDonald set about to crowd Reuther from the center of the stage.

So, in 1954, McDonald teamed up with John L. Lewis, whose power for mischief had outlived his power in Labor, and with Dave Beck, then new as Teamster president. Reporters soon were calling the loose alliance the Lewis-McBeck axis.

The Lewis-McBeck Axis was to strike a blow at its enemies Walter Reuther and George Meany in September, 1954, at the Steelworkers' biennial convention at Atlantic City. Here, so McDonald's critics allege, he planned to take his union for a walk out of the CIO—then into a new federation with Lewis and Beck. The delegates, however, didn't want to leave the CIO. To many of them, the titles CIO and United Steelworkers were interchangeable.

When McDonald discovered that he was a general without an army, he announced an about-face. Instead of taking the Steelworkers out of the CIO, he urged that all Labor close ranks by

86

merging the CIO with the AF of L. Pressure by McDonald on the hesitant Reuther did indeed speed the merger.

When the CIO and AF of L merged, Reuther stepped down as president of the CIO and became a vice-president of the new AFL-CIO—just like McDonald. At last he was out from under the shadow of his rival, Reuther.

Storm

Considering the well-being that unionism has brought to the Steelworkers in twenty brief years, you'd expect contentment and gratitude among rank-and-file members—and tranquillity in the union.

It seems only yesterday that employers were hiring private armies that shot down strikers as at Homestead, Pennsylvania. Today, steel executives tour the steel plants arm in arm with McDonald. To the union worker, this is a sign that he is at last a first-class industrial citizen with a voice over the conditions of his work.

This voice, expressed through his union, has quadrupled the steel worker's earnings from an average 66 cents an hour in 1936 to $2.68 an hour in 1957. He has been transformed into a middle-class fellow who owns his own home, has a car. The union has won him as much as three weeks' paid vacation plus seven paid holidays as well, including Labor Day and Good Friday. In case of layoff, the millhand with two years seniority gets 65 per cent of his regular pay—the year round under a Supplemental Unemployment Insurance Plan—that is a big foot in the door toward an annual wage.

And where millhands once crowded into squalid company towns, dominated by company police and hostile company politicians, the steelworker today is often a solid citizen who sits on his town's school board, heads blood bank campaigns—or even runs the town as Mayor.[2]

Many of these boons were won during fifteen years of Phil Murray. More had been added in the five years of David McDonald.[3] In

---

[2] At Aliquippa, Pennsylvania, once known as "Siberia" because of company domination, the Mayor and most of the town's council have been Steelworker members.

[3] In labor circles, much of the credit for the Steelworkers' gains is given to the bargaining acumen of the union's lawyer, Arthur J. Goldberg, who is also counsel of the AFL-CIO Ethical Practices Committee.

fact, the contract he signed in 1956 was hailed as the "best contract ever." Soon after, in 1957, a revolt was kindled against McDonald. In a tight election race, an obscure millhand, Donald C. Rarick, almost swept him from office. Why?

"He's a fancy Dan," one steel worker said of McDonald. Another described how once, coming to the International office on a pension matter, he found himself in the elevator with McDonald, but couldn't get up the nerve to shake hands with his own union president. The well-tailored, distant figure was as awesome to him, he said, as the company president. "He don't get to us," the rank and filer said. "He might as well be a man from outer space." Others simply say, "He ain't one of us, and I hate his guts."

Some of the restiveness is not of McDonald's making. The men have long been taught to believe that the employers were out to destroy their union. This, for the most part, is no longer true. Still, as time passes, employers regain some of the confidence they lost in the initial great defeats at the hands of the unions. They tend to assert managerial authority more confidently and fight harder over yielding to employee grievances. This leaves union committeemen and representatives bewildered and frustrated and revives the old fears about employer enmity. It stores up rank-and-file wrath against the union. The men are also jittery about the spector of automation.

Father Owen Rice, a wise and seasoned labor priest of the steel towns, summed it up: "The men in the plants are restless just as the teen-agers are. And it's turned them against their union."

Late in 1956, McDonald lighted the fuse to the members' discontent—and almost blew himself out of office.

At the union's convention, he asked the delegates to increase his pay from $40,000 to $50,000. He also asked for a virtual doubling of dues—from three dollars per month to five dollars. You couldn't convince the steel worker that his added two bucks per month weren't only for McDonald.

So, when the Steelworkers' convention heard the resolution for a dues boost, all hell broke loose. Delegates, instructed by their locals to fight the dues increase, milled around the floor microphones sixty deep.

But they could have saved their breath. McDonald had prudently made those preparations which assured victory. Although most of the USA locals lie east of the Mississippi, the convention was held in Los Angeles, California. Many locals, lacking the expense money to send delegates, had turned over the delegates' proxies to International staff men—who are hired by the president. The convention, consequently, was generously stacked with International men, which is nothing unusual in union conventions.

McDonald shrilled at the anti-dues-hike delegates, cut off debate before the boys had warmed up to their wrath and so mishandled matters that his dues victory was bound to leave scars that in turn could lead only to revolt.

It did.

One frustrated dues protestor was a six-foot, four-inch furnace tender from McKeesport, Pennsylvania, named Donald C. Rarick. Known to his friends as Rip, he is an unlettered, uncomplicated fellow of thirty-nine who earns his living with his hands and is innocent of even the most rudimentary skills needed to administer a big union.

Rarick plunged, with the valor of ignorance, into the most quixotic of all adventures: rebellion against intrenched union power.

First, Rarick buttonholed convention delegates as they were packing for home. Dispersed in locals throughout the land, rank and filers present little threat to those in union power. But, gathered in one place, as in convention, they can complain and conspire. Rarick laid the foundation for a dues protest movement.

The aim at first was simply to sign up 25 per cent of the union's locals to a petition for a new convention. Faced with such a petition, says the union constitution, the president must call a convention. Here Rarick learned the first fact of union life. The president interprets the union constitution. So McDonald had no trouble at all in ruling there could be no new convention. A new convention could only consider new business—not old business like dues.

So Rarick vowed to take the dues fight to the members. He decided to run for president of the Steelworkers.

89

Alas, Poor Rarick!

How do you run for president of a union of 1,000,000 men? It's like seeking proxies from a half million stockholders to upset the management of American Telephone and Telegraph—only more so. To reach each of the million-odd members of the USA with one postcard—just to acquaint them with the name Rarick and let them know your hat's in the ring—would cost $25,000. Where does a millhand get that sort of money?

Yet Rarick did run, and thereby lies a tale. It is a short, short story that dramatizes our unions' most serious illness: the hardening of the unions' democratic arteries. It is virtually impossible, as matters now stand in most unions, for rank-and-file "outs" to oust the "ins" who control the union machinery—including the balloting, the treasury and the favors.

Rarick and his rebels passed the hat at the steel-mill gates in and around his home town, McKeesport, and neighboring Pittsburgh. The dimes, quarters and dollar bills so garnered came to a total of a little more than $8,000. Less than enough, remember, to send that one postcard to the USA's members.

President McDonald, who has not been seen at a plant gate for lo! these many years, passed no hat. He had, for his personal use as candidate, the full resources in men, money and publications of the Steelworkers Union.

First there was the union newspaper, *Steel Labor,* which reaches every member free. Although it is the newspaper of all the members, it saw no Rarick and heard no Rarick in its pre-election edition. The photogenic face of candidate McDonald, on the other hand, beamed from the front page and the entire issue lauded his records and aims.

From the union's treasury came money for local radio programs for McDonald and for full-page ads in local (private) newspapers. And from the treasury came a cool million for a round of regional conferences, in which candidate McDonald—using chartered four-engine planes—made the regional rounds to build his political fences. McDonald protested, of course, that these junkets were not political.

For poor Rarick, even getting on the ballot was a problem. The Steelworkers elect their president by referendum vote. But to get on

90

the ballot the candidate must be nominated by at least forty locals. This meant that the unknown Rarick had to go before this many local meetings—and there, in the face of opposition from local officers allied with McDonald, run against and beat McDonald in a nominating election. This is one of the requirements that Phil Murray—copying the authoritarian United Mine Workers—prudently worked into the USA constitution to keep power in his hands.

Still, Rarick managed to win nominations in ninety-one locals—or fifty-one more than was needed to get him on the election ballot.

McDonald—who had scorned to notice Rarick and his sweaty rebels down below—said that he'd "take off the gloves."

His gloves off, McDonald branded Rarick a "Trotzkyite," which would have startled millhand Rarick if he knew what a Trotzkyite was. Rebels were threatened with expulsion and generally treated as conspirators against the security of the union.

A spy was dispatched to infiltrate Rarick's meetings—in the same way the boss used to plant spies inside union-organizing meetings.

The campaign next was rocked with sensational charges. Rarick reported that he was approached by one Armand Carlomagno, an ex-convict who heads the Teamsters' taxi local in Pittsburgh. First, said Rarick, Carlomagno hinted he, Rarick, "was in a lucky position" to command considerable cash if he withdrew from the race. Rarick says he has witnesses to this meeting, and it has not been denied by Carlomagno.

By the time election day, February 12, 1957, rolled around, rebel "Rip" Rarick had gotten his name before a good many of the steel workers—largely through newspapers in Pittsburgh and elsewhere that looked on the union election as news and assigned reporters to cover it.

Now, Rarick had to cope with the machinery by which the union elects its president. The steel workers vote on printed ballots at their union halls. Local officers tally the votes and send a result to the International offices at Pittsburgh. Here Honest Ballot Association representatives add up the tallies sent from the locals. Whether the local officers have sent honest counts, the Honest Ballot people of course don't know.

In his home-town Pittsburgh area—where he and his friends

91

could roughly check the balloting—Rarick piled up a three to one lead. Even McDonald's own local at Jones & Laughlin went to the rebels.

But reports released later from the hinterland brought a different story. From Chicago, the district director, an ally of McDonald, reported that McDonald had received 34,500 votes to Rarick's 1,400—a twenty-four to one tally. "We have more Rarick committee people working there than the votes the district director credited us with," the agonized Rarick cried.

When the International announced that McDonald had won by 404,172 votes to Rarick's 223,516, Rarick demanded that the union publish the results local by local. The International refused.

In despair, Rarick appealed to the McClellan Committee. The Committee held no hearings on the election.

Panic

McDonald's reaction to Rarick's tidal-wave vote was one of panic. As Big Rip Rarick demanded to see the returns, local by local, the International office tried to quiet him. Communication was set up between McDonald's personal lawyer and Rarick's lawyer, a young man by the name of James Ashton, who had worked his way through law school with a full-time job in a steel mill.

James Ashton is a warm and intelligent young man, and McDonald was soon putting his arm around "Jimmy's" shoulder and pouring out to him his most intimate hopes and fears. McDonald berated his own staff, charging some of them with incompetence and disloyalty and drunkenness.

Most of all, McDonald wanted to know from Jimmy Ashton who on his own board of directors aided the rebels and gave damaging inside union information to them. When Rarick and two fellow rebels were elected presidents of their locals—so putting three big locals into insurgents' hands—McDonald moved to salvage his prestige. At the next convention in September, 1958, which was generously attended by staff members on the Steelworkers payroll, McDonald staged a show of strength aimed at crushing the rebel rank and filers.

92

McDonald played the role of determined leader. He delivered his lines with dramatic flourish, making the most of his gifts as a handsome figure.

"This cancer [the Rarick opposition] must be ripped out of your bowels," he thundered. The pro-McDonald delegates howled their Ja's happily.

The untutored Rarick, little skilled in organizing a disciplined speech or addressing a large audience, was no match for McDonald.

The convention voted to order Rarick's local to try him on charges of "dual unionism":—a capital union crime carrying the sentence of expulsion. Rarick's local acquitted him. But he may be tried again—by the International's executive board.

The picture of a big union quelling a rank-and-file uprising is legitimate news. When Abe Raskin of the *New York Times,* who is highly respected as dean of the labor reporters, chronicled this news, McDonald caught up with him at the convention hotel bar one night.

"After all the years I've known you, Abe," McDonald complained lugubriously, "I don't understand why you don't like me." After McDonald had left, some of his understrappers crowded around the mild-mannered Raskin and wanted to know how he'd like to pick himself off the street someday. McDonald, who had nothing to do with these threats, came off the convention rostrum the next day to apologize to Raskin. But the incident disclosed what no apology could hide. McDonald, although in the public eye, could not face other men's appraisal of his value as a union leader.

Uneasy Head

Phil Murray had left McDonald a going concern: a well-oiled and smoothly functioning union machine. In five short years, McDonald had embroiled himself in civil war.

As McDonald broods over these disasters, the ghost of Phil Murray keeps him wretched company. For McDonald is not permitted, for one minute, to forget that, had Phil Murray lived, these rebellions would never have happened.

McDonald, interviewed, was an edgy man, and the nervous facial

93

tic that has afflicted him for several years was more pronounced than ever. I found him snappish, unresponsive to questions and sensitive about the Rarick incident to the point of rudeness.

McDonald's troubles unfortunately, are not his own private affair. They concern the 1,000,000 men in his union. It also concerns the steel industry with whom McDonald must bargain and from which he will demand wage boosts to improve his union position, and this concerns the economy of the whole country.

When storms lash a powerful union in a basic industry, tidal waves are bound to be raised elsewhere.

CHAPTER 7

David Dubinsky:
He Bosses 400,000 Women

The International Ladies' Garment Workers Union is probably the most famous in the world. Abroad, it's known for the schools and hospitals it built near Paris, at Palermo, Italy, in China and in Israel —and for the rebellion it financed against the Communist bosses of Italy's unions. At home it is celebrated for its workers' homes and summer resorts, for health centers that dot twenty cities; for model arbitration machinery that has made strikes virtually obsolete.

The ILG's president, David Dubinsky, a stooped little tailor of a man in his late sixties, is one of the three or four best known and respected union leaders.

In all this lies one of the strangest of Labor's strange-as-it-may-seem stories. First, the ILG is a woman's union, and only 20 per cent of its members are men. The women flow in and out of the union in great streams—about 200,000 or half of the membership came and went in the last three years—so that the union has to organize like mad simply to stand still. The members, mostly immigrants, speak so many tongues that the union's paper, *Justice,* has to be published in English, Yiddish, Spanish, Italian—and in Canada, in French.

The soil from which the mighty ILG and Dubinsky sprang adds to the believe-it-or-not flavor of the story, too. It is New York's Garment Center—a murderously competitive commercial jungle where cloak and suiters, working on a 1 per cent margin, die like flies; where Communists made their first great bid for union power, and nearly won; where gangsters have so woven themselves into the very fabric of the garment industry that neither the full might of the federal government, nor New York County District Attorney Frank Hogan, nor the mighty ILG itself has been able to rip the racketeers out.

In the air the Garment Center breathes are tension, suspicion and struggle. The struggles Dubinsky has seen have been mighty ones. David Dubinsky is forever taking on Goliath. First, there was the Goliath of man's inhumanity to man—symbolized by the sweatshop. First thing that greeted Dubinsky when he arrived at nineteen in New York in 1911 was the horror of the Triangle Company fire, in which 146 garment workers—locked into a sweatshop—lost their lives.

Then there was the Goliath of Communism. The Reds had seized strategic posts in the ILG in the mid-1920's, and plunged the union into a disastrous strike. Only a civil war, in which the then young Dubinsky played a key role, could drive the Reds out. The union emerged so broke it couldn't even pay its telephone bill and could get only incoming calls. Dubinsky, taking over as president in 1932, was called "undertaker"—there was only one thing to do with the union, to bury it.

Goliath No. 3 was and is—the gangster. Often, in the Garment Center, the ILG has been able to organize only after pitched battles with hoodlums in which Dubinsky could never know which of his people were loyal—and which had infiltrated from the mobs.

Outside the Garment Center—on the national stage—Dubinsky has been the gadfly, strategist and counselor to George Meany in the larger union struggle with the racketeers.

This, as we shall see, makes Dubinsky one of the most significant figures in Labor.

Diffident Dictator

A visit with David Dubinsky is likely to be pulse-quickening, if not altogether hair-raising.

The Garment Workers Building in upper Broadway—about a stone's throw from the hubbub of Times Square—once belonged to the Ford Motor Company. But any resemblance between the way the Garment Workers' president Dubinsky disports himself and the decorum that must have prevailed under Ford Motor Company president Edsel Ford is purely impossible.

Dubinsky doesn't rise from his chair to greet you. He bursts from it. His diminutive body—he's five feet five—is made even smaller by a stoop he says he acquired as a boy when he carted his baker-father's bread on his back to stores in Lodz, Poland. The posture makes his large head seem even larger.

Dubinsky has the round face of a Herbert Hoover or a Winston Churchill, but there all similarity ends. As incandescent as an electric bulb, the face lights up at the flick of the slightest emotion. And the emotion can range from childlike glee accompanied by joyful cackles to purple rage. So animated by perpetual emotion, his face has an unlined, youthful look.

The air of youthful vigor is deepened by Dubinsky's constitutional inability to sit still. An uninitiated visitor, new to Dubinsky's ways, watches with amazement as Dubinsky levitates about the room, his great head bobbling on his round body, and his voice raised to a shout. For Dubinsky doesn't talk, he yells—his voice rising to a falsetto shriek when he really warms to his conversational task.

The volcano flow of words is peppered with earthy S.O.B.'s—pronounced "sonsapitches"—and, whoever the visitor may be, with earthy Yiddishisms which Dubinsky doesn't pause to explain. And should the telephone ring, he'll talk into it, for security reasons, in Yiddish. Until Dubinsky was forty, when he became the ILG's president, Dubinsky spoke more Yiddish than English, because virtually all of the union hierarchy and most of the members then were of immigrant Jewish origin. Only when Dubinsky's resolute secretary, Hannah Haskell, locked him in his office with an English instructor did Dubinsky begin to change his lingual ways. But his talk is still heavily accented.

96

Dubinsky's Polish-Jewish childhood and youth helped mold a complex, and often baffling personality. As a persecuted minority, the Polish Jews sought refuge in a wry humor that mocked their oppressors—and irreverently respected nobody. So Dubinsky, meeting the world's mighty as the head of a great union, takes everybody in stride—with a soupçon of deflating humor.

When the late Albert Einstein pressed Dubinsky to set up a utopian worker's village in New Jersey—and kept on pushing the idea over Dubinsky's repeated no—Dubinsky finally ended the discussion with, "Dr. Einstein—when it comes to physics, you're the professor. When it comes to tailoring, I'm the professor."

As a onetime immigrant boy, too, Dubinsky has absolutely no side. Most labor leaders, except the flashily dressed racketeers, are indistinguishable from their opposite members on the management side. But Dubinsky has the rumpled look of the man who's slept in his clothes. His baggy pants are belted precariously around an ample belly. He wears $7.50 ties, but they're knotted informally beneath a crumpled collar.

Dubinsky pursues informality relentlessly to the point of originality. While other labor giants arrive in style at conferences, Dubinsky is likely to ride up to the meeting place on a bicycle. At a Miami Beach session he made one concession to the vacation resort air of the place. He wore sneakers.

Before food and drink—especially drink—Dubinsky is equally informal, and as a tippler has built a reputation as solid as his other reputation, that of labor leader.

Late for a dinner appointment with Dubinsky, I found him not long ago intrenched behind a zombie, a murderous drink composed of a tumblerful of assorted rums. I ordered a daiquiri which Dubinsky sampled and liked. Dubinsky downed his zombie in several gulps, ordered a daiquiri, then another and another—polishing off four in noisy and gleeful succession. Then coherently, and with sober shouts—after all, this was an interview—he proceeded to give a lucid exposition of life among the labor leaders at an Executive Council session that day.

Dubinsky talks of his drinking as other men boast of their golf scores and loves to tell of the time when Thomas E. Dewey, then a rising young prosecuting attorney, invited Dubinsky to his apartment to discuss Garment Center rackets.

"He puts out a bottle of brandy," Dubinsky recalls happily. "And I go to work on it, and finish it. He puts out another, and I work on that—and still I'm not saying what I shouldn't."

Despite the two bottles of brandy Dubinsky—as Dewey later put it—was "honest but not frank."

When a man has held union power for twenty-five years, is addressed humbly as "D.D." by understrappers, and hobnobs with other holders of great power, he is likely in time to take himself seriously. Dubinsky, no less egocentric than any other significant leader, does take himself seriously at times and will often refer to himself in the third person—as men conscious of their fame sometimes do.

Still, Dubinsky's Polish immigrant background has saddled him with a diffidence, too, so that he thinks twice about intruding himself openly in the current power politics and power struggle of Big Labor. This doesn't stop Dubinsky from playing a key role. But he's likely to do it through back-of-the-scenes counseling and intrigue rather than open maneuvers and knockdown debate.

Early in 1957, for instance, George Meany startled his fellow elders in the AFL-CIO Executive Council by making a revolutionary proposal. Meany had done his homework, seemingly, was well prepared and had his proposition written out in careful and lucid English. It was the famous proposal that no labor leader henceforth be permitted to take the Fifth Amendment before Congressional Committees, courts or government agencies—as a means of hiding his union affairs. This was a truly revolutionary move, because it meant that the Federation was butting into the hitherto autonomous and sacred private preserves of the constituent unions.

The twenty-nine members of the AFL-CIO Executive Council swallowed hard and took the historic plunge—away from national union autonomy. And no one at the meeting suspected that the real sparkplug of the move was David Dubinsky, nor that Dubinsky had discussed it with Meany.

Dubinsky had conceived the idea while listening to early Senate Committee hearings on union corruption. "If we don't do something about those crooks that are hiding behind the Fifth Amendment, what can we say to the public?" he wanted to know from his lawyer.

98

"We will have to run away and hide our head in shame." So Dubinsky's lawyer prepared a draft of a proposal—barring union men from resorting to silence. And it was this proposal, modified by Meany and his lawyer, that Meany read.

Diffident or not, Dubinsky—to use a Garment Center word—is a *Kuechleffel,* a stirring spoon, who mixes in everywhere and knows most everybody's business. At meetings of Big Labor, Dubinsky knows unerringly where the policy winds are blowing, who is doing what to whom—and in what direction some mighty labor cat is likely to jump. Reporters who gain Dubinsky's confidence find him an incomparable guide—and a gold mine.

Once at a San Francisco convention of the old American Federation of Labor, Dubinsky heard John L. Lewis make a seemingly innocuous speech before the local press club. He turned to Victor Riesel, the labor columnist.

"Does the speech tell you anything, Victor?" Dubinsky asked.

"Not much," Riesel said.

"Put a word together here, a word together there, and it still tells you nothing?" Dubinsky pressed.

Then, to the baffled Riesel, Dubinsky explained, "I think he's saying he's going to take a walk; he's going to pull the Miners out of the Federation."

Such a move in 1947 would be page-one, black-headline news. Hesitantly, Riesel flashed the Dubinsky tip to his editors and with misgivings saw the San Francisco papers announce the story in extra editions soon after.

Sure enough, three days later, John L. Lewis strode theatrically to the convention platform, thundered his defiance at the Federation and led the United Mine Workers out of the House of Labor.

Riesel, the trained reporter, had sensed nothing in John L.'s press club speech.

But Dubinsky, "listening with my insides," had "had a hunch."

Papa Knows Best

To his union family of 913 officers and 769 staff members, Dubinsky is the jealous father. Or, to be less charitable, the absolute monarch.

99

When a man's elected to ILG office—whether to a local job or to the International's General Executive Board—first thing he does is to sign an undated resignation. (This is a constitutional requirement initiated by Dubinsky. Resignation follows a two-thirds vote by the ILG board—which Dubinsky controls.) With this ceremonial he hands his official head on a platter to Dubinsky. For the undated resignations hang over official heads like a Damocles sword. It's as if a United States Senator, elected by the people of his state, were to submit an undated resignation forthwith to the President. ILG apologists say the strange device is needed to combat possible official corruption. If a man is caught cheating, his head can be quickly lopped off, without the need of making out a court case against him—is the way one vice-president explained it. But Dubinsky himself signs no such sudden-death device. Nor do the elected officials of any other union, as far as I have been able to ascertain.

Although union members are entitled to elect their own manager-administrators, an election that displeases Dubinsky may bring swift intercession. When the ILG's New York Embroidery local's manager died not long ago, the local's executive board promptly named a successor—all according to Hoyle, i.e., the local's bylaws. Dubinsky, getting the news while out of town, stormed back and roared his disapproval at the local board's choice. The cowed board reconvened, promptly unfrocked the newly named manager and, hat in hand, asked Dubinsky to name his own man. Which he did, bringing in a manager from another local.

The dictation extends to employers too. The ILG gives itself the right to check the employer's books. It's to keep him honest in his dealings with the union, says the union—and we'll take a closer look at this when we explore the Garment Center's underworld. But the fact remains the cloak and suiters don't like it—and can't do anything about it.

Dubinsky is the acknowledged top dog of Seventh Avenue (as the Garment Center is sometimes known). And a curious rite not long ago underlined this fact.

It was the day on which Dubinsky celebrated his twenty-fifth year as president of ILG. All over the Garment Center, just before noon, the sewing machines whirred to a halt, the steam in the pressing

100

irons cooled. All hands took a half day off to celebrate Dubinsky's quarter-century reign. Can you imagine General Motors or Chrysler slowing their assembly lines, when Walter Reuther marks an anniversary as the Automobile Workers' president?

Union-Made Utopia

For all of his baffling interior and bumptious exterior, Dubinsky is one of the passing breed of great founder-revolutionaries who were to Labor what a Henry Ford, say, was to industry.

Both were world changers. Ford did it by mass merchandising a complicated piece of machinery, the Model T Ford, and so making it possible for the average American to buy it. Dubinsky did it—in the early organizing stages of his union, at least—by merchandising mass discontent. Both were builders and doers. Ford built his car to fit his image of a new world in which the man who labors can afford to buy the product he helps create. Dubinsky built his union in the image of his world too—a Socialist world.

The story of the ILG really begins with the story of David Dubinsky, teen-age agitator and conspirator. Unions today are businesslike affairs with money to invest, insurance to buy; some worry conservatively about rocking the economic boat. Yet, only yesterday, the unions were agitational institutions. They organized the discontent of the wage earners in order to build union power and bargain with employers—from strength. So, the great leaders of even the recent past—John L. Lewis and the late Phil Murray, the younger Walter Reuther—were agitators and rebels. In fact, a hero's record of agitation or struggle against the "bosses" or even society, generally, was as vital a piece of equipment to the earlier labor leaders as administrative ability is today.

Dubinsky is the proud owner of what is probably the most picturesque and radical record of them all. He was a conspirator against Czarist oppression at age fifteen. At sixteen, he was languishing in jail as a union ringleader. At seventeen, he was a political exile in Siberia. At nineteen, he was a Socialist agitator, haranguing passers-by from street corners in New York.

101

Born in Brest-Litovsk, Poland, Dubinsky grew up in Lodz, an industrial town then savoring the miseries of the early industrial revolution compounded by Czarist oppression. Wage earners worked twelve to fifteen hours daily and were barred from organizing or striking by the Czar's secret police. So ugly was Lodz and so barren the life of its 500,000-odd people that two novels were written about it: one, *The Bad City;* another ironically titled *The Promised Land*.

It was the perfect backdrop for a young reformer. So, when Dubinsky went to work in his father's basement bakery at fourteen, he promptly helped form a union and became its secretary. (He was the only baker who could read and write.) He also joined the Jewish Socialist party which was known as the Bund. At fifteen, he was cooling his heels in the Lodz jail for illicit union and political activity.

In jail, young Dubinsky had enemies—and friends. The enemies were the swarms of bedbugs that infested the jailhouse mattresses. Seeking sleep, Dubinsky tried lying on the hard cell floor; to frustrate the bugs he improvised a moat, pouring a ring of water about himself. But war techniques—even in the war between man and insects —are forever advancing. The bugs, as bright as they were ravenous, would climb up the walls, make their way to the spot on the ceiling just above the recumbent prisoner, Dubinsky, then let themselves drop like dive bombers on the unhappy youth. There was nothing for it but to stay up until daylight (when the bugs vanished) and spend the night in long discussions with the politically sophisticated older prisoners or in reading. Books were available, and Dubinsky grounded himself in the Socialist and Marxist texts of the time.

At seventeen, Dubinsky, now old enough for adult treatment, was packed off by the police to Siberia—marching a good part of the way under conditions of near starvation and exhaustion.

This teen-age introduction to tyranny turned many of Dubinsky's radically minded contemporaries to Communism. But with young Dubinsky, curiously, it had an opposite effect. He was fed up with dictatorships of any sort, including the promised dictatorship of the proletariat.

So, when Dubinsky escaped from Siberia and immigrated to New York in 1911, he breathed the air of political freedom and found it good. The government was no longer the enemy. Why seek the overthrow of the government, as the Communist firebrands urged? The real enemy was social injustice: sweatshops, onerous working conditions, poor wages. And this enemy could be fought best under a democracy.

Dubinsky first tried to win reforms through the Socialist party—once a great favorite with New York East Side immigrants. But when the Socialist millennium proved slow in coming, Dubinsky plunged into unionism.

Ten men organized for collective bargaining in a shop could pry more social benefits from the boss than two thousand citizens could pry from a legislature. This was the philosophy of Sam Gompers, father of the AF of L. In time, it was to become the dominant, and saving, philosophy of America's unions.

Dubinsky stopped being an active Socialist about ten years after he came to America. He stopped voting Socialist when Al Smith ran for President in 1928—and he dropped out of the party altogether when the New Deal came. But Dubinsky never stopped building his "union welfare state."

Let's take a panoramic peek at it.

Pins and Needles and Health Clinics on Wheels

The ILG's 450,000 members, spread through 332 cities in 40 states and 5 Canadian provinces, work a 35-hour week.

The union and employers have jointly handled a half billion dollars of health and welfare funds for members. These have earned $18,000,000 interest in ten years.

The ILG operates health centers in twenty cities. In New York, the health center occupies six stories of the union's own twenty-two-story skyscraper. In Harrisburg, Pennsylvania, the "health center"—on wheels—brings nurse, technician, doctor and diagnostic instruments to members' homes.

The union has given away $23,000,000 to worldwide good works since 1940, including a $1,000,000 hospital in Israel.

103

ILG's summer resort for members, Unity House, includes a $1,000,000 summer theater.

The ILG's own "labor college" graduates some fifty future union leaders yearly.

The ILG's "co-operative village" cost $22,000,000 to build, houses 1,660 families on a slum-cleared thirteen-acre site where sweatshops once flourished.

The union produced a musical comedy, *Pins and Needles,* which packed them in on Broadway for two years, then toured the country in road companies. The ILG's movie, *With These Hands,* has been shown by the State Department abroad.

Most of the above were "firsts" among the unions. The ILG led the pack with the first employer-contributed unemployment compensation plan (1919).

The ILG was first with a Management Engineering Department which helps inefficient employers step up output, cut costs—and stay in business. The union was first to publish its balance sheet and expenses down to paper cups and towels at headquarters. It was the first, too, to build a factory for an employer.

This is the bright side of Seventh Avenue. For the seamier side of the Garment Center you must meet "The Boys."

Gangsters discovered the Garment Center when employers and unions alike hired hoodlums during the bitter organizing wars of the 1920's.

The employers paid off the gangsters in cash. But the Garment Workers Union, lacking cash, had to pay off with favors.

The hoodlums who fought the union's battles emerged as owners of dress firms.

And while the mighty ILG made most dress men toe the union line, many hoodlum shops operated non-union. Or they enjoyed "concessions." They didn't pay the 7 per cent—now 8½ per cent—of payroll welfare fund contribution. They enjoyed more "flexible" union regulations.

Dress men say the union was paying off for past favors. The union said the underworld—known in the Garment Center as "the Connections" or simply as "The Boys"—were too tough to handle. If you sent an organizer into a shop owned or protected by The Boys, you signed his death warrant.

Inside the underworld Trojan horse—which the union itself had let into the Garment Center—were some of the country's most lurid cutthroats.

One was the mousy and diminutive Louis "Lepke" Buchalter, who kept eight killers on a weekly payroll and was said to have ordered seventy murders. His loot from garment and trucking extortion alone was a million yearly.

The FBI called Lepke the most dangerous criminal in America. And when he died in the Sing Sing Prison electric chair in 1941—for the murder of a garment trucker—he left the Garment Center an evil legacy: the gang of lieutenants who had filled his murder contracts, collected his extortions and hid him for two years while state and federal sleuths hunted him.

The men Lepke left behind him were among the Garment Center's biggest businessmen.

As a businessman, Albert Anastasia[1] owned a string of apparel factories in Pennsylvania that produced thousands of dresses yearly for New York jobbers (also called manufacturers). He was secret owner as well of a great fleet of garment trucks. As a gangster, Anastasia was the Lord High Executioner of Murder, Inc., and assigned the killers who filled the orders for assassination from mobs all over the country. Twice jailed as a killer, Anastasia twice walked out when witnesses "disappeared." When Lepke gave himself up, it was Anastasia—the man who hid him—who drove Lepke to the rendezvous with J. Edgar Hoover.

Johnny Dio—whose name has become a household word synonymous with union racketeering—got his start in the Garment Center, too. Extortion from Garment Center truckers earned him a seven-year Sing Sing sentence. He came out to become a non-union dress manufacturer and merchant of "protection" against the union.

Please note that each of the foregoing—Lepke, Anastasia and Dio—was somehow mixed up with Garment Center trucking. This is no coincidence. It's through the garment trucks that the underworld sits in the driver's seat in dressmaking.

---

[1] Albert Anastasia was murdered in 1957, seemingly in a gang war over Cuban gambling.

To understand why, let's visit the Garment Center.

Go west off Broadway into any of the crosstown streets from Thirty-fifth to Thirty-ninth. In Thirty-fifth Street, known as "Garment Center Chinatown," because the cheapest dresses are found there, you are plunged into a head-reeling world of swarming activity. Great vans line both curbs, hub to hub, choke the street and permit only a trickle of traffic. On the sidewalks, equally choked, youths push hand trucks laden with dresses and coats. Elderly manufacturers, salesmen, clerks, models battle their way through the tangle. If it's after lunch, salesmen are drifting back from their rounds in the nearby department stores. In knots, they talk wistfully of "clickers"—dresses that click.

As far as the eye can see toward the Hudson stretch the near-skyscraper buildings through whose portals pass 80 per cent of all the dresses, coats and suits American women buy.

Now look back at the trucks that choke the streets. These are the jugular vein of the apparel industry. For only a few of the dresses that flow through the Garment Center are produced in it. They are finished by sewing "contractors," in Brooklyn, the Bronx, in New Jersey, Pennsylvania and elsewhere. So into the making of each dress or suit go four truck trips in and out of the Garment Center.

First, a truck fights its way in with the piece goods. Truck trip No. 1.

The manufacturer cuts the piece goods from patterns, loads the "cut work" on trucks, and sends them out to the contractor-factory. Truck trip No. 2.

The contractor sews the dress, and it is returned to the manufacturer's showrooms. Truck trip No. 3.

Store buyers from coast to coast order them, and Truck trip No. 4 hauls the apparel to the store, or to a rail terminal.

"It's a crazy, complex system," said a dress man. "But the store buyers want us all in one place. And we want to be near our competitors to smell out what they're doing. Are they making up the A line? Is the H line a dog?"

The wheels of the trucks make the system go around. And it's The Boys who own the big truck firms openly or in the names of close kin. Many of their business partners and ex-crime associates are active in the truckers' trade associations. They have their hooks

106

in the Drivers Union of the ILG that supplies drivers and helpers.

With the trade associations and Drivers Union as "enforcers," The Boys run the garment-trucking like an underworld racket. None can cut in without an O.K. from The Boys to "Go"—i.e., operate. Territory and customers are parceled out. The customer is stuck with his trucker for life.

This is the picture the United States Justice Department painted in an anti-monopoly suit against the Garment Center truckers. The Boys used "violence and threats of violence" to force all truckers into trade associations, charged the government. They "fixed and maintained trucking rates at high and uneconomic levels."

The truckers didn't even dispute the picture the Justice Department painted. They pleaded "*nolo contendere*" (we do not contest) and paid fifty-five thousand dollars in fines. To The Boys, this was peanuts. Trucking is the surest profit maker in the industry. Apparel manufacturing is a fiercely competitive business in which a wrong fashion guess may mean sudden death. One of every five firms folds yearly—and others take their place. But the trucks go rolling on. They haul some $4,500,000,000 of women's apparel yearly. And the trucker gets a sure seven to ten cents per garment hauled.

So the truckers paid their fine cheerfully. That was in 1944. Then many went right on running their trucking like a racket. Today, the Justice Department is investigating the truckers again. And the charges add up to the same picture of a tight, fenced-off racket-like preserve.

To maintain this preserve The Boys gained influence in an ILGWU local—the drivers' local—and point it like a pistol at the heart of Dubinsky's empire.

Connections in the drivers' local is a life-and-death business necessity for the underworld. Control of the drivers is vitally important to the ILG too.

The "Edge"

The Boys must control the drivers to safeguard their most profitable traffic—the sale of "protection" against ILG organizing. Such protection gives the protected employer a competitive advantage through substandard costs. This is known in the Garment Center as "the Edge."

107

"The Edge" is the garment industry's biggest headache. It hurts the workers who must work in substandard shops to make it possible. It hurts the ILG whose agents are corrupted or killed by hoodlums to maintain substandard shops. It hurts the majority of manufacturers who abide by agreements with the union—then must face unfair competition. It hurts those manufacturers who make deals with hoodlums for an "edge"—then fall into gangsters' clutches for life.

But The Boys have made great fortunes from it. In every deal involving an "edge" there are three participants: the sewing contractor who runs a "protected" substandard shop; the manufacturer who uses him—and the trucker. The trucker brings them together and gives "protection" to both.

The payoff is a commission to the trucker—three to ten cents a dress. Or the manufacturer pays the trucker by putting him on his payroll. Or gives him a piece of his business. So, with the "edge," "the Boys" have pried themselves into scores of companies.

Former United States Attorney Paul Williams of the New York area, estimated that some two hundred firms—truckers, contractors, jobbers—are involved in racketeering.

The racketeers are so firmly rooted that one trade association executive despaired, "They're an evil growth on the body of the industry. And I tell you, they'll never be eliminated."

Just ten minutes' subway ride from the Garment Center lies the biggest law-enforcement office in the world, that of District Attorney Frank Hogan. He commands 250 racket busters—sleuths, lawyers, accountants, laboratory technicians. These have kept Garment Center hoodlums under surveillance for years. From time to time Hogan sends some to jail for extortion. But, like the Garment Workers Union, he has achieved no major breakthrough.

There is no crime in operating a non-union shop. And the bribery or threats that make it possible are hard to detect and harder to prove. Dress men won't give testimony. They're afraid they'll be dead witnesses.

Once District Attorney Hogan's men swooped down on the Garment Center, subpoenaed truckers' and dress men's books, and grilled one hundred manufacturers.

"We suspected the manufacturers were paying tribute to hood-

108

lums for protection against the union," Rackets Bureau chief Al Scotti said.

"But prove it?" he despaired. "That was another thing."

The dress men had rewritten their books to hide payments to The Boys. Some told the District Attorney of tribute payments. But, when asked to testify in court, they became ill. Some collapsed and required hospital treatment.

Hoodlums, facing jail, were just as loath to talk. The District Attorney had found a dress man's canceled check made out to a notorious hoodlum. On it was the telltale notation, "pro." To the racket busters this spelled "protection." Confronted with the check, the recipient, one "Scarface Louie" Lieberman, pleaded guilty to extortion.

When Scarface Louie was pressed to tell with whom he split the protection loot, he blurted, "Put me in jail. Keep me there for life. But I won't talk."

Garment Jungle

Sharing the Garment Center with hoodlums is, for Dubinsky, an agonizing problem in coexistence.

Hardly a week passes but that some dress man pleads, "The racketeers' competition is driving me out of business." Then the dress men get into a hassle with the union.

"You've got to do something about the racketeers. Or let us get down to their cost levels," they storm.

"Every waking moment," replies some weary union man, "we're devoting to the problem of eliminating the racketeers."

When the union launched an all-out drive in 1949 against the shops "the Boys" were protecting, a reign of terror ensued. It was the Lepke days all over again.

First, hoodlums invaded the union's office and sent three officials to the hospital. "We'll cut your ears off," they threatened others over the telephone. Roving gangs beat up strike pickets. The union called for help to the Seafarers Union which sent fifty huskies to the Garment Center to protect the picket lines.

Then the union organizer, William Lurye, was murdered. To this terror was added betrayal. An underworld ally then heading the

109

garment drivers' local permitted his drivers to cross the picket lines—so breaking the strike of their fellow ILG members.

In 1952, when unionized dress manufacturers kicked up another fuss, the Garment Workers Union returned to the attack. This time they brought several dozen protected shops into the union fold. But The Boys continued to offer "protection" to the unionized employers and so encouraged them to chisel on their contracts. This required further knock-down and drag-out fights by the union.

If the ILG controlled the truck drivers' local, it could wipe out the evil of the "edge," since the trucks would no longer haul garments to substandard or non-union shops.

Yet it's a fascinating measure of gangster staying power—once they've dug in—that the racketeers, not the mighty ILG, have controlled the ILG's own drivers' local. The ILG local doesn't even have a written contract with the truck owners.

Until he was indicted on charges of extortion, this local was bossed by one Sam Berger. Tried, he was freed, but two union aides were convicted. His office was a hangout for hoodlums from all over the country.

I once asked Dubinsky, "Why don't you fire Berger?"

"Fire him?" Dubinsky screamed in his most excited falsetto. "How would that solve anything? I couldn't ask another man to take his place. He'd be killed."

"If I was twenty years younger, I'd go in there and risk my life and straighten it out," sighs Dubinsky.

Recently Dubinsky has talked of putting an ex-cop or FBI man in charge of the local.

"Could he clean it up?" Dubinsky was asked.

"Don't ask foolish questions," Dubinsky shouted. "The government with the FBI couldn't clean it up. The state with the electric chair couldn't clean it up.

"The only thing that will clean it up," he said, "is when people talk. But people are afraid to talk."

Once the manufacturers refused to give the usual pay raise at contract-signing time.

"Not another penny, until you clean up," they said.

Today, the ILG is still struggling with The Boys.

Uneasy Marriage

The ILG is famed for its peaceful relations with employers. Arbitrators kept the Garment Center free of major strikes until the brief walkout of 1958. Yet, because of underworld infiltration, suspicion hangs like a foul cloud over the marriage between the ILG and the employers.

Since some of the dress men are gangsters, or reformed gangsters or grew up with gangsters, the ILG, like a cat at a rathole, is forever sniffing for evidence that some of its officers and business agents are being bribed by the boss to sell out the union.

"Let me give you an example," said an ILG vice-president. "One of the companies we have a contract with is Studio Frocks. Do you know who owns Studio Frocks? Well, I'll tell you. 'Nig Rosen,' the racketeer. What sort of fair dealing do you expect from him?"

Several days later, as if to underline the ILG official's words, Nig Rosen, whose real name is Harold Stromberg, was seized by Federal Narcotics agents. He was convicted of a narcotics charge, and is appealing. Nig Rosen, dress manufacturer, was accused by the government of heading an international narcotics syndicate that netted between $18,000,000 and $20,000,000 a year.

With manufacturers like Nig Rosen to deal with, the ILG maintains accountant watchdogs who regularly pry into employers' books. They check up on cloak and suiters to see whether they're paying their full share of welfare benefit money to the union, whether they're sneaking out cut garments to non-union, substandard sewing contractors in violation of union agreements.

But in the Garment Center even watchdogs have to be watched.

"Not long ago," a vice-president told me, "we heard that some of our accountants had been corrupted. Instead of reporting that a dress man owed, say, ten thousand dollars in welfare contributions, they'd falsify the books to show he owed only five thousand dollars —then split the difference with the manufacturer."

What to do?

The vice-president held a secret, after-hours huddle with the head accountant and a handful of trusted aides. They sifted rumors and prepared a list of suspects. When trusted accountants checked up on the untrusted ones, they found four (out of thirty-five) were

111

cheating the union. They were turned over to the District Attorney.

Once Dubinsky hired a former FBI man and instructed him to build a union FBI that would keep the union bunch honest. For two years the ex-FBI man collected dossiers on union officials, snooped in offices and generally scared the hell out of everybody. The cure for corruption seemed more drastic than the ailment—so Dubinsky let the man go.

So much for Dubinsky and of the world in which he built and rules the ILG. From this world, with racketeers in his own back yard, Dubinsky has emerged on the national stage as a central figure in the struggle against racketeers in all unions. And so we'll meet him again in other chapters.

112

IV

Looking backward—and forward. How America's unions got that middle-class way, as seen through the lives of the unions' two fathers: Samuel Gompers and John L. Lewis.

The American Federation of Labor is a rope of sand.

V. I. LENIN

This Rope of Sand will prove more powerful than chains of steel.

SAMUEL GOMPERS

CHAPTER 8

Sam Gompers:
Father with Labor Pains

A country, an institution or a movement usually has but one father. The American union movement had two. In fact, the union child was born in two stages—one set of birth pangs lasting fifty years. The baby nearly died. The second father took over with a new idea for its survival. Revived and regenerated, the union child shot up like a beanstalk to its present giant size.

The two fathers were Samuel Gompers and John L. Lewis.[1] The two men had many similarities. But they also had one great difference. Gompers passionately believed in organizing skilled workers of the same craft—to build unions of plumbers, or carpenters or cigarmakers. If the wages of the skilled were raised, the wages of the unskilled would take care of themselves, Gompers felt. With the craft union instrument, Gompers established a Labor movement beachhead—against incredible opposition. But it was only a beachhead. It remained for Lewis, who passionately believed in another method of labor organization—the industrial union which embraces everybody in a plant or industry—to make the breakthrough—organizing the mass industries—that transformed the unions. From a minority, tolerated movement, they became a major participant in

---

[1] A good case might be made for including a third father—Franklin Delano Roosevelt, whose Wagner Act broke the mass industries' resistance to unions.

the mainstream of American life.

Still, Gompers had to come first and make the one great contribution that would make possible John L. Lewis' vast organizing drives of the late thirties.

Gompers' contribution was to divorce the American unions from the class struggle. He forged a "pure and simple" unionism: "pure" of any revolutionary isms, and "simple" in that the union concerned itself solely with "more now" rather than with social panaceas and politicking for pie in the sky later. Gompers made the American unions a middle-class movement unlike any other in the world, a partner rather than a deadly enemy of the growing young American capitalist giant. He therefore made unions respectable to a people who had always regarded labor organizations with suspicion.

When Gompers died after wandering for thirty-eight years in the wilderness of hostile public opinion, he was buried with military honors. A postage stamp was struck off in his honor. A monument was erected to his memory at Washington, D.C., and dedicated by the President of the U.S.

New York's East Side, where Gompers grew up toward the end of the last century, was an intellectual melting pot that stewed with every ism of protest then known to man. Socialism, anarchism, Communism—imported by refugees from European oppression— were in the air that Gompers breathed.

The sweatshops, the killing dawn-to-darkness workday, the poverty and hunger imposed on wage earners by early factory owners provoked agitation for social panaceas. Under these conditions, the Labor movements overseas had cast their lot with the politicians of protest and sought the better life through class "solidarity" and government by and for the proletariat. Yet here, Gompers threw in his lot with a free economic system on the ground that a free union movement could survive only under free capitalism.

How did Gompers get this way?

In the answer lies the fascinating story of the growth of a trade union idea that fitted America. But, first, let's get acquainted with Gompers.

116

"But I'm President of the AF of L"

In aspect as in ideas, Sam Gompers was an original. He was, in fact, on first acquaintance—as his own secretary put it—"startling." Depending on how you felt about him, Gompers could be described either as a squat frog or as a pouter pigeon. His great chest and torso, those of a big man, moved on a little man's legs. He had the rough, boulder-like head of a peasant, but the knowing blue eyes and face of a man of great sensitivity. His long arms reached almost to his knees, but his hands were as finely shaped as those of an artist. And, to top this list of incongruities, there was the Gompers voice: rich, sonorous as a pipe organ and quite up to filling a Madison Square Garden or a cathedral.

The great chest and the greater voice gave Gompers an importance he took no trouble to dispel. Like many a small-sized man who makes a splash in the world, he bristled with humorless dignity and self-assertion. His two-volume autobiography has hardly one light word in it. It is stiff and formal and with perfectly straight face will picture Gompers attending an early union conference at which "practically every man [including Gompers—then as poor as a church mouse] wore a silk hat and a Prince Albert coat."

Gompers didn't unbend even in his most intimate letters to his family. The stiffness was due in part to Gompers' lifetime love affair with the English language which he courted with the passion of a stranger who goes on discovering new resources in it all his life. Gompers seldom used a colloquial word where a "prose" word would do. Even his conversation had the rolling, elegant quality of a sentence from Gibbon.

At a time when every man's hand was raised against the unions and against the union leader, Gompers' humorless dignity was armor against a hostile world. Once when the then President Theodore Roosevelt tried to cut short an argument with Gompers with the assertion, "But, Mr. Gompers, I'm President of the United States," Gompers shot back, "But I'm president of the American Federation of Labor." When Teddy Roosevelt roared with laughter, Gompers didn't know what the other President was laughing about.

Gompers' rounded, fancy prose was highly effective on a platform. Once Gompers so shook up a Madison Square audience that the

117

crowd started breaking up chairs. Gompers was thundering out against unemployment. Alarmed at what he had wrought, Gompers called on other oratorical powers to calm down the frenzied crowd. "Never again," Gompers vowed in his autobiography, "would I give such free rein to my emotions."

This oratorical talent, coupled with the showmanship and quick presence of mind of a carnival barker, helped Gompers through many an AF of L crisis. Once, during a convention, an exasperated Socialist foe leaped to the rostrum and thrust a pistol into Gompers' ample belly. A man with less self-importance might have panicked. But Sam owed it to his audience not to. With several hundred eyes fixed on him, Gompers placed his left arm on the pistol-packer's shoulder. Then in a stage voice he intoned, "Sir, hand me that pistol." The sonorous demand, repeated with increasing volume and dignity, was too much for the gun-toting wretch. He handed the pistol over. This, of course, brought down the house.

Another time, when radical foes heckled Gompers from the convention floor for patronizing a non-union barber, Gompers challenged one detractor to rise and state his grievance.

"Who shaves you?" the critic demanded.

"Who shaves me?" Gompers intoned in his cathedral-organ voice.

"Yes, who shaves you?" the man wanted to know.

"Sam Gompers shaves me," said Gompers with dignity. Gompers, as usual, was dead serious. But he broke up the house anyway.

Since much about Gompers had a touch of the unexpected, it was logical that his private life should provide the greatest contradiction of all. For, here, Sam was the playboy of the union world.

The corner saloon, when Gompers was building the AF of L, played an important role in a worker's life. The bartender cashed his checks and had the latest news on jobs. During strikes there was the free lunch. Since the fledgling unions had no meeting halls, the saloon's back room served as a meeting place. Here in the dear dead days of the nickel schooner of beer, the boys nursed their drinks and talked union business. If the bartender complained about the beer nursing, the union meeting adjourned to another saloon.

118

To succeed as a union leader, then, a man had to develop the belly and kidneys of a brewery dray horse. Sam Gompers was equal to the challenge. In fact, Gompers' drinking exploits in time became a public matter that got into the newspapers and were aired before an AF of L convention.

"I love life and enjoy living," Gompers once admitted in a rare lapse into candor. "I have always rebelled at conventions that merely repress . . . and have hated hypocrisy."

"On any night," as one biographer painted the picture, Sam— lover of life—"might be found leading a crowd of men into a saloon where, far into the night, they would make merry with foaming beer and sometimes with more potent liquor."

Gompers was a man who hated to be alone. Solitude, as he put it, "had no joy or comfort for me. A companion with the love of life added pleasure to the day's work."

So when Sam was in some strange city on a union mission and evening fell, he'd become restless. "Let's take a walk and get some fresh air," he'd say.

Then, with the instinct of a homing pigeon, he'd set a course for some side street lined with workmen's saloons. There he'd find the "fresh air" he sought: the yeasty—sometimes miasmic—air of the saloon's back room.

"Many a time over a mug of beer or a drink of whiskey," Sam Gompers recalled, "I won men for the cause of trade unionism when I would fail in every other way."

In his early days of grinding poverty, Gompers could make a meal of soup created from flour, salt, pepper and water. Gompers and his burgeoning family (he had eight children in all) knew hunger even after Gompers became AF of L president and had a hard time collecting his twenty-two-dollar-a-week pay. But when the AF of L became stabilized and per capita revenues poured in from the constituent unions, Gompers turned to good living with gusto.

Gompers got to be so well known as a night-life figure that comedians in New York's old burlesque or girlie shows would signal his arrival by patting their bellies affectionately and calling them "my Sam Gompers." After the show, he'd play the role of jolly host at supper and, flanked by pretty girls—as one biographer relates it—he'd consume endless drinks and cigars.

119

Naturally this lust for life was not lost on Gompers' enemies. The Knights of Labor, a bitter rival of the AF of L in the 1890's, broadcast a pamphlet which declared: "The General Executive Board [of the Knights of Labor] has never had the pleasure of seeing Mr. Gompers sober."

Gompers' anguished protests never did catch up with this canard.

Hard work—Gompers sometimes got by with one hour's sleep at night—harder play and even harder knocks from a bitterly anti-union world showed on Gompers toward the end of his life. At seventy-four he was almost blind; his hair had come out in great patches, accentuating the ill-health and homeliness of his rugged face. His body was racked with diabetes.

"I have been tried and seared as few men have," Gompers wrote at the time. "I have almost had my soul burned in the trial of life."

Being no angel contributed to the searing. The times in which Gompers built his union contributed even more.

It was Gompers' fate to arrive in America as a thirteen-year-old immigrant boy when the Civil War was ending and the curtain was going up on America's explosive rise toward world industrial leadership. The new age of invention was creating great industries and turning millions of farmer boys and small-town Americans into industrial workers and potential union recruits. The machines also brought social chaos and unrest. The times were tailor-made for the labor organizer role Gompers was to play. But they also held obstacles that were to limit this role.

Between young Gompers' arrival in 1863 and his founding of the American Federation of Labor in 1886 (when he was thirty-six), some 400,000 new patents poured forth. The Westinghouse air brake, interlocking block signals and George Pullman's palace car had revolutionized rail travel and freight hauling by 1870. The refrigerator car, making its debut in 1875, created a new meat-packing industry.

By 1900 Edison's incandescent lamp, Alexander Graham Bell's telephone, Hoe's rotary press that could print and fold 240,000 eight-page newspapers in an hour and Christopher Shole's type-writer had changed the lives of city dwellers and businessmen.

By 1900, too, thanks to the Bessemer open hearth process, electricity and chemistry, America's great ironmasters were producing as much steel as Great Britain and Germany.

So, by 1910—when Sam Gompers was a vigorous sixty—more than 50 per cent of Americans lived in towns and cities. And the United States had become the leading manufacturing and industrial power in the world. Factory workers had swelled to an army of nine millions.

No other country offered such a market for the union organizer's services. Although machinery in time made the American worker the envied home- and gadget-owning aristocrat of the Western world, few of machinery's early benefits went to the worker. Floods of immigrants—18,000,000 poured in between 1880 and 1910—competed for jobs and depressed wages everywhere. In the basic industries workers were idle 20 per cent of the time.

"A large part of our industrial population," a Presidential Commission reported at the turn of the century, "are living in a condition of actual poverty." With indignation seldom found in a government document, the Commission report went on: "Between one-fourth and one-third of male factory and mine workers 18 years and over earn less than $10 a week; from two-thirds to three-fourths earn less than $15 weekly." This was less than was needed to keep body and soul together. The difference was made up by hunger or by the labor of women and children.

Nearly half of women workers in factories, shops and laundries work at less than six dollars a week, the President's Commission found.

"Last of all are the children," the report continued, "for whose petty addition to the stream of production the nation pays a heavy toll in ignorance, deformity of body or mind and premature old age. The competitive effect of the employment of women and children on men's wages can scarcely be overestimated."

It wouldn't occur to anybody today to pay a fireman only when he goes out to a fire, and to keep him unpaid as he waits in the firehouse. Yet, when streetcars first appeared on New York

121

streets, motormen and conductors reported at dawn at the car barns, then waited their turn to take a car out. "Often," as Gompers told it, "days passed without their obtaining more than one round trip."

As late as 1923, the year before Gompers died, steel mills operated on a twelve-hour day and a seven-day week. Trainmen worked seventy hours a week, and textile mill operatives, most of them girls and women, worked sixty to seventy hours.

When Gompers set out to organize worker discontent, he found he had a lifetime war on his hands.

The union curbs the owner's absolute control over his producing property through the "work rules," wages and working conditions it bargains out. To the early industrial giants, the idea that the worker could exercise this power was a revolutionary one to be resisted at all cost.

"You are willing to let . . . killings take place rather than settle conditions?" John D. Rockefeller, Jr., was asked during the Ludlow, Colorado, mine strike of 1913.

"We believe so sincerely . . . that the [mining] camps shall be open [non-union], that we expect to stand by our officers at any cost," Rockefeller replied. The cost was the lives of seventeen miners, their wives and children.

Some employers, like railroad man George F. Baer, had a divine right explanation for it.

"The rights and interests of the laboring man will be protected and cared for, not by the labor agitators, but by the Christian men to whom God, in his infinite wisdom, has given control of the property interests of the country," said Baer.

So the struggle for a voice over the conditions of one's work, i.e., industrial freedom, plunged America into a half century of violent industrial war which at times flared into something akin to revolutionary class struggle.

The difference was that, in the class struggles of older countries, an oppressive government was the target. Here, the target was the employer. The worker's weapon was the strike and the boycott. The employer resisted with the lockout, the black list, with private

122

armies, detective agency spies and with compliant police and state militia.

The history of the unions, then, is largely a fighting history with its own Bunker Hills, Gettysburgs and Waterloos.

One battle had for its battlefield virtually the entire continent. This was the railroad workers' revolt, now known simply as "the Great Strike of 1877." It started when Eastern railroad executives ordered firemen then working for five dollars and six dollars a week to take another 10 per cent cut. The men struck and were soon joined by mobs of unemployed who blocked rail traffic and destroyed rail property. Riots and pitched battles with militia spread from New York to San Francisco. More than one hundred rail workers were killed. Several hundred were wounded. For the first time during peace, federal troops were called out to suppress a strike.

At Homestead, Pennsylvania, in 1892, strikers fought it out with an army of rifle-bearing Pinkerton detectives imported by the Carnegie Steel Company. The strikers suffered three dead and won that battle from the Pinkertons, who lost seven men. But the strikers lost the war. They couldn't cope with continued use of force. The pattern of armed suppression (to break picket lines) introduced at Homestead helped bar unions from the steel mills for forty years.

The names of the industrial war's battles are as gory as those in any military history. "Bloody Ludlow" describes the fight between the Colorado Fuel and Iron Company and its miners. "The Herrin Massacre" is the name by which Illinois disorders, bordering on civil war are remembered. "Bleeding Harlan" described similar struggles between miners and owners in Kentucky.

The industrial war even included a "children's strike."

When textile millowners at Lawrence, Massachusetts, precipitated a strike with a wage cut in 1912, they faced professionals in the class struggle. These were strategists sent by the radical Industrial Workers of the World, who took over the strike and welded the twenty thousand untutored immigrant strikers into a disciplined resistance group.

Chief problem was to feed the strikers' families—some fifty thousand mouths. To meet it, the strike leaders appealed to families all over America to take in the strikers' children. Soon, trainloads of children were pouring out of Lawrence to eager foster parents in

Boston, New York, Philadelphia and other cities. Each trainload removed hundreds of mouths that needed feeding. And wherever the children went, they aroused public indignation against employers who had forced the separation of mothers and babies. The employers tried to stop the exodus by force, obtaining court injunctions against the removal of the children. When the migration persisted, state militia men invaded the trains, clubbed mothers and children and hauled them to detention centers. This, of course, fanned public indignation further, and the millowners had to settle on the strikers' terms.

In twenty-five turbulent years—from 1881 to 1906—the country was rocked by 38,000 strikes and lockouts in which some 9,500,000 wage earners battled for union recognition or better conditions against 200,000 resisting employers.

If Sam Gompers were to build an enduring union movement where none had survived before, he had the triple job of overcoming resistance from employers on the right, radicals from the left— taking care meanwhile not to scare the living daylights out of the fearful middle class in the middle.

Rope Trick

Into a bare, brick-floored shed near New York's East River docks one day in 1886, Sam Gompers and his schoolboy son, Henry, lugged a kitchen table borrowed from their home. From the grocer across the street, they brought some tomato crates. From a school nearby they borrowed ink. Gompers and son were furnishing the first "headquarters" of the American Federation of Labor.

The shed, eight by ten feet—the size of a dentist's anteroom— had been donated by Gompers' Cigar Makers Local 144. It had a door and a small window. Gompers looked about him with pride. At thirty-six, he had just been elected president of newly founded AF of L. Gompers balanced his chunky body on an up-ended crate, dipped his pen into the borrowed ink and thoughtfully composed a letter—so transacting the AF of L's first piece of business.

At the AF of L founding convention at Columbus, Ohio, several weeks before, Gompers had presented a blueprint.

This blueprint Gompers had drawn by studying the rise and fall of prior attempts to unite workingmen.

124

Led by intellectual reformers, some of these early "unions" had been curious catch-alls. One, the National Labor Union, had not only embraced local and national unions but women's suffrage leagues and farmers' groups as well. Another, the Knights of Labor, was open to all workers, skilled and unskilled, as well as to farmers, merchants, capitalists. Only "professional gamblers, bankers, liquor dealers and lawyers" need not apply.

Then there were the Sons of Vulcan, the Knights of Industry, the Followers of Lafayette, the Washington Guards, the Lincoln Leaguers—all with secret passwords and rituals, boyish handshakes, and vague, political reform goals.

Into these, workers in quest of better conditions poured, in and out as through great sieves.

Gompers introduced two simple, but then novel, ideas: The first was "autonomy." He convinced fellow unionists that the AF of L should be patterned on the federal principle of the United States government. National unions could join and (unlike the states) withdraw voluntarily. The unions could elect their own officers, make their own deals with employers, call their own strikes—without interference from the Federation government at the top.

The second principle was that only trade unions working for economic goals—more pay, shorter hours, better working conditions—could belong.

The AF of L founding convention voted its president a thousand-dollar yearly salary. For a staff, Gompers had a treasurer at $100 a year and an office boy, his son Henry, who worked after school and summers at $3 a week. The AF of L started with 25 affiliated unions embracing some 317,000 members who, it was figured, would bring the AF of L some $5,000 operating money the first year.[2]

Since there was no president's salary until the AF of L constitution became effective several months after the convention, Gompers, his wife Sophie and their six children had a hard time of it to eat and pay the rent. But Gompers had a solution. He asked his family to make believe he was on strike.

---

[2] In 1957, the AFL-CIO collected $8,663,335 per capita dues from 144 international and national unions, plus another $1,300,000 from directly chartered federal locals.

When Gompers took to the road to organize unions, he became even poorer. In contrast to the $128-a-day luxury hotel suite Dave Beck of the Teamsters was to lavish on himself later, union provision for traveling expenses was sketchy in Gompers' day. From one cross-country trip Gompers returned "$90 out of pocket." A trip through New England left him "$35 short."

Gompers had as little power and authority as he had money.

He could advise or persuade; he could arbitrate. But he couldn't order or compel. This was done by the officers of the autonomous, constituent unions.

The public couldn't understand that the leader of all of America's unions had no direct power. So Gompers spent a good deal of time explaining to the public he was no "labor generalissimo," as some newspapers described him.

"I have never ordered a strike, I have never decreed a strike, and I have never had the power to call off a strike after it is called,"[3] he once said.

Gompers' job was to give the AF of L permanence, make it a force in the industrial life of the country, and to win for it the loyalty of the American workmen.

Gompers coined a slogan, "organize the unorganized." As the AF of L's treasury grew, he built an army of recruiting sergeants (union organizers). He helped organize twenty-eight new international unions, among them such future giants as the Garment Workers and the Carpenters. The army of union organizers also became Gompers' eyes and ears around the country, and was the foundation on which he built a political machine which kept him in power for thirty-eight successive years.[4]

Gompers showed how a Federation could endure. But, to make the lesson stick, he had to develop a type of unionism that fitted the America of his time. And to win a bitter, eighteen-year civil war

---

[3] The Federation president's role is still so little understood that, in the fall of 1957, George Meany was still explaining to Senators Barry Goldwater and Carl Mundt that the Federation had no power to negotiate contracts or settle strikes.

[4] With the exception of 1895, when the Socialists and Single Taxers ganged up on Gompers and sidelined him until the next annual convention.

in which the Socialists, boring from within the Federation, tried to take the unions away from him.

Anti-Radical Radical

The man who was to build a middle class, conservative Labor movement in America was born into a world in which everything cried for change. The time was 1850, the place was London's East Side. Gompers' home was a single tenement room where his Dutch-Jewish immigrant parents and their five children ate, slept, bathed and pursued such family life as was possible.

In the neighborhood lived silk weavers then losing their jobs to new machinery. They tramped the narrow streets, wringing their hands and filling the air with a cry that was burned into young Gompers' mind.

"God, I've no work to do," the men wailed. "Lord, strike me dead; my wife, my kids want bread, and I've no work to do."

Sam was taken out of a Jewish religious school at ten and apprenticed to a shoemaker, promptly begged off, because he couldn't stand the noise, and asked his father to apprentice him to the quieter cigarmaking trade instead.

When the Gompers brood migrated to New York and Sam found jobs at his trade, the shops were so quiet that the cigar-makers would choose one among them to read out loud—or spend the time debating the problems of the day. The reading and debating naturally turned to schemes for social change. Much of the talk concerned unions, then little more than social clubs.

Young Gompers, then approaching twenty, was a sight for startled eyes. Eager to get on with the job of being a man, he had cultivated a walrus mustache. This, on a face lighted by dancing blue eyes, gave Gompers a half-bumptious, half-prankish air. Eager to get on, too, Gompers had married at seventeen when a friend had imprudently entrusted his best girl to Gompers for a summer. So, emerging from his teens, Gompers was already a paterfamilias with four mouths to feed.

He was also an assertive figure among his cigarmaking shopmates. He learned to think on his feet, to use every trick of showmanship and timing and so become one of the most effective orators of his

127

time. From the worktime discussion searches for the millennium, Gompers graduated to an inner circle of workmen-thinkers who called themselves the "Ten Philosophers." Out of their orgies of talk into the early morning hours, according to Gompers, "came the purpose and the initiative that finally resulted in the [modern] labor movement."

Two of the "Ten Philosophers"—older men than Gompers—became his mentors, helping him pick his way through the forest of Socialism, anarchism, greenbackism, single taxism, toward the idea that in the trade union lay the workers' best hope for a better deal. One was Ferdinand Laurel, a big and powerful Swede, known for his practical longheadedness as *Ferdkopf,* horse head. The other, a taciturn, blunt man and Jewish immigrant like Gompers, was Adolph Strasser. All about Gompers on New York's Lower East Side were rebels and revolutionaries. When everybody's a leftist, it's radical not to be one. That's the kind of radical Gompers became.

Laurel had an insider's knowledge of Europe's revolutionary movements—and an insider's disillusion. This had turned him from politics to unionism.

Strasser, also a disillusioned radical like Laurel, helped distil the slogan for which Gompers is perhaps best remembered: "More, now."

Testifying before a Senate Committee in 1873, Strasser, then president of the Cigar Makers Union, was asked, "What are your ultimate ends?"

"We have no ultimate ends," Strasser replied. "We are going on from day to day. We are fighting only for immediate objects—objects that can be realized in a few years."

Question: You want something better to eat and to wear and better homes to live in?

Strasser: Yes, we want to dress better, and to live better, and become citizens generally.

Gompers boiled all this down to one sentence: "It takes no philosophy to see that $3.00 a day is better than $2.50 a day." Then, to one phrase: "More, now."

The first task that practical men Gompers, Strasser and Laurel set themselves was to turn their local Cigar Makers Union—the

128

famous Local 144—into a guinea pig.

Strange as it may seem, the pre-Gompers unions had no formal method or machinery for making demands on the employer.

Sam Gompers introduced the union contract and so put the union's relations with the employer on a stable and continuing basis. The discovery of the union contract was to modern unionism what the discovery of the wheel was to civilization. It made unionism go by solving problems raised by two central actors in the union drama: the boss and his worker.

The boss's dilemma was this: how do you accept and live with a union which, after all, is a device for curbing your control over your own property? The contract made possible a working partnership. The boss continued as property owner, risk taker and profit taker. The union, through the contract, became the administrator of the job. The contract set wages, conditions for overtime, for seniority (priority to the job). The contract stipulated who could become an apprentice and how he'd be trained; it even set the conditions for introducing new machinery. While the union didn't own the job, it established control over it.

The wage earner's dilemma was this: in older countries, where a man was born into a class and remained there, it made sense to fight for improvement through "class solidarity," i.e., by allying one's self with others in the same boat. But in the land of the American Dream where a man could strike it rich, move out of his class through education or energy, class solidarity and the class struggle held little luster. What could a class organization like a union do for you that you couldn't do for yourself? The answer, as Gompers worked it out through the union contract, was that a union protected your rights to the job. The American worker who wouldn't buy "class solidarity" would buy "job solidarity." He would band together with others to protect his job.

So the union contract became the taproot from which a Labor movement could flourish in free enterprise soil.

Soon, full-time officials and staff men arose to serve the contract: to study the market for the labor of union members so that it could be sold, in a businesslike way, for the highest price; to police or enforce the contract; to settle disputes arising from it. With the contract as the local's backbone, the union became the business agent

129

for the workers. This was pure and simple unionism, business or fundamentalist unionism, built around the contract.

On Guinea Pig Local 144 of the Cigar Makers, Gompers tried other ideas. One was the payment of regular, substantial dues. A man who gave little to his union would have little interest in it, he felt. Nor could he expect anything from the union in time of need, because it had no treasury. Gompers also pioneered with out-of-work benefits, union death and sickness insurance. He wanted the worker to rely on his union for the security he might otherwise seek from the government. A Jeffersonian Democrat with a distrust of government, Gompers felt so strongly that the worker should make his own security through his own unions that he helped kill Social Security legislation when it was first introduced in 1916.

Gompers' pure and simple unionism was tested in the depression year of 1877 when cigar manufacturers dismissed many of their workers and cut the wages of those who remained, bringing on a strike. Gompers and his practical philosophers led a disciplined strike in which, for the first time, the united strength of the strikers approached the solid front of resisting employers.

The times were against the strikers. Unions were not popular or even respectable. Gompers' cigar strike ultimately collapsed when the employers—who knew a thing or two about organizing, too—joined hands to lock out those workers whose earnings were supporting the strikers. Unions used to blossom forth during strikes to die when the strike was over or succumb during depressions. But Gompers' Local 144 survived the strike and the depression.

Gompers thought through a union fundamental to which he adhered with the religious fervor of a true believer. It was this: Americans are essentially conservative and property-conscious, and labor unions can't afford to arouse public opinion by threats to private property.

Gompers learned this precept at first hand in 1874 when he narrowly escaped death under the hoofs of mounted police who were suppressing a New York workers' demonstration that had been captured by leftist fire-eaters.

"I saw how professions of radicalism and sensationalism concentrated all the forces of organized society against the labor movement," he wrote. It was a lesson he never forgot.

The Socialists, who battled Gompers for AF of L control for almost two decades, regarded the unions as mere palliatives and useful only as spearheads in a war for social change. So, to Gompers, everything they stood for was a threat to his fledgling unions.

The first big battle came over the Socialists' notion that sections or cells of the party had a right to affiliate with the AF of L—as a party. It was as if Tammany Hall, the Democratic organization in Manhattan, wanted to affiliate today with the AFL-CIO.

The showdown came about when unions in New York asked Gompers for a charter to form a citywide "Central Trades Federation." On the list of petitioning "unions" was the New York section of the Socialist party.

Gompers gave an indignant no to the charter petition; then beat the Socialists three to one in a test at the next convention.

Year after year, the Socialists would propose at conventions that the AF of L harness itself to drives for the collective ownership of industry—or the "co-operative commonwealth."

To this Gompers once replied, "I want to tell you Socialists that I've studied your philosophy and read your works. I declare to you: economically you are unsound, socially you are wrong, industrially you are impossible."

About Rewards and Punishments

Sam Gompers drew about him a hard-drinking and hard-fighting group of Irish huskies. The Irish took as naturally to union politics as they took to big city politics, soon built union machines that kept them in office for years and were Gompers' solid underpinning in the Federation.

By 1905, only two decades after the founding of the AF of L, Sam Gompers—still beleaguered by enemies—could nevertheless look about him with some satisfaction. His pure and simple unionism dominated the union field with 1,500,000 members—by far the largest agglomeration of union power ever assembled.

Politics, in Sam Gompers' union book, was something to be

131

scorned altogether—or used sparingly. It could be used, for instance, to pressure state legislatures to help those workers who could not help themselves, say women and children.

Then, suddenly, Gompers plunged head over heels into politics.

The enemy, the employer, had wheeled up weapons which had turned Sam Gompers' economic artillery of boycott, strike and picket line into pea shooters. One employer weapon was the court injunction which could spike a strike—the union's ultimate weapon —by banishing the picket line or barring the boycott. The union man who dared defy the injunction went to jail for contempt of court, without jury trial. If the union appealed, it faced years of treasury-draining lawsuits.

Another weapon was the Sherman Anti-Trust Act. Passed by Congress in 1890 to curb business monopolies, the famous law had gathered dust until the government turned it against unions—a use that must have surprised many of the Congressmen who voted for it.

For instance: When hatmakers struck against a Danbury, Connecticut, employer in 1903 and urged a boycott against his products, the Hatters Union was prosecuted as a monopoly in restraint of trade. The punishment was a $250,000 fine which cost the hatters their homes and their life savings. The famous Danbury Hatters Case—upheld by the U.S. Supreme Court—exposed the unions to widespread suits and impotence in the battle with anti-union employers.

When St. Louis metal workers struck the Bucks Stove Company, Gompers put the company on the "unfair list" published in the AF of L magazine. This meant that good unionists would boycott its products. The stove manufacturer obtained an injunction which not only forbade the strikers to boycott the company but also barred published comment on the dispute. Gompers defied the order, was held in contempt of court and ordered to jail for a year.

The judge belabored Gompers as "a leader of the rabble who would unlaw the land, bring hideous pestilence and . . . subordinate the law to anarchy and riot."

Gompers took this with controlled rage. Then in tones that Patrick Henry might have used, Gompers orated, "If I cannot discuss grave problems in which the people of our country are interested . . . I shall have to bear the consequences. . . ."

132

Gompers never went to jail, because the Supreme Court held, seven years later, that the issue was moot, i.e., the strike was over.

For ten years Gompers battled to win laws that would curb the use of the injunction and exempt the unions from the Sherman Act. But, being Gompers, he devised his own kind of politicking: Don't get married to any one party. Don't give birth to a Labor party of your own. Play the field. Reward your friends and punish your enemies—whether they are Republicans or Democrats or whatever. Gompers launched campaigns to unseat hostile Congressmen and stumped Maine in a drive against a Republican officeholder. The campaigns had mixed results, but they did scare some hostile Congressmen into a more cautious attitude toward Labor. In time Woodrow Wilson helped Gompers win the Sherman Act curb he wanted, which the courts promptly emasculated; and it remained for the New Deal to bring the relief that Gompers had sought.[5]

But Gompers had laid down a principle which the unions still religiously follow: No matter what the provocation, don't be drawn into Labor party or other third-party adventures.[6]

The Summing Up

The time was the fall of 1924; the place was El Paso, Texas. The chief actor: Sam Gompers. Now, seventy-four, ravaged by disease and incredibly hard work (and play), and almost blind, he sat huddled on the rostrum while the Labor movement bade its "Grand Old Man" good-by. Men who rise to the leadership of the Plumbers, or the Miners, or the Stone Cutters, don't burst into tears easily. But on that day—the last of the AFL convention—there wasn't a dry eye in the house.

Delegate after delegate rose to pay homage to Gompers' forty years of service to the unions. For the last time, friends and critics alike cast a unanimous ballot for Sam Gompers for president. With tears rolling down his cheeks, Gompers said his last words of farewell.

---

[5] The Norris–LaGuardia Act.

[6] At least not on a national scale. David Dubinsky of the ILGWU and Alex Rose of the Hatters Union helped form and run a Labor party, later renamed a Liberal party, that plays a balance-of-power role in New York City and State politics.

This tearful praise for Gompers' lifework—coming in 1924—had an ironic twist. For here was the state of the unions at that moment:

In five years—after hitting a membership peak after the First World War—the unions had lost more than a million members. Now, although the AF of L still mustered 2,800,000 dues payers, it was relatively worse off than in 1910. Then it commanded one-tenth of the country's workers. Now, it had only 5 per cent.

Not only that. The AFL also seemed permanently barred from the one great reservoir of workers that could make it a significant movement—the mass industries: autos, steel, rubber, cement. In a great industrial nation, the AF of L mustered virtually no industrial workers, drawing its members from the building trades, clothing manufacture, printing, mining.

The unions couldn't even retain the minority position to which their impotence doomed them. They faced disintegration through a new counterattack from anti-union employers. At the very moment that Gompers was receiving the tearful kudos of his followers, employers were wooing away union members through the "American Plan," i.e., through company unions.

The unions were crumbling, and resisting industries seemed impregnable.

Had Sam Gompers failed?

No one could give the answer in 1924 when Sam Gompers "went out into the silence." The answer—that he had not failed—came a decade later when the Labor movement's other father, John L. Lewis, backed by the New Deal sentiments of a depression-battered people, picked up where Gompers had left off and forced the mass industries to accept unions.

CHAPTER 9

John L. Lewis:
Labor's Rogue Elephant

One day in 1955, the elders of the AFL-CIO Executive Council—whose ponderings cover lots of territory—had an argument over oil paintings. At the entrance to their oak-paneled conference room atop the new AFL-CIO Washington headquarters building, they had already enshrined on canvas four labor greats: Samuel Gompers, William Green, Philip Murray and George Meany. Now the debate swirled around a painting that wasn't there, that of John L. Lewis, boss of the miners, father of the mighty auto, steel and other mass-industry unions, and, all in all, the most resplendent figure the unions have yet sprung.

Bouncy David Dubinsky, who has a forthright New York Garment Center English all his own, rose to ask, "Are you fellas trying to rewrite the history books just like the Russians? Trotsky is kicked out of Russia, so you don't find him in the Communist encyclopedias. Lewis kicks himself out of the Federation. So are you going to treat him like Stalin treated Trotsky?"

The "fellas" on the Executive Council nevertheless decided against sanctifying Lewis with a painting. They declared, in effect, "To hell with him. He ain't one of us."

The incident of the missing painting points up Labor's grandest enigma, the life and works of John Llewellyn Lewis. It was Lewis who broke the mass-industry barrier to unionism, recruited millions and so transformed a dead-end, minority Labor movement into a major factor in American life. Lewis, in the late thirties, was a popular leader who swayed multitudes of men, gave Churchillian phrases to their aspirations and bent foes outside of Labor—and inside—to his will. For a brief moment, Lewis gave the unions excitement, drama and purpose. Men pinned their hopes on him, and in millions

135

of homes his picture hung side by side with that of the Virgin Mary or Franklin D. Roosevelt. Then, on a caprice, Lewis dropped the reins of the CIO he had founded.

Lewis said farewell with "I have done my work." That was in 1940 when Lewis was sixty, at the height of his powers, and with the union-organizing job by no means finished. Since then, the man who has done so much for the unions has been outside the pale of Labor's councils. Still head of the Miners, he has played the role of a great rogue elephant, using his declining strength to harass the labor world he once dominated.

Man on a Mountain Peak

Few men, dubbed great within their own lifetimes, have accepted their own grandeur as unquestioningly as John L. Lewis.

He could couch it in sublime terms:

"The heights are cold," Lewis confided in his farewell speech of 1940. "Who ascends to the mountaintop finds the loftiest peaks encased in mist and snow."

Or go to the ridiculous:

"Even the posterior of a great man is of interest," he said, after stooping over to tie a shoelace and straightening up to find a busload of Washington rubberneckers watching him.

Such is the awe that Lewis casts upon his office family that a visitor to the United Mine Workers Building in Washington is likely to feel he is in the hushed temple of some feared tribal deity.

Toward the rear of the spacious entry hall, an elevator operator sits silently, like a guard.

"Mr. Lewis," he repeats with seeming incredulity. "You mean you want to see Mr. John L. Lewis?"

On the second floor the visitor passes through two anterooms, each easily the size of a Washington Cabinet member's office. In the first, two stenographers work silently beneath a John L. Lewis that scowls down upon them from a portrait in oils on the wall. There are tension and a damn-your-eyes look about Lewis—from the gray mane of hair to the turned-down, firm mouth, the broad, out-thrust chin and the dewlaps. This is the face that launched a thousand jibes when Lewis was the symbol of massed union power.

136

It is the face of an angry man and of one who is playing a part in the grand manner.

Does Lewis ever smile in public, you wonder as you look up at the famous dark cliffs of eyebrows that overhang and recess the steel-gray eyes.

Through a second anteroom you go, where a union functionary shrinks silently behind a bare desk and outstretched newspaper.

Now you enter the lair—or shrine—of the great man and begin the trek, dubbed the "last mile," to the outsized desk in the farthest reaches of the depot-like room. The office, some forty by forty feet, is weighted down with overstuffed leather furniture once favored in corporate executive suites and men's clubs. The ceiling is vaulted like that of a small church, and from it hangs a magnificent crystal chandelier. Behind a giant desk that has been described as "the throne" sits John L. Lewis, massive, silent and portentous like a great Buddha.

The first time this writer walked the "last mile" to Lewis' desk was on the delicate business of asking questions about the "provisional" system with which Lewis has abolished elections for key posts in the UMW and runs the show with appointees.

The brief interview yielded more insight into John L. Lewis than it did into autocracy in his union.

After a few questions, Lewis said, "If you want to paint John L. Lewis as a tyrant, go ahead and paint him as a tyrant. You aren't going to get any help from Lewis."

He referred to himself in the third person with the same lack of self-consciousness that Charles de Gaulle does.

But, as a subsequent interview proved, Lewis can be charming too, and, again, in the grand manner.

When the Lewis scowl unfreezes, the Lewis smile can warm the visitor all over. He can perform virtuoso feats of conversation, clothing his speech with so picturesque and literary a quality that the visitor feels Lewis is putting on a show especially for him. An ordinary labor man says, "If you raise the wages of the lowest paid, the wages of the higher paid will take care of themselves." Lewis says, "If you raise the valleys, the peaks will take care of themselves."

Face to face, Lewis can melt the most determined critics. Columnist Westbrook Pegler was so warmed over by a Lewis tête-à-tête that he wrote a laudatory report, confessing later—when distance had lent disenchantment—that he had been taken in. Even labor leaders important in their own right are awed. David Dubinsky once sat down with Lewis for a two-hour talk right after F.D.R. had honored Dubinsky with an hour's White House audience—during wartime.

"Nothing that has ever happened to me," vows Dubinsky, "not even that hour's interview with the President, has ever given me as much pride as the two-hour talk with Lewis."

This is the Lewis power over acquaintances. Over those closely associated with him, the effect is likely to be that of a Svengali over Trilby. Associates (even the closest couldn't be called friends in the sense of a shared relationship) who broke with Lewis suffered emotional torments and couldn't leave him without looking back at him as the most memorable experience of their lives.

Although Philip Murray achieved distinction in his own right, his break with Lewis after twenty-five years of association was like that of a baby who has to cut its own umbilical cord from its mother. First, when Murray got out from under Lewis' shadow and accepted the presidency of the CIO, he told himself as much as he told the CIO convention.

"I think I am a man. I think I have convictions. I think I have a soul, and a heart and a mind. With the exception of course of my soul, they all belong to me. Every one of them."

And when Lewis tried Murray before a United Mine Workers Board and ousted him as vice-president, Murray broke down and cried like a child.

"I don't wish to go," he sobbed.

"When John L. came into a room, you knew it," men said of Lewis. And when occasion required he could wring the ultimate drama from even the most prosaic incident.

Once, when Lewis wanted to embarrass the AF of L's leaders before their own convention, he asked permission to present two resolutions. Delegates usually don't interrupt their chatter and socializing while a brother drones off a motion. But as Lewis edged his 240-pound bulk out of the Miners' delegation and into the aisle, the chattering lessened. Then a hush fell as Lewis, head down, seemingly lost in thought, moved ponderously toward the platform, bearing, to all appearance, a most fateful message. The distance to the platform was but fifty feet, one witness recalls, but Lewis moved with such deliberation that it seemed to the hushed hall that he would never get there.

Arrived, he took little more than a minute to intone two resolutions which together added up to twenty-six words—one barring anti-union employers from advertising in the Federation journal, another barring labor leaders from associating with such employers.

Lewis so dominated his own UMW conventions that for years he performed near miracles in bulling down open revolts.

Once, when Lewis had turned the convention over to the then vice-president Phil Murray, a delegation of rebellious miners set up a clamorous demand to be heard and wouldn't stop.

"You couldn't hear yourself think," one witness recalls. "It sounded like a riot, like a bunch of madmen." Lewis meanwhile sat silently toward the rear of the platform with his head down, looking up now and then to stare some of his critics in the eye—or draw reflectively on his cigar, then blow out the smoke contemptuously as if he were blowing the smoke into the face of the howling delegates.

Then, as the observer tells it,[1] John L. Lewis, who was some twenty-two feet away from the lectern and the gavel-wielding Murray, suddenly seemed to leap from his chair and face the convention with one bound.

"Of course, it was an impossible thing to do," one witness reported, "and we didn't know how he did it."

"This beating of breasts like savages in Africa pounding on their tomtoms must cease, you understand?" Lewis shouted. And it did.

"I am somewhat of a man," Lewis liked to say of himself. Which nobody could deny.

John Llewellyn Lewis was born in Lucas, Iowa, on Lincoln's Birthday in 1880, the son of an immigrant Welsh coal miner. As a boy and young man, he suffered injustices at the hands of mine owners, so creating a reservoir of emotion which he could tap as mine leader for the rest of his life. Young John's father, a brawling scrapper of a man, was blacklisted for leading a strike. This barred

---

1 In Saul Alinsky's *John L. Lewis, an Unauthorized Biography.*

him from work in his home town and followed him like the mark of Cain from minehead to minehead, bringing hunger and insecurity to Lewis' family. Too restive to remain in school beyond the eighth grade, young Lewis was digging coal at fifteen—putting in agonizing ten- and eleven-hour days in air so "thin," lacking in oxygen, that often he had to give up and go home.

It was obvious—not only to Lewis, but to those around him—that he was destined for bigger things. So in his early twenties Lewis began to calculate his chances and make those lunges for power which he was to repeat time and again until he reached old age.

Here Lewis had the help of the only person he probably ever respected and lastingly loved—his wife.

Myrta Bell Lewis, whom John L. Lewis married at age twenty-five, was a doctor's daughter and schoolteacher with resources of will that led family friends to describe her as stronger, even, than her redoubtable husband. The young wife took her young spouse in tow in the manner of the schoolteacher in *How Green Was My Valley*. She taught Lewis to read Dickens and Shakespeare and the classics. *Time* magazine remarked wryly that later she tried to stop Lewis from quoting them. The young wife also served as audience and critic as Lewis practiced his oratory.

So armed, Lewis took his first fling at power. He ran for Mayor of his home town of Lucas, Iowa, and was licked because his father-in-law, the doctor, persuaded the townsfolk to give their votes to another.

Lewis and his wife decided his career lay in labor leadership. So the Lewises moved to the mining country around Panama, Illinois. Conscious of his Lincoln's Day birthday, Lewis might have felt that John L. Lewis of Illinois had a finer ring to it than John L. Lewis of Iowa.

Within a year, Lewis was the president of the Panama, Illinois, UMW local. Soon after, the regional or district organization of the UMW sent young Lewis to the state capital at Springfield as a lobbyist, where he gave the first hint of the Lewis powerhouse to come by winning a State Workmen's Compensation Law and mine safety legislation.

Now, through a curious twist of fate, came the most significant event in Lewis' life. Sam Gompers, the AF of L's founder and president, spotted Lewis and took him under his wing as lobbyist and organizer. So, unwittingly, Gompers prepared Lewis for his later revolt against Gompers' own cherished craft unionism and for his role as reviver and second father of a greater Labor movement.

Lewis, thirty-one, vigorous and on the make, fawned on Gompers and studied the Grand Old Man, thirty years his senior, as a student might study a textbook. He mimicked Gompers' grand manner, deliberate speech and oratorical flourishes. Lewis watched Gompers at work as Labor's ambassador to the public—and learned that "labor leadership is 90 per cent showmanship." But the most important lesson Lewis learned stemmed from his assignment as organizer in the steel, glass and rubber industries.

"I got the measure of that problem," Lewis later told this writer.

Lewis found that these great industries—hostile to unions—could not be organized with the tools of the time, the craft unions of skilled workers.

After nine years of apprenticeship with the master, Sam Gompers, Lewis performed a masterful stroke of his own. With lightning speed, and without the benefit of an election, he rose in 1920 to the presidency of the Miners, then the country's most powerful union.

Lewis helped the then Miners' president to get a government post, and in turn was rewarded with a job as statistician and UMW journal editor at headquarters. When the president resigned and was succeeded automatically by the vice-president, Lewis moved up, by appointment, to the vacated vice-presidency. The new president soon dropped out of the picture, and Vice-President John L. Lewis automatically became President John L. Lewis.

At forty, Lewis was the youngest leader of a big international union. He had an oaklike body and the driving energy of a bull. "See this desk?" he told a visitor. With one bound, the 250-pound Lewis was atop his desk looking down triumphantly on his startled guest.

Hardly had Lewis made his somewhat similar leap atop the UMW than he tried again for greater power. Sam Gompers had ruled the AFL for thirty-four years. Lewis ran against Gompers and was trounced two to one.

141

Worse defeats followed. As coal lost its dominance after World War I, the coal operators fought each other fiercely for business, squeezing wages to the lowest levels since 1878. Thousands of miners quit the union that could no longer protect them, and the UMW —500,000 strong when Lewis took over—tobogganed to 75,000 by the early thirties.

To hold power during this descent into the economic maelstrom, Lewis waged war against self-rule in his union—winning victories against his own people that he couldn't win outside, so setting a pattern of union autocracy later copied by less imaginative men.

Lewis destroyed self-rule through a species of union martial law. UMW locals are usually small, sometimes numbering little more than several dozen miners. The effective unit of union representation, then, is a district union government—embracing the locals within a region—and having its own president. As district officers got into money or negotiating difficulties, Lewis replaced them with appointees. Most International Union presidents have the power to name "trustees" to take over locals for the duration of an emergency. Lewis called his appointees "provisional" officers—but kept them on for years.

Outraged miners fought Lewis' "provisional" officers in the union hall, in the courts and—as in Illinois—on bloody local battle-fields.

UMW conventions were wild and turbulent, but Lewis and his machine rode down the opposition.

In answer to one near riot, Lewis roared, "May the chair state that you may shout until you meet each other in hell, and he will not change his ruling."

For thirty-six years, right through the last quadrennial convention in 1956, eloquent pleas for self-rule have been laughed down by delegates much in the manner that Mussolini's followers once shouted, "We spit on freedom."

Let's listen as one unsung Patrick Henry pleads for union liberty. The time is October 1956; the place is the UMW convention at Cincinnati, Ohio.

"Delegate Komchak: 'This may be amusing to some of you. I came here as a representative of my local that sent me here to do a job, and I'm going to do it. They sent me here for the fourth time to

142

try to convince the members and our officers that we want democracy in our union. Do you believe in democracy? If you do, I am not a laughing subject.

" 'I want to say whether or not some officers in some districts have mulcted the funds twenty years ago is no reason why their members today shouldn't have democracy in our union. If any member doesn't want democracy, does that deprive me of it? Everyone knows that men who are appointed are there on sufferance of those who appoint them. I am pleading with the delegates. . . . Give the districts the right to elect their own officers.' "

To which a pro-Lewis delegate replied that this reminded him of "Gabriel trying to run the heavens better than God could."

"If there is one way to get Communism in the Mine Workers it is to have elections," the delegate said.

Another delegate once summed it up, "Mr. Lewis don't want it [autonomy]. So why fool around with it?"

Man at the End of a Lifeline

By 1933, when Lewis was fifty-three—an age when men are usually resigned to whatever life has brought—Lewis seemingly was headed for oblivion. The coal industry and its union, sick even during the 1920 boom, seemed at a dead end. Worse, the entire Labor movement—the greater stage on which Lewis once hoped to play a part—seemed at a dead end too.

The unions in the AF of L, which could boast a World War I peak membership of 4,500,000 dues payers, had lost more than half of their members by 1933. Worse, industrialists had unleashed a counteroffensive against unionism that threatened to grind all unions out of existence.

Few realized the Labor movement's precarious position in 1933, except the scared labor leaders themselves. At this juncture of the unions' sinking fortunes, a lifeline was thrown them by the federal government.

This was the famous Section 7A of the National Recovery Act (NRA) with which Franklin D. Roosevelt's New Deal set up codes to regulate and revive industries. It stated that employers must bar-

143

gain with unions of their employees' choosing.

Lewis pounced on Section 7A, calling it "Labor's Magna Charta," and says today that he conceived it and "it was written right here in the Mine Workers' offices." Professor Philip Taft, the labor historian, says he has proof that the AF of L Executive Council insisted on such a provision as a condition of supporting NRA.[2]

Still, Lewis was the first to seize the lifeline.

He scraped $75,000 from the bottom of the UMW barrel, hired organizers and deployed them in the mining towns with the fighting slogan: "The President [Franklin Delano Roosevelt] wants you to join the union."

Miners sang a jingle:

> *In nineteen hundred and thirty-three*
> *When Mr. Roosevelt took his seat,*
> *He said to President John L. Lewis*
> *In union we must be.*

Thousands who had dropped out of the UMW poured back in. Membership rocketed to 400,000 in a matter of weeks. A union was reborn. So was Lewis' power inside Labor. He looked about for new fields to conquer, and chose the anti-union mass industries and their millions of unorganized workers as his target.

When Lewis tried to harness the AFL to his organizing dream, he collided with two obstacles deeply imbedded in the Labor movement: craft unionism and union imperialism.

Sam Gompers had built a lasting union movement with skilled workers organized in craft unions. But assembly lines had reduced skilled workers to a splinter of the labor force, and no modern Labor movement could carry weight unless it embraced the new millions of partly skilled, or totally unskilled industrial workers. For the new assembly line plants, the craft union of Gompers' day was obsolete. If you organized a five-thousand-man Ford plant on a craft union basis, you'd have thirty to forty trade unions bargaining

---

[2] The Railway Labor Act already contained such a provision affecting railroad employees, but for industry generally, the stricture was revolutionary.

for men working on the same assembly line. In a word, chaos.

A different organizing idea was needed: industrial unionism. In an industrial union, all the skilled electricians, carpenters, sheet-metal workers as well as all the unskilled assembly-line tenders and plant sweepers belong to one big union, and bargain as a unit.

But here is where union imperialism came in. The heads of the craft unions—Big Bill Hutcheson of the Carpenters, John Posehl of the Operating Engineers, Dan Tobin of the Teamsters—had staked out empires of dues payers based on craft jurisdictions.

Anybody who handled wood, be he a woodsman felling a tree or a carpenter installing a windowframe, belonged to Bill Hutcheson by right of a charter granted by the AF of L. With jurisdictions like these, Hutcheson and other craft-union barons had job patronage to dispense, deals with employers to fatten on. And, although Hutcheson, for instance, had virtually no members in the auto, or steel, or rubber plants, he didn't want someone like Lewis to organize them into an industrial union. They belonged to him, said Hutcheson—and the AFL backed him.

Besides, the craft-union lords of the AF of L had another fear. If new millions poured into great new industrial unions, these would outnumber and outvote the dominant craft-union politicians and shift labor power and emoluments to a new, upstart breed of unionists.

Lewis had none of these fears. For one thing, his UMW was an industrial union embracing all crafts employed in the mine and at the minehead. Besides, Lewis had urgent fears of his own.

Unless the steel industry was unionized, Lewis' own United Mine Workers was in mortal danger. The United States Steel Corporation had kept the UMW out of its own "captive" coal mines—and so menaced UMW's position in all mines.

So Lewis pleaded with the AF of L's president, onetime coal miner William Green, to put men and money into the field to "organize the unorganized." When Green and his high command temporized, Lewis plunged the Labor movement into a civil war. His Fort Sumter was the 1935 AF of L convention at Atlantic City.

Lewis' oratorical effort in 1935 has come down as a classic, and no story of the rise of the unions is complete without it. He was the popular leader rallying his people.

145

Lewis said, "The Labor movement is organized upon the principle that the strong should help the weak. Isn't it right that we should contribute something of our own strength, our own knowledge, our own influence toward those less fortunately situated, in the knowledge that if we help them and they grow strong, in turn we will be the beneficiaries of the changed status and their strength?"

Lewis warned of the unions' precarious position.

"The strength of a strong man is a prideful thing, but the unfortunate thing in life is that strong men do not remain strong. And that is just as true of unions and labor organizations. And whereas the craft unions may be able to stand upon their own feet and, like mighty oaks before the gale, defy the lightning . . . the day may come when these organizations will not be able to withstand the lightning and the gale.

"Prepare yourselves by making a contribution to your less fortunate brethren. Heed this cry . . . that comes from the hearts of men. Organize the unorganized."

Inaction would encourage the enemies of Labor, Lewis said, and "high wassail will prevail at the banquet tables of the mighty."

To the oratorical punch, Lewis added a blow that landed the unions' family row on page one of the newspapers. In a brawl on the convention floor, he knocked down and bloodied up the human symbol of intrenched opposition to fresh union ideas: Big Bill Hutcheson of the Carpenters.

But neither Lewis the orator nor Lewis the pugilist prevailed.

John L. Stirs the Multitudes

On the day after the convention, Lewis called a council of war in an Atlantic City hotel lobby. Surrounded by Sidney Hillman and Dave Dubinsky of the needle trades, and Charles P. Howard of the Printers, Lewis pledged money and men from the UMW for an organizing drive. So was born the Committee for Industrial Organization which later became the Congress of Industrial Organizations (CIO). In four tidal years, some 5,000,000 men washed into the new Federation.

First targets were the two chief citadels of anti-unionism, U.S. Steel and General Motors.

Yet General Motors fell in forty-two days, and U.S. Steel signed up with Lewis two weeks later.

Some 400-odd organizers, led by Lewis' aide, Phil Murray, and paid almost wholly by UMW cash, poured into the steel towns. When steel companies took $500,000 worth of advertising space to warn of "CIO coercion," Lewis thundered back on the radio, "Let him who will, be he economic tyrant or sordid mercenary, pit his strength against this mighty surge of human sentiment now being crystallized in the hearts of thirty million workers who clamor for . . . industrial democracy. He is a madman or a fool who believes that this river of human sentiment can be dammed by the erection of arbitrary barriers of restraint."

Lewis was, at long last, playing the massive role for which, he felt, his talents and energy had cast him. He was a leader stirring the multitudes. He was a man to whom a nation listened. He was a giant who would grapple with other giants—the lords of industry, for instance.

Before Lewis' army could come to grips with "Big Steel," the war shifted unexpectedly to the automobile industry.

Without consulting their generalissimo, Lewis, the buck private auto workers launched an offensive of their own. They locked themselves into their plants and vowed they'd sit there until General Motors recognized a union.

The plant seizures were not part of Lewis' master plan. They burdened him with unexpected anxieties and doubts. The key to the mass-industry drives was the hands off policy of a newly benevolent government. But could the New Deal withhold troops if men forcibly seized other people's property? Besides, how could Lewis square these acts with his rock-ribbed Republicanism and his orthodox views on property rights? The property problem Lewis put to the leftist professionals who had flocked to his organizing standard—who knew their way around in the class war, in union organizing and in slogans. The leftist brains whirred, and came up with a rationale to answer the capitalists. The sitdown strikers have property rights in their jobs, was the slogan.

The threatened use of bayonet-wielding troops to evict the strikers, Lewis blocked with his finest moments—as a ham actor.

"All right, you've got the National Guard," he told Michigan

Governor Frank Murphy as the Governor agonized over public pressure to use troops. "What kind of bayonets do you think that you'll use? You know, if they use the flat, sharp kind, they can push them in a long way, but they can't twist them. . . . On the other hand, if you use the square kind, they can twist them around and make a big hole, but they can't push them in so far."

When Murphy felt he could no longer stay the troops, Lewis told him, "Tomorrow morning, I shall personally enter G.M. Plant Chevrolet No. 4. I shall order the men to disregard your order and to stand fast. I shall then walk up to the largest window in the plant, open it, divest myself of my outer raiment, remove my shirt, and bare my bosom. Then, when you order your troops to fire, mine will be the first breast that those bullets will strike."

The troops remained outside the plants. Instead, Roosevelt secretly intervened to persuade G.M. to meet with Lewis.

With the solemnity of a President embarking for a Summit Conference, Lewis entrained for Detroit accompanied by a carload of reporters who wired hourly bulletins on the journey. At Detroit, the combination of a scowling Lewis plus the realization that you can't fight City Hall (i.e., the federal government) brought the General Motors executives around.

Victory in the steel industry came almost as an anticlimax soon after. The human key to Lewis' success here was Myron Taylor, Big Steel's Chairman of the Board. Lewis met Taylor, so one story goes, when Mrs. Taylor spotted Lewis in a restaurant and said, "What an interesting man. I'd like to meet him."

In any case, Lewis and Taylor closeted themselves in Lewis' Washington hotel suite and, after ten days of generous breakfasts and lavish lunches (one menu included oysters Rockefeller and pheasants under glass), ate their way to agreement.

"Within one year we organized 5,000,000 men in the basic industries," Lewis told this writer. "They had contracts, were paying dues and their unions were going concerns. . . ."

It took Sam Gompers forty laborious years to build an AF of L of 4,000,000 members. Lewis bettered this in one roaring year. The difference, of course, was that Lewis had the government with him while Gompers had the government against him—something Lewis won't concede to this day.

A Niagara Falls of fame washed over Lewis. At one time the *New York Times* devoted 5 per cent of its space—roughly sixteen columns or two pages per day—to activities in which Lewis was involved. All heads turned when the well-caricatured figure of Lewis entered a restaurant. When he addressed a Labor Day meeting at Pittsburgh, some 200,000 wildly cheering unionists turned out for him. Men scrawled his name on fences as an act of defiance against anti-union employers. And Lewis' Washington office rivaled the pressroom in the White House nearby as a journalists' hangout.

"Remember you are in the center," Lewis is reported to have told an aide at the time. "The world will come to this office."

Not long after, the world was going elsewhere. Lewis' office was an Elba, and Lewis was an embittered spectator to great events rather than an actor in them.

Lewis' Biggest Mistake

In a conversational post-mortem over his career, Lewis once confided to David Dubinsky his biggest mistake. It was the mistake, he felt, of surrounding himself with Communists during the early CIO days. These caused him to exaggerate his own political strength, plunged him into the fatal break with F.D.R. and led to Lewis' self-exile from national labor leadership.

John L. Lewis' "biggest mistake," however, was to be born with —or acquire along the way—a fatal flaw: inordinate vanity and pride.

Arguing with Lewis once, Labor Secretary Perkins exclaimed, "But that's the sin of pride!"

"That's my pride," Lewis bristled. "It's as good as the pride of the Vanderbilts."

This pride led Lewis to make an initial mistake in 1940.

As Roosevelt later told the story (with relish), Lewis came to the White House and asked for a place with Roosevelt on the third-term Democratic presidential ticket.

"We are the two most prominent men in the nation," Lewis is supposed to have said. "It will be an invincible combination."

"Which place will you take, John?" Roosevelt replied. Roosevelt and Lewis had needed each other. Now Lewis, miffed, broke the alliance. He threw in his fortunes with the extreme isolationist groups that fought American aid to the Western allies. On the eve of the third-term election, Lewis went on a radio network that reached an estimated sixty million Americans and urged his labor following to vote for Roosevelt's opponent, Wendell Willkie. If Roosevelt was elected, Lewis vowed, he'd step down as president of the CIO.

Thirteen days after Roosevelt was elected for his third term, on November 5, 1940, Lewis went before the CIO convention at Atlantic City and redeemed his pledge to step down as leader. Neither Lewis nor the delegates expected this abrupt ending of his CIO career. Lewis had watched with tear-filled eyes as the delegates opened the convention with an hour-long ovation and floor demonstration for him. He felt this would inevitably be followed by an insistent and unanimous draft to remain.

Yet the hoped-for draft never came. The men who hadn't followed Lewis in his crusade against Roosevelt wouldn't get down on their knees to Lewis now. They chose, instead, to follow Sidney Hillman, who blocked the Lewis draft and brought Phil Murray to power.

As many hardbitten labor men cried unashamedly in a stilled, vast auditorium, Lewis recited his own funeral oration over his career as CIO president—and finished himself off as leader.

Until the great divide event of his life—his capricious resignation as president of the CIO—Lewis had moved with sureness and grandeur toward the greatest prizes of fame and power America could offer. *Time* magazine wondered in the late thirties whether "this vast and glowering Welshman would wind up in the White House." Instead, it now seemed, in 1940, as if the tidal forces that had created Lewis cast him aside when the need for him was over. The CIO which he had founded no longer needed an imperious leader to summon the working host and battle the lords of industry. That battle won, the CIO needed a Phil Murray to conciliate the brawling elements within it and hold the CIO together.

Lewis, the ex-CIO president, was still president of the United Mine Workers and so held strategic control over the nation's coal pile. At sixty, he was in the full pride of his manhood; he had achieved much, and he had dreams of doing more. This was not a man who could bottle up his explosive power within the confines of one union.

So Lewis, who had been running with the grain of events when he led the CIO, began in 1940 to rub history the wrong way. Like a gambler who tries to retrieve his fortunes with reckless tosses of the dice, Lewis made lunge after lunge for grand prizes of his own devising. Being Lewis, his flounderings made a great splash. He even managed, from time to time, to scare the country—and the unions— out of their wits. But he never regained the glory that was his during the three brief years from 1937 to 1940.

In his new role as national gadfly, Lewis' first adventure was to try and organize the nation's 3,000,000 milk farmers in the midst of war in 1942. The drive was a bust, and the catch-all union Lewis formed for the purpose—District 50 of the UMW—remains like a tombstone today to mark the grave of a $3,000,000 Lewis folly.

Next, disregarding the wartime need for coal and the freeze on wages and prices, Lewis shut down the coal mines with demands for pay boosts and kept shutting them down every spring in leonine defiance of the President, the Army, the Congress, the Justice Department, the courts, the press and the people.

Lewis succeeded in prying higher pay for his coal diggers, and, as a scholar of the classics, had a glorious time playing the role of Titan battling the gods of Olympus. As soon as Congress could get around to it after the war, it passed a law to cut leaders like Lewis down to size. This was the Taft-Hartley Act.

Ironically, the man whom Congress chiefly had in mind when it passed the Taft-Hartley Act over Harry Truman's veto was already a spent locomotive, shunted off the main track of union events.

Lewis still sat atop the nation's coal pile, but it was a shrinking pile as oil, gas and electric power provided an increasing share of the nation's energy. From a union 750,000-strong in 1920, the United Mine Workers had shrunk to 200,000 by the mid-fifties. Lewis, without power of his own, could only fish in troubled labor waters to annoy those who held power.

When George Meany forced the gangster-ridden International Longshoremen's Association out of the American Federation of Labor and then spent $1,000,000 of Federation funds in a drive to woo the ILA's members away, Lewis lent the beleaguered dockers' union $300,000 and so helped it survive.

When David McDonald toyed with the idea of pulling his 1,000,000-man Steelworkers out of the CIO and so wrecking it, Lewis met portentously with McDonald and Dave Beck of the Teamsters and encouraged reports that a new Federation was being born. Nothing came of it.

In between these sorties, Lewis used the ample time on his hands to win a model welfare plan and build a chain of modern hospitals in coal country which had few doctors and fewer facilities. He used UMW money to buy control for the union of the second biggest bank in Washington, D.C. He put the UMW into the shipping business.

Although seventy-eight as this is written, Lewis seemingly has not resigned himself to the role of outsider. The old bitterness against the younger men who did what Lewis couldn't do—hold on to leadership—doesn't mellow. It grows more rancid. So while the AFL-CIO struggles with the corruption crisis and declining membership, Labor's once most eloquent voice is raised in piping derision.

To Lewis, George Meany is "an honest plumber fighting sin." Walter Reuther is a "Marxist who is inebriated by the exuberance of his own verbosity."

To those reporters who still seek him out, Lewis likes to hint that he must not be counted out of further adventures, say, like intervening in the struggle between the AFL-CIO and the Teamsters.

"There's a fight going on down the street," Lewis told this writer, "and for the first time in forty years we're not in it. But we have the knowledge we can get into it any time we want to."

"At age seventy-eight?" I asked.

"I am as free to move today as when I first came into this office," Lewis replied.

Labor leaders stopped taking these threats seriously at least a decade ago. Lewis has, for years now—as A. H. Raskin of the *New York Times* put it—been a "glorious anachronism."

Yet the hold that Lewis has on union men's imagination won't die.

I asked the president of a world-famous union recently what the unions could do about their gravest problem: that of recruiting new members.

The labor man shook his head.

"What we need today," he said, "is another John L. Lewis."

V

The troubles the unions have seen.

The rank and file have let their servants become
their masters and dictators. The workers have now to
fight not alone their exploiters but likewise
their leaders, who often betray them.

MOTHER JONES, union pioneer, 1925

We knew there was corruption,
but we didn't know it went so deep.

GEORGE MEANY, 1958

It wasn't extortion—they paid me the money as bribes.

JOE FAY, ex-union vice president

CHAPTER 10

The Corrupters

One of the country's big industries—just how big no one really knows—is so hush-hush that you won't find its representatives in the yellow pages of your telephone book. And yet there are many who know just where to find it. This is an industry that sells a secret service: the corruption of union leaders. It consists of an underground network of middlemen or union influence peddlers who, for a fee, will get the employer a favorable union deal. This deal may be to keep the union out of the plant—or to come in under a "sweetheart" contract.

Everyone now knows about the labor leader who steals from the treasury, or the racketeer who extorts from an employer. But little is known, because he hides in the background, of the man behind the most serious union corruption of all: the collusion between employers and union men.

It is hard to spot this fellow, because he doesn't openly display the wares he sells, i.e., influence with unions. The protective coloration behind which he hides is that of "industrial relations consultant" or "labor relations" lawyer.

Taming unions, through middlemen, is big business. One middleman we'll soon meet collected $2,480,000 in seven years. He had clients in almost every state in the union.

The middleman's influence can reach high, and cost the wage earner much. One labor man, so reached, was Dave Beck. The former Teamster boss was found by the McClellan Committee to have taken, "not borrowed," $370,000 in union funds. But his

155

greater corruption got less attention. Beck connived—the McClellan Committee also found—with one influence peddler-middleman to permit some employers to have no unions at all, and others to have "sweetheart" deals. To union members, the dues Beck misused were peanuts compared to the loss of pay resulting from substandard contracts. Of all the union problems I've investigated, that of the middleman-influence peddler is most loaded with woe for the worker. For in the deals the go-between arranges, the union's function is perverted. Instead of serving as an instrument to win better wages and working conditions, it becomes a tool for keeping the worker in line. Thus it performs a function similar to that of the unions in Communist Russia.

Good Old Reliable Nathan

One spring day in 1957, an elderly fast-talking witness before the McClellan Committee chortled and wise-cracked his way through a sordid story.

Serving as a "purchasing agent," the witness, according to testimony, had been used by the then Teamster president Dave Beck to drain off $85,000 of union funds—on love seats and roofing for Beck's home, knee drawers for his ample person, on hosiery for his wife, on deep freezes, cameras, guns, garden hose for his son, Junior. And on diapers for his niece's baby.

The witness who could get it for Dave Beck wholesale (Senator John McClellan called Beck's end of it "theft") was Nathan W. Shefferman, who described himself as a "labor relations consultant." Obviously a big operator, Nathan Shefferman worked chiefly for employers—some four hundred of them from coast to coast. His "Labor Relations Associates of Chicago, Inc." also had offices in Detroit and New York.

The most that Senators could get out of Shefferman was that he "created good will" for employers and "made surveys." Try as hard as they could, the Senators could not learn from the sixty-nine-year-old Shefferman precisely what it was that he did.

The Senators had a right to be puzzled. For a man who advised employers, Shefferman led a curious business and personal life. His entertaining was not for employer-clients but for labor leaders. His

156

closest friend was labor man Dave Beck. Shefferman traveled yearly from Chicago to Seattle to spend the Christmas holidays with the Teamster boss, went on European junkets with him, never permitted Beck to pick up a dinner check—was his "clown prince" who regaled Beck with dialect stories.

For an employers' man, Shefferman's friendships with other labor leaders while less close were equally impressive. Shefferman was much in demand for speeches before union conventions—where he gave out with catch phrases, Edgar Guest poetry and soporific clichés. Shefferman and his son threw costly dinners for members of the old AF of L Executive Council at their annual meetings. They took the boys sea-fishing or to the races. Shefferman worked hard at making labor friends. His pockets bulged with gadgets: a wrist-watch alarm clock, a spring-driven self-powered razor, a miniature camera. A one-man purchasing agency, Shefferman bought some $478,000 of goods at wholesale for 421 persons over a nine-year span, using his connections with employer-clients as supply sources. Among those who benefited—besides Beck—were some ninety labor leaders and labor lawyers.

Shefferman's expenses for new business were equally puzzling. He testified he gave Dave Beck $24,000 "out of friendship," but prudently charged it as a business expense. He gave another Teamster boss $750 for referring an employer client to him.

Why did Shefferman—labor relations consultant to employers—spend so much money and lavish so many favors on union leaders? Where did he get the money? And what could the labor men do for him?

The answer came some months later—in the fall of 1957—when the McClellan Committee paraded a host of witnesses—employers, lawyers, union members and its own investigators—to piece together a startling picture of employer-labor leader conspiracy with middle-men as the catalysts. Disguised as a "human relations" expert, Dave Beck's friend, Nate Shefferman, was a union wrecker straight out of the old world of industrial espionage exposed by the La Follette investigation of the 1930's. With an added service: he could sell his influence with labor powers like Beck and others. Shefferman, who had talked volubly about his purchases for Beck when first questioned by the McClellan Committee, pleaded the Fifth Amendment when recalled for questioning about his middleman role. His testimony about his "labor relations" activities "might tend to incriminate me," he pleaded.

Nevertheless, from Shefferman's own records and other sources, the investigators learned that his Labor Relations Associates of Chicago, Inc. sold $2,480,000 of labor services in seven years. Chief client was the country's leading store chain, Sears, Roebuck & Co. Sears helped put Shefferman in the union-busting business, gave him access to goods at wholesale so that he could do favors for dozens of labor leaders and footed some odd expense bills. (Among these was $96.50 for entertaining Dave Beck on his 1955 trip from Chicago to Indianapolis to attend the funeral of Beck's predecessor, Dan Tobin.)

For the case-hardened Senators who thought they had seen everything in the way of labor rackets, the dramatic hearings on the middleman were a short, short education into the root cause of union corruption. The late Lincoln Steffens once found that for every crooked political boss who gave away a valuable franchise, there was a crooked businessman who bribed him to do it. Now, the Senators learned that, where there's union corruption, there are the corrupters as well as the corrupted.

"It has come as a profound shock to see men acting on behalf of American business take the Fifth Amendment before this Committee," Senator John McClellan observed.

"Are there sufficient laws to deal with businessmen who knowingly pay off money to union officials to prevent or discourage unionization?" he wanted to know.

How to Tame a Union

As depicted in Senate testimony, Shefferman's methods, employed by other middlemen as well, added up to a blueprint for draining away a union's power or taming the union and turning it against its members.

First and crudest was the "conduit" method. Here, for a fee, Shefferman aides turned themselves into human pipelines through which employers funneled money and gifts—Senator McClellan called them "payoffs"—to union men.

158

When automobile and electric appliance distributors and other businessmen at Flint, Michigan, faced Teamster unionization, they knew exactly what to do. They testified:

They got in touch with Shefferman's man in Detroit, George Kamenow. "The fee is $100 a month," Kamenow would tell his client-businessman, "and another $2,000 to entertain union officials. I'll need the money to take the boys to the Rose Bowl Game," he'd explain. Once the fee and "entertainment" costs were paid, immediate results followed.

"So you paid $2,000 to have the pickets removed?" Committee Counsel Bob Kennedy asked an electrical supplier.

"That is correct," the supplier replied.

One Flint car dealer testified he paid labor relations advisor George Kamenow the usual fee and "entertainment-for-the-boys" contribution. Then, when the Teamsters withdrew, he said he went right on paying money to take the union boys fishing in Canada and buy airline tickets for them for union conventions in Seattle and for Christmas presents.

"You were paying to entertain union officials, when they had nothing to do with your plant?" counsel Bob Kennedy asked the employer.

"It looked to me like a good investment," said the employer.

The Senate Rackets Committee transcript here reads:

Bob Kennedy: And this payment was worth while to keep you from being unionized?

Mr. Graff: [Max H. Graff, the employer] Well, you can turn it around that way.

Some employers stuck to their story that they had hired middleman George Kamenow to give them "labor relations advice." But others were more forthright.

One builder, fighting a strike of carpenters, knew that he could win if he could get the local Teamsters to bring supplies through the Carpenters' picket line. So he called for Shefferman's man, Kamenow.

"And did he tell you that he wanted $2,000 in cash as well as a $2,000 check?" asked Committee counsel Bob Kennedy.

"That is correct," replied the builder.

159

LABOR U.S.A.

"And the $2,000 in cash was to be passed on to certain of the Teamster Union officials?" asked Bob Kennedy.

"It was told to us that the $2,000 would be passed on to Teamster officials; that is right," testified the builder.

These well-laid plans went agley when rank-and-file Teamster members refused to cross the Carpenters' picket line, anyway. But when employer money enters the middleman pipeline, it stays there.

"Did you get your money back?" Chairman McClellan asked the builder.

"I didn't ask for the money back," was the reply.

Nine Flint employers testified they paid $27,700 to middleman Kamenow and Shefferman's labor relations firm to regale the union boys with fishing trips, football and baseball junkets, pocket money for labor conventions, Labor Day and July Fourth celebrations and gifts. On the receiving end, they said, were friends of Kamenow in Flint Local 332 of the Teamsters. One chief friend was Frank H. Kierdorf, business representative and organizer for the local. As is sometimes the case in the Teamsters, Kierdorf had unusual qualifications for his job. He was appointed business representative by Jim Hoffa when Kierdorf came out of prison where he served a stretch for armed robbery. He burned himself fatally later while setting fire to a shakedown victim's store.

In an illuminating affidavit to Senate Committee investigators, Kierdorf stated that "Kamenow was active in combating union influence," but this seemingly didn't prevent union man Kierdorf from being pals with Kamenow and going on "five- to eight-day fishing trips" with him—during which Kamenow supplied the boat and provisions. Nor did it prevent Teamster Kierdorf from buying goods at discount through Kamenow's charge accounts at Sears, Roebuck and other stores in Flint. He said he paid for the goods and denied that he withdrew pickets or did any other similar favors for Kamenow.

Questioned before the Senate Rackets Committee, Kierdorf did not repeat the denials in the affidavit. He refused to answer any questions—except to give his name—on the ground that it might tend to incriminate him.

George Kamenow, too, sought refuge in the Fifth Amendment on the ground that he might otherwise be incriminated.

Senator McClellan summed up the testimony involving the employer-middleman-union-man triangle:

". . . It looks to me like we are developing a pattern of what amounts to a payoff to union officials to have them disregard the rights of the workingmen; to be reluctant, if not to refuse, to press any drive for unionization.

The Mysterious Strangers

Or, to keep a union out, middleman Nathan Shefferman would simply copy the methods of the old labor spy agencies. This sort of union busting is now outlawed by the Taft-Hartley Act. Here, according to Senate testimony, is how Shefferman turned the clock back for his chief client, Sears, Roebuck, at its stores in Boston. We'll call this episode the "case of the mysterious strangers"—a drama that began to unfold in Sears stores when employees voted three to one to affiliate their independent union with the Retail Clerks International.

First, a balding stranger who called himself James T. Guffey arrived from Chicago, put up at a Boston hotel—and from his hotel room began to play an important role in the stores' and employees' affairs.

A National Labor Relations Board examiner pieced together this story:

To Guffey's room, reluctant employees soon began to trek, during working hours, on orders from their superiors. "These meetings are top secret," Guffey hush-hushed his visitors. They were violating the Taft-Hartley law, Guffey told them. So mum was the word. At the same time, new faces began to appear in the Sears, Roebuck stores. About a dozen in all, and scattered through several stores, these newcomers did no selling but described themselves as "public relations" men from Chicago. This "public relations," it soon turned out, consisted in gathering dossiers on employees, spying out their union sentiments, visiting their homes and—as the Retail Clerks Union later charged—there trying to brain-wash them.

So hidden was Shefferman's hand that nowhere in the subsequent NLRB investigation does his name appear—nor that of his labor relations firm. But Shefferman had left his traces. The man who called himself Jim Guffey or Fred Warren was an old reliable Nathan Shefferman hand. He drew his pay from Shefferman under the name James T. Neilsen—and was a confessed embezzler.

As part of Shefferman's campaign, one employee allowed his car to be damaged. A brick shattered a car window, and the tires were ice-picked. The Retail Clerks were blamed. The car owner got three new tubes—paid for by Sears.

Shefferman's aides stirred up so much confusion that, when a new election was held, the employees reversed themselves and voted against the Retail Clerks Union.

Sears, Roebuck has since dropped and repudiated Shefferman. But the benefits gained from his efforts were substantial. Of 205,000 employees in Sears, Roebuck, only 14,000 belonged to unions at the time of the McClellan disclosures. Half of these were in the Teamsters.

About Collective Bargaining and Unions at a Bargain

When Nate Shefferman couldn't keep a union out altogether, he'd turn to a second technique: the union-you-can-live-with method.

This brought some strange bedfellows into the factories of Shefferman's clients. Mattress manufacturers usually sign with the Upholsterers Union. But in the Indiana, Illinois, Washington, Texas and Alabama plants Shefferman served, teamsters stuff the mattresses. And, in New Jersey, retail clerks do the sewing.[1]

There was method in this strange melange. The collective bargaining of these locals would lead to a bargain for the employer only.

In a New Jersey plant of a Shefferman client, the Englander Company (mattresses), women sewing and stapling machine operators earned (in 1957) an average $1.27 an hour against the $1.88 average of the industry as a whole. At such a bargain, Shefferman's client didn't fight the union—a local of the Retail Clerks. He welcomed the union in. In fact, as the National Labor Relations Board found, the Englander Company assisted the union's leader in organizing the plant. Naturally, the local's boss, one Abe Lew, was a pal of

---

[1] The Retail Clerks, a union with a fine reputation, is fighting valiantly to clean up spotty local situations.

Shefferman. (When Lew died in 1958, it was found that he had looted his local union welfare fund reserves of some $220,000.)

Union leader Lew was entertained lavishly by Shefferman and his son in New York—at Englander Company expense. He'd come running to Chicago and Miami Beach when the Sheffermans beckoned.

In 1955, the Englander Company signed nine of its plants into the Teamsters at one stroke. The contract was signed with Jim Hoffa's Central Conference of Teamsters. The Western Conference of Teamsters, run by other officials, wouldn't have anything to do with it.

The agreement was a top-down contract, i.e., it was signed between the Englander Company and the Teamsters—as Bob Kennedy put it—"without any consultation with the employees whatsoever."

The Englander Company's labor relations lawyer, Sidney Korshak, explained why the contract was signed—and so let the cat out of the bag:

"The papers were calling attention that the merged [AFL-CIO] federation was going to . . . unionize every unorganized company in the United States. We were fearful of that, and we felt we could live with the Teamsters," Korshak said.

That the Englander Company was right in assuming it "could live with" Jimmy Hoffa's Central Conference of Teamsters emerged from the terms of its contract.

The Teamsters Union is the most powerful in America. Elsewhere it uses its power to win some of the highest wage rates enjoyed by union men anywhere. But in the plants of Shefferman clients, the Teamsters—tamed—were content to accept wages that, in some instances, barely exceeded the dollar per hour minimum required by law.

In Michigan City, Indiana, as Senate investigator Pierre Salinger testified, a porter-janitor was paid $1.27½ per hour in 1955. The contract in Seattle (signed with the Western Conference Teamsters which had refused to go along with the Hoffa contract) paid the porter-janitor thirty cents an hour more.

In the Hoffa contract, female production workers were paid from $1.12½ an hour to $1.42½ an hour. In the Western contract—by

163

contrast—women's wages ranged from border makers at $1.62½ to floor girls at $2.02 an hour.

For his services, it was testified, the Englander Company paid Shefferman $76,400 in a little more than three years. After the company signed its "we-can-live-with-the-Teamsters" contract, Shefferman's job was considered done, and his employment by the company ended.

Tangled Skein

For a fascinating moment, Senate investigators glimpsed the outlines of an interlocking league of labor influence peddlers, some from the underworld, who called on each other when their own connections didn't reach far enough.

This picture emerged when investigators looked into the circumstances under which a Shefferman client "ran away" from one union and into the arms of another.

The unraveling of this episode began routinely enough. A Connecticut bathroom fixture manufacturer who had dealt with a local of the Jewelry Workers faced organization by the United Automobile Workers. He preferred to do business with the Jewelry Workers Union, some of whose locals are notorious for their sweetheart deals.[2] While the company resisted the UAW for months, it signed a contract with the Jewelry Workers on the same day it was approached.

But when the UAW refused to withdraw and went, instead, to the National Labor Relations Board to demand an employee election, curious things began to happen. A varied assortment of influence peddlers materialized who tried to get the Auto Workers to withdraw.

As McClellan Committee testimony showed, a shadowy figure with inexplicable friendships among labor leaders appeared: one Phil Weiss, described by Counsel Bob Kennedy of the McClellan Committee as "being foremost in the country . . . as far as selling . . . racket connections." Kennedy also characterized Weiss as having the most far-reaching effect on labor racketeering of anybody in the United States." To all questions before the McClellan

---

[2] See Chapter 13, "Cruel Sweetheart."

164

Committee, including the date of his birth, Weiss refused to answer on the ground that it might tend to incriminate him.[3]

Up in Weiss's Room

In early 1956, there trooped to Phil Weiss's suite at the Essex House, in New York City, a number of men. One, according to McClellan Committee testimony, was Hyman Powell of the Jewelry Workers, who testified that UAW regional director Charles Kerrigan came there too.

Hymie Powell told the McClellan Committee why.

Counsel Bob Kennedy [questioning Powell]: Did you make arrangements to meet with Mr. [Charles] Kerrigan to see if he would withdraw [his organizing drive]?

Powell: I did.

Bob Kennedy: Where did you meet with him?

Powell: At the Essex House.

Bob Kennedy: Where?

Powell: Phil Weiss's suite.

Bob Kennedy: Why did you meet in Phil Weiss's suite?

Powell: I was going to ask Phil Weiss if he could use his influence with Charles Kerrigan to get him to withdraw.

Bob Kennedy: What does Phil Weiss do?

Powell: I haven't any idea at all.

Powell also went to others who, as he said, had influence.

Bob Kennedy: Did you go out to see Sidney Korshak [a lawyer for one of Shefferman's clients]?

Powell: I did. . . . I made it my business and I especially went out to Chicago . . . and I asked Mr. Korshak whether he could use his influence since he dealt with a lot of . . . people connected in the Labor movement to get the UAW to withdraw.

Bob Kennedy: Whom did you want Mr. Korshak to speak to?

---

[3] Phil Weiss was convicted on charges of transporting stolen goods, sentenced to five years in prison and fined $10,000. On appeal, the case was remanded to the lower court. As this is written, Weiss, still under indictment, awaits a new trial.

Powell: I wanted him to speak to everybody, but I mentioned to him Phil Weiss's name.

In Hymie Powell's curious union world there's nothing odd about asking an employer's lawyer in Chicago to intercede with a shadowy figure in New York for help against a rival union.

The McClellan Committee then heard Powell testify that up in Phil Weiss's room, Weiss spoke to UAW man Charles Kerrigan. Extortionist Johnny Dio also was "interested in getting [the UAW] to withdraw," Powell said.

Senate investigators suspected that Phil Weiss and Johnny Dio were trying to bribe UAW man Charles Kerrigan. This was never proved, and, even if the attempt were made, it didn't succeed. The UAW refused to withdraw and continued to press for an employee election. Four days after the NLRB ordered such an election, the company moved its plant to Chicago. There it signed a contract with the Teamsters to represent employees who make bathroom fixtures.

The Senate Committee focused, of necessity, on Nathan Shefferman. So it didn't pause to explore the new vistas of investigation opened up by the case of the runaway fixture manufacturer. This was a pity, for many tantalizing questions were left unanswered.

How wide was Phil Weiss's influence? To what extent were racket figures involved in the union middleman industry? And how widespread, and what were the ramifications of the middleman network anyway?

Still, the investigation was an eye opener for the Senators and for the country. Union corruption, it turned out, was a two-way street in which some businessmen and labor leaders walk hand in hand and must share equal guilt.

"The tale of Nathan Shefferman has given business its worst publicity since the La Follette hearings of 20 years ago," Daniel Bell wrote in *Fortune*.

More than 70 per cent of Shefferman's "top money" clients—as Senator McClellan pointed out—used Shefferman's services to fight unions. "It was management who paid the bills," said the Senator.

166

CHAPTER 11

Journey to the Underworld

Side by side with the great unions that perform legitimate services for their members, there exists today a nationwide shadow federation of secret labor bosses. Always in the background, they wield power over unions in their own bailiwicks and exchange favors through a subterranean network of influence that spans the country.

Although seldom visible, these phantom wielders of power are real enough. They are the regional overlords of organized crime— the survivors or heirs of the Prohibition era rackets who today are men of substantial business interests, lawful as well as unlawful.

Staking out city and state domains, these men rule cartels of crime that have woven themselves into the very fabric of their communities. In the Midwest, the Chicago Capone mob, bossed chiefly by Tony Accardo and Paul (the Waiter) Ricca, dominates the numbers and policy gambling, the jukebox and pinball racket monopolies and has infiltrated legitimate businesses: laundries, hotels, auto agencies. The gangsters wield great political power and even have their own anti-crime lobby at the state capital.

In the East, a New York-New Jersey criminal axis cuts so wide a swathe in business, politics and crime that the names of some of its bosses have become household words: Frank Costello, for instance, and the late Albert Anastasia. Detroit has its Angelo Meli; Cleveland has its Babe Triscaro.

Stacked about me, as I write this, are the interview notes and documentary materials gathered during a decade of investigative reporting into the underworlds of our big cities. Running like a persistent thread through these annals of crime is the gang boss's back-of-the-scenes influence in unions.

How did bigshot gangsters get into unions?

Why do they stay in them?

How do they use unions in their rackets?

When these questions are clearly answered, it will be seen that the present weapons with which union corruption is being fought—and even those weapons contemplated in proposed laws—are as pea-shooters pelting peas off a concrete wall.

The gangster uses unions to police and protect deeply intrenched, lucrative monopoly rackets.

"Extortion? Shakedowns?" a veteran prosecutor exploded at me one day. "That's not what gangsters are chiefly in unions for. More and more, they are using them as a wedge to pry into legitimate business and turn them into rackets." The prosecutor was Al Scotti, Rackets Bureau Chief in the New York County District Attorney's office who has spent his working life fighting racketeers.

Anatomy of a Racket

Of all the strange dramas that Robert Kennedy has pieced together as counsel for the McClellan Committee the "Case of the Golden Garbage" was the strangest, and it spelled out today's pattern of underworld enterprise policed by union power.

As portrayed by the testimony, this cast of characters included:

A crime overlord known as "Lord High Executioner" of Murder, Inc., whose union power qualified him for the title of Secret Labor Boss. He was never on stage, but cast a menacing shadow over the action.

A professor with a criminal record who tutored the children of the biggest names in mobdom and served as "watchdog" over the crime overlords' racket interests.

A union man with a wooden leg and a rubber conscience.

A "labor relations advisor" once accused of peddling dope. He used business firms as "whips" and unions as "clubs" to keep racket victims in line.

A corpse—that of an honest union man, "rubbed out" in the line of racket business duty.

Also hoodlums with such names as Joey Surprise, Pasta Fazula (Italian for beans and macaroni), cowed businessmen and cheated union members.

Act I opened in Westchester County, a rich suburban community bordering on New York City. Here, as in other New York suburbs, there flourished a lowly but lucrative service industry: the private collection of waste and garbage from homes, restaurants, stores. Several hundred firms describing themselves as "carting companies"—and sometimes as "sanitation engineers"—operating in New York and its suburbs divided some $50,000,000 of business yearly.

There's gold in those hills of garbage, and the smell of it attracted to genteel Westchester some cold-eyed gents with prison pallor and Lower East Side New York accents. These bought their way into a garbage-carting firm, and this soon brought to garbage collecting an excitement that store owners never expected of it.

First, there came to one store manager the private garbage collector who carted his refuse.

"I want to get out in one piece," he said, giving up the business. "I don't want my trucks burned to the ground."

Next, as was testified, little men in suède shoes and pulled-down hat brims showed up in behalf of the garbage firm.

"You been paying $15 a week for service; now you pay $28," they said.

When the leading stores went out and found themselves a new garbage collector, another new face appeared on the scene. It belonged to a businesslike fellow who walked jerkily because of an artificial leg. This was Bernard Adelstein, one of the two bosses of a Teamster local in East Side Manhattan. The other boss was Joseph Parisi (now dead), a convicted rapist and underworld figure—whom Adelstein described as "a fine labor leader—may his soul rest in peace."

Adelstein gave the word that the merchants could not use the garbage man they preferred (whose prices, incidentally, were lower);

169

they must use a firm the union dictated. When one chain store company, Safeway Stores, resisted, Adelstein quickly taught the chain store the power of the Teamsters. They coerced the store in Westchester County by refusing to pick up the refuse at Safeway Stores in the Bronx and Manhattan. Attacked on the flank, the Westchester Safeway Store yielded. Its refuse was soon being collected again by a mob-owned carting company.

And death by murder wrote a footnote. When an honest union man who headed the Teamster local in Westchester County disputed the invasion of the underworld union from Manhattan, he was told by its bosses, Adelstein and Joe Parisi, it was testified before the McClellan Committee, "Don't think you are too tough and that we can't take care of you. Tougher guys than you have been taken care of." Adelstein denied making any threats.

Three weeks later, the honest union man was shot twice through the head and killed.

In Act II the scene shifts to another rich New York suburban area, Nassau County. Here in one of the fastest growing communities in America, big and little owners of trucks were peaceably collecting refuse, bidding against each other for business and meeting occasionally in a county trade association.

Into this business paradise there entered a serpent. This was Vincent Squillante, a saturnine man of few words who described himself as "labor relations advisor." "Hire me," he tempted the garbage men, "and your union troubles will be over." As a clincher, he picked up the phone and talked intimately with Bernie Adelstein, whose Manhattan Teamster local also operated in Nassau.

Squillante has been accused by the Narcotics Bureau of being a major source of supply for narcotics. Now he went to work for the refuse carting companies—on union matters—and soon catapulted himself to executive director and boss of the cartmen's trade association. He then introduced some novel business ideas.

First he taught the garbage firms—let's call them cartmen—the fundamentals of "property rights." Once a cartman had a customer, he always had that customer—and no one could bid against him or try to take him away. If that customer, a store, say, moved, the cartman who had served "the stop" would serve whoever moved in.

Next Squillante taught the cartmen how to bid on business. Designate one cartman to make the winning bid; then others don't bid. That way, there'd be no nonsense about competitive prices.

Naturally, there soon sprouted in Nassau County—as there had in Westchester—new carting companies owned by some of the most lurid rascals known to the New York police. These were the companies that enjoyed favored treatment from the association, according to the McClellan Committee, and were the ones chosen to bid on plush business. When some legitimate cartmen refused to go along with the monopoly association and competed, defiantly, for business, Squillante, ever resourceful, formed "whip" companies. Troublemakers who stepped out of line were beaten right back again by the "whip" companies that raided their customers, underselling them when necessary. It was easy to crack the whip, too, because Squillante worked as a team with union man Adelstein, and so could deprive the rebel of truck drivers. Whip companies were permitted by union boss Adelstein to operate non-union. Adelstein even loaned the non-union carters union pickets to coerce stores into taking his service.

To control the carting firms even more tightly, Squillante—with an assist from union man Adelstein—forced the businessmen to take out cards in Adelstein's union, thus creating the phenomenon of a Teamster local that derived one-third of its revenues from dues-paying and card-holding employers. The employers might pull out of the association and make a fight for their business lives. But if they pulled out of the union—or were booted out—they were branded "unfair to organized labor" and deprived of drivers.

The narrative up to this point has shown you the pattern of underworld business operation: seize control of a trade association and transform a legitimate business into a monopoly racket controlled by a closed ring of insiders. A captive union—whose resemblance to a legitimate labor organization is purely coincidental—enforces the monopoly by keeping insiders in line and outsiders out through its control of the drivers.

We now come to Act III of our racket drama, the one in which the master criminal and brains of the dirty business is dragged from the shadows and into the light.

When Squillante had established himself as czar of the private garbage collection in Long Island (which embraces Nassau County),

171

he introduced a new trade association activity: "public relations."
He brought into the Nassau cartmen's association a little, bespectacled man in his sixties who spoke the English of a college professor.
Which was not surprising, for that is what the stranger once was—a
college teacher of English. The "professor," C. Don Modica by
name, instituted a trade association paper which he dubbed *The
Hired Broom*. In it he sometimes ran essays, headed: "Out of garbage grows a rose." It was testified he also lectured the trade association members on the "three E's"—Education, Enforcement and
Engineering. (The Enforcement, of course, was the enforcement of
the racket monopoly. The Engineering concerned the collection of
garbage.)

Nassau cartmen who came to conferences held in Squillante's
office on Madison Avenue in New York City found the "professor"
engaged in still other activities. As the cartmen talked business, the
"professor" quietly busied himself writing mathematical symbols on
a blackboard and explaining them to a boy of twelve.

One cartman, who could not contain his curiosity, asked a neigh-
bor, "Who's this fellow?"

"Don't you know? That's Albert's boy," was the reply. "Albert"
was the redoubtable Albert Anastasia, probably the most awesome
name in the underworld. Anastasia once assigned killers to handle
mob underworld executions—and was reputedly responsible for
several score slayings. On the side the professor was coaching the
boy in his math.

The professor, as the Senate Committee later showed, tutored
the children of such bigshot gangsters as the deported Joe Adonis
and the late Willie Moretti.

The professor, according to the Committee, had served time for
practicing medicine without a license and for grand larceny and was
watchdog over the garbage racket for Anastasia. And Anastasia, not
Squillante, was the boss of the racket.

Senate investigators testified that the professor reported regularly
to Anastasia by telephone concerning the garbage business. They
found that Squillante boasted that he was a "godson of Albert Anastasia." And they found that when one of Squillante's "whip companies" needed capital to expand, an emissary went into New York
to see some of "the Boys" with the object of raising $250,000. One

172

of "the Boys" was Anastasia.

Anastasia is dead. He met the same bitter end—a shot in the head —to which he had consigned so many others. Nassau County Prosecutor Frank A. Gulotta, now a judge, sent Squillante to Sing Sing for extortion, along with Teamster official Adelstein. But first, in 1957, Adelstein went down to Miami Beach as a delegate to the Teamsters' convention and there—as part of the Hoffa machine—rose and nominated a Hoffa crony for vice-president.[1]

Mother of Rackets

Underworld access to union power in turn spawns virtually every other labor racket: boodling of welfare funds, making lucrative deals with employers to lock wage earners into substandard wage contracts. And, as long as the underworld dominates some unions, others are in danger of invasion.

Not long ago, the broker who handled the welfare fund insurance for the Distillery Workers Union looked up from his desk and into the mugs of two big-name gangsters.

"We control the Distillery Workers' insurance," they said. "Cut us in."

And, as New York County District Attorney Frank Hogan found, they did indeed control it. For, as he also discovered, they were part of a New York-Chicago underworld axis that had got its hooks into the Distillery Workers Union.

One of the gangsters was Little Augie Pisano, a bigshot in the Eastern gangs. The other was George Scalise, the Chicago Capone mob's labor front. They not only controlled the Distillery Workers but had connections in other unions and so could channel so much business to their captive insurance broker that he set up offices in Newark, New Jersey, Chicago and Los Angeles to handle it.

Please note: the gangsters didn't get into the Distillery Workers Union merely to boodle the welfare funds. They already had influence in the union.

The racketeer with union power can also sell a service to employers.

In Chicago, where the Capone gang has influence in a score of

---

[1] As this is written Squillante and Adelstein have appealed.

173

unions, the gang helps fight legitimate unionism in the city's restaurants.

Enter any of Chicago's seven thousand restaurants, and you are likely to find—in that highly unionized town—that your waiter does *not* belong to a union and probably works for subunion pay. As any Chicago newspaper reader knows, there is a union in the field: the Hotel and Restaurant Employees and Bartenders International Union (AFL-CIO). And, as the newspapers have often reported, and as McClellan Committee testimony corroborated, some locals of the union are controlled by gangsters.

The Capones have the resources, if they wish, to organize most of the restaurants in jig time and raise working standards. One of these resources, according to the McClellan Committee, is Joey Glimco, a power in the Chicago Teamsters, through whom the gang could shut off anti-union restaurants' meat and bread and so bring them to book.

The Capones apply this sort of pressure from time to time, to be sure. But it isn't to organize a union house and win union pay. That isn't what the underworld is in the union business for. The occasional blockades against restaurants enforce the gang's deal with restaurant owners and so turn the restaurant union into a meal ticket for the underworld.

Testimony before the McClellan Senate Rackets Committee painted this pattern: On one side of the deal were the owners of 20 to 25 per cent of Chicago's restaurants—who belonged to the Chicago Restaurant Association. On the other side were locals of the Restaurant Workers Union, harboring Capone gangsters. The union's "organizers" rarely talked directly to the restaurant workers, the kitchen help and the waiters. Instead, they went directly to the boss. "Put three of your workers into the union," the organizer would tell an employer of, say, twenty workers. The owner would give the union man the names of three employees, who might not even know they'd become union members. For the employer paid the union initiation fees and dues—and kept on paying them for years—even after the workers had left, or had died. The union made no further demands on the boss, nor did it discuss pay or welfare benefits. The employer paid off with dues for several of his employees.

The Senate Rackets Committee heard that as a further, more

substantial, regular payoff the Restaurant Association maintained a "voluntary fund" to which employers contributed—and from which came a $125,000 fee for "labor relations" lawyers closely associated with the Capone gang.

The lawyers, testimony strongly hinted, didn't keep the lavish fee but sluiced it to gangster shadow bosses behind the Restaurant Workers locals.

When you hire robbers to serve as cops, you must be prepared to protect yourself against the "cops." The gangster, if opportunity affords, will move in on the employer as well as the worker.

So the voluntary fund, from which the $125,000 "labor relations" fee came was also a war chest to keep the Capones at a safe distance. When hoodlums demanded that one restaurant chain sign over its employees, the Association's voluntary fund poured out $247,000 to help the restaurant chain resist a ten-week blockade.

The McClellan Committee's exposures forced the retirement of some of the Restaurant Union's more lurid bosses—but there's no assurance that the Capone gang now has no hold on the union.

As long as the underworld dominates some unions, others are under the ever-present danger of invasion. Detroit gangsters shot and almost killed Walter Reuther, president of the United Automobile Workers, because—as one theory has it—they sought to end Reuther's war on a multimillion-dollar numbers gambling racket in the automobile plants.

All for One

The underground network along which the gangs' secret labor bosses interchange favors and union influence is rarely glimpsed by outsiders. Yet sometimes a criminal trial, or a grand jury hearing or a chance wire tap, will expose it to view.

One revealing glimpse was provided when five Capone gang chiefs were tried and convicted of extorting $1,000,000 from Hollywood. Testimony showed that when underworld bosses seek favors from other gangsters around the country, these hasten to "fulfill the contract" with a zeal that points to an unsung solidarity within the underworld.

175

For instance:

First step in a Chicago gang plot to shake down Hollywood via a racket union was to seize a union. So when Capone gang bosses Frank (the Enforcer) Nitti and Paul (the Waiter) Ricca wanted to install a puppet to run the Movie Projectionists Union, they simply sent word to gangland colleagues around the country to line up convention delegates for their man.

Gang chiefs from the big cities lined up delegates in the locals in their towns, then sent hoodlums down to the convention at Louisville, Kentucky, to make sure the boys voted right. The Capone puppet won hands down.[2]

Hoodlums whose own connections in Labor don't reach far enough have access to a central underworld clearing house of influence: a figure who is a labor power openly, and is the underworld's ambassador or back door to the unions as well.

Two union powerhouses have served in this ambassador's role in recent years: one was Joe Fay of the Operating Engineers. Today, it's Jim Hoffa of the Teamsters.

Fay, a stocky, hammer-fisted man, was only a fourth vice-president of the Operating Engineers Union, but actually bossed that union and so dominated the building trades that he was known in the East as "Mr. Labor."

At conventions of the old American Federation of Labor, Fay made no bones about representing underworld interests. Fay—controlling building trades convention votes—helped raise George Browne, the Capone puppet, to vice-president of the AF of L with a seat on its policy-making Executive Council.

Labor boss Fay's best friends included racketeers—such as the late Longy Zwillman of Newark, New Jersey, who spent long evenings at pinochle with him and called himself Fay's "public relations advisor."

So powerful was Fay that, even after he went to jail for extortion in 1948, he continued to run his labor empire from a Sing Sing cell, sending out orders via a lieutenant who visited him regularly. So many big wheels in Labor and politics beat a path to

---

[2] This was Georgie Browne, now in hiding from underworld vengeance, for spilling the beans at the trial that convicted the Capone chiefs.

Fay's cell door that it became a public scandal, and Fay was removed to a remote prison upstate.

The Meaning of Jimmy Hoffa

Fay's successor as "the man to see" when gangsters wanted union favors was Jim Hoffa, then an obscure ninth vice-president of the Teamsters.

I first met Hoffa in 1955, long before he had become a household word. And so there began for me a fascinating hunt for clues which, laid end to end, spelled out the significance of Hoffa and the Teamsters to underworld activity.

I spent several afternoons in interview-conversations with Hoffa and watched him at work at a trucker-union conference.

As revealing as the talks was the awesome respect with which those around Hoffa treated him. But most revealing of all was a freckled, redheaded, slight man in his mid-fifties who dogged Hoffa's heels in the hotel lobby, carried his luggage to and from airport cars, waited for him outside conference rooms.

Hoffa introduced the genial redhead.

"Meet Paul Dorfman," he said. Dorfman became president of a waste collectors' local after a predecessor was murdered—then was kicked out by the AFL-CIO as a "corrupt influence." Earlier, I had spent several weeks trying to catch up with Dorfman to ask him about the Dorfman family insurance business, which in three years had collected some $1,000,000 in commissions and fees from Teamster welfare fund insurance. Dorfman had evaded me, just as he evaded questions before Congressional investigators. I had written critically about him in a *Reader's Digest* article on union welfare funds scandals.

But now Dorfman had no hard feelings.

"You should have given me a chance to answer," he said, with no reference to the weeks he spent dodging my calls.

Locked behind that freckled forehead were many answers that Dorfman could give—if he dared.

A Senate committee investigator described Dorfman as "a major figure in the Chicago underworld" and an "associate of most of the leading gangsters in the Chicago area." Then Robert Kennedy, coun-

177

sel for the McClellan Committee, put Dorfman on the stand. Counsel Kennedy wanted to know whether Hoffa Teamster insurance had been channeled to the Dorfman family insurance agency as part of a deal. Did Dorfman use his influence in Chicago to help Hoffa extend his Teamster power there, in return for the insurance business? Kennedy asked.

"I refuse to answer on the ground that it might tend to incriminate me," said witness Dorfman.

"Weren't you with Mr. Hoffa continuously at the trial in New York [on wire-tapping charges]? And weren't you at the [Hoffa] trial here in Washington [on bribery charges]?" Bob Kennedy asked Dorfman.

Dorfman pleaded the Fifth Amendment.

"And weren't you in a hotel room in Chicago when Mr. Hoffa and several of his colleagues were selecting those officials who would run on his slate at the Teamster Convention in Miami, Florida?" Bob Kennedy asked. Again Dorfman pleaded the Fifth Amendment. "And isn't this one example and probably the most serious of Mr. Hoffa's tie-up with the underworld?" Bob Kennedy asked.

"I refuse to answer on the ground that it might tend to incriminate me," Dorfman said.

Hoffa's relations with the Capones—most powerful crime organization in America—raise fascinating questions. For instance: when Paul (the Waiter) Ricca, elder statesman of the gang, faced deportation and needed quick cash, he got the money—$150,000—from two Hoffa-controlled locals in Detroit. In a tangled transaction Ricca first gave the Hoffa locals half title on his Long Beach, Indiana, estate—which meant that Hoffa's locals owned a twenty-room mansion, half of a swimming pool and half of a tennis court. How did the Capone chief come to be selling real estate to Teamster locals? Hoffa explained that Ricca's estate would be used as a "school for Teamster business agents." But why a school at Crown Point, Indiana, for business agents in Detroit?

Was the Capones' elder statesman, Ricca, a secret labor boss with influence in the Teamsters?

Hoffa has played the role of secret back door into legitimate labor. This is how the back door opens:

When New York extortionist Johnny Dio (later indicted in connection with the blinding of columnist Victor Riesel) and other racketeers wanted Teamster charters with which to set up locals in New York, Hoffa helped get the charters for him. Dio got into difficulties for selling protection against union organization and went to jail for extortion. He is appealing.

When Samuel (Shorty) Feldman, one of Philadelphia's most notorious criminals, wanted to go into the restaurant union business (with the same object as Dio: piracy), Hoffa undertook to help him too. The Philadelphia District Attorney Victor H. Blanc was tapping Feldman's telephone and overheard Hoffa's promise to deliver a restaurant union charter. But Feldman got his restaurant union charter anyway.

How was Teamster Hoffa able to help racketeer Feldman get a charter in another union not his own—the Restaurant Workers?

This brings us to the most important facet of Hoffa's own power and the influence he's able to place at the service of the underworld: Hoffa's power reaches beyond his union, because of the help the Teamsters can give in organizing and in strikes. Some unions depend on the Teamsters for their very existence.

When the Distillery Workers demanded that the big Eastern distillers recognize their union, and the distillers balked, "the Boys" knew just what to do to bring them into line. They telephoned Hoffa in Detroit, who was soon on the phone to New York.

"Sign your salesman into the union," said Hoffa. Distillery executives, fearing their liquor wouldn't move, signed.

This control of the wheels makes Hoffa the Indispensable Man—to the secret labor bosses from the underworld, and to the unions they control. And so around Hoffa and the Teamsters there rotates an assortment of satellite unions in whose ranks may be found the rascals that have given Congressional investigators their most lurid hearings.

The Mug who Came to Dinner

The gangsters got into the unions virtually by invitation.

Let's look in on two scenes enacted several decades ago.

The time is 1926. The place is a lavishly appointed office in an expensive New York midtown hotel.

179

The actors, left of stage, are a group of taut-faced garment union leaders. To the right is an easy-smiling, handsome gent, Arnold Rothstein, the then king of New York crime and financier-overlord of a host of gambling, narcotics and prostitution rackets.

The little tailors had asked an audience with the underworld monarch—and a boon. Could Rothstein use his underworld influence to call off the gorillas—hired by the employers—to crack union strike pickets' skulls? To be specific, could Rothstein call off the notorious Legs Diamond and his gang? Obligingly, Rothstein picked up the telephone. In a matter of minutes, the dreaded Legs Diamond and his Boys were shaking the dust of the Garment Center from their feet. Rothstein said he was glad to do this as a favor to his aging father, a retired and highly respected dress manufacturer.

Now came a more delicate problem. The Garment Union leaders confessed that they, too, had hired gorillas—Augie Orgen's gang to be exact, to stink-bomb employers' lofts and combat employers' thugs. Once hired, Augie wouldn't be fired. Could Mr. Rothstein do something about that too?

Why not? All that was needed was just another telephone call.

The little union men, watching the suave Rothstein, had a blinding flash of truth. Both gangs of gorillas—those working for the employers as well as those working for the union—were working for the same underworld boss, Arnold Rothstein.

Some nine hundred miles away in Chicago, another underworld chieftain, Scarface Al Capone, also gave an audience to union emissaries. The union men had come, hat in hand, from a high official in the American Federation of Labor, now dead. Would Al Capone work for the unions? Would he supply the troops to fight the employers' mercenaries and help introduce unionism into a number of service industries? Al Capone would—and did.

The men who came to the New York Garment Center as thugs remained to become powers in business and the rackets who defy all efforts to dislodge them. In Chicago, Al Capone gangsters worked for the unions. Today unions work for them.

If we've learned anything from our journey to the underworld, it's this: the gangster is a deeply rooted fixture of American big-city life. The unions can fight him by refusing to let criminals or known hoodlums hold union office. But more is needed: a war on the gangsters' business rackets. This is essentially a police matter.

Prosecuting the gangster is a backbreaking task. Victims and collaborators won't talk. They'd rather be live collaborators or victims than dead witnesses. Yet New York County District Attorney Frank Hogan and his chief racket buster, Al Scotti, have shown that it can be done. They uncovered the $500,000 welfare fund boodling in the Distillery Workers Union and sent a gang chief and a union puppet to jail. The convictions led to a Senate investigation of union welfare fund frauds and a chain reaction of further exposures. The New York District Attorney also sent Hoffa's friend, Johnny Dio, to jail as a labor racketeer.

Frank Hogan's war on racketeers seems to be the exception to local law enforcement rather than the rule. Chicago has witnessed some nine hundred gangland murders in forty years. There have been only seventeen convictions. Hoodlums who get away with murder get away with much else too.

Although the McClellan Committee has uncovered scores of instances of thievery and other lawbreaking, local prosecutors have followed through in only a fraction of the cases. This is disinterest bordering on abdication of duty. Or it could be that the gangster has such political influence in his community that he is too hot to handle.

Is the gangster a member of a privileged class? And are his organized rackets the protected evils of a privileged class?

If they are, it's obvious that the war on the hoodlums is one that can't be waged by unions alone.

CHAPTER 12

The Union That God Forgot

In all the annals of perverted unionism, there are—to my mind—few unions that can match the record of the International Union of Operating Engineers—whose members drive tractors, cranes and earth-moving equipment. It is my candidate for America's worst union. In support of my nomination I offer these:

Item: The Operating Engineers' affairs in the East were run for some years from a cell in Sing Sing prison. Vice-president Joe Fay, imprisoned for extortion, sent out orders to local union bosses, discussed contracts, settled threatened strikes.

Item: The Operating Engineers' president until 1958, one William Maloney was twice indicted on racket charges along with Capone gangsters (one dismissal, one acquittal). The McClellan Committee accused him of achieving local dominance with the aid of gangster guns and of conspiring with employers to cheat his own members. Asked once about racketeers in his union, President Maloney blurted, "It's true they bring the union into disrepute, but that's no reason for throwing them out."

Item: Today's president, Joseph J. Delaney testified at a New York State investigation of union welfare fund insurance graft. Asked how he earned three hundred dollars weekly as "labor consultant" to a union man–insurance broker, Delaney replied, "Every time he seen me, he'd always ask, 'What's new?' "

Item: The union's secretary-treasurer, Hunter P. Wharton, was excoriated by a U.S. District Judge for harboring hoodlums in the union's Philadelphia local—and by the McClellan Committee for playing a "key role in the brutal assault" on a member. Wharton's assistant, when acting boss of the local, was indicted on charges of taking bribes from employers but was continued in his job until he died twenty months later (without being tried).

Compared with other construction unions, say the 800,000-man Carpenters, the Engineers, with their 280,000 dues payers, seem small shakes. Yet, since the sitdown of one hoisting crane operator

182

can immobilize some one thousand other building trades craftsmen and laborers on a job, the Engineers command a jugular-vein power over a construction job. The national highway program alone comes to $40,000,000,000. Which gives you some idea of racket opportunities.

An unscrupulous Operating Engineers' boss can exact "strike insurance" from the contractor—a bribe to prevent strikes. Or he can make side deals with the contractor not to enforce the tough written provisions of a contract—and so permit the employer to short change the men.

As an Engineers' vice-president, Joe Fay did both. Brought to trial on charges of extorting $370,000 from contractors, he had a unique defense:

"It wasn't extortion," he pleaded. "The contractors paid me the money as bribes." For part of the bribe, Fay turned his back as contractors cheated his members on pay and working conditions.

As president, William Maloney, the McClellan Committee found, had an "under-the-table" relationship with one of the country's biggest construction companies, permitting it to forego overtime payments, among other things.[1]

Control over an Engineers' local opens broader vistas of opportunity than extortion and bribe taking alone. The man who controls an Operating Engineers Union can control the contracting work in the area. Alone, or in cahoots with a contractors' association, he can say what contractor can get the job. He can keep outsiders out by withholding the crucial engineers from them.

So, in the Engineers, the relations between some employers and union bosses are the coziest of any in America.

On Long Island, contractors held cards in the Engineers' local, attended meetings, sat on the union's policy-making executive board. In fact, such was the influence of the contractors that a National Labor Relations examiner found that they dominated the local and recommended it "disestablished"—i.e., forbidden to bargain for the employees.[2]

---

[1] This is the S. A. Healy Company. Its founder and head, Stephen A. Healy, pleaded the Fifth Amendment before the McClellan Committee.

[2] The National Labor Relations Board agreed with the examiner on his findings of fact (employer domination) but didn't act on his suggestion to disestablish the local.

In Newark, New Jersey, the palship between union and employer is such that the local's boss, an ex-pug by the name of Pete Weber, or Moszcaski, is business partners with contractors, with whom he's supposed to deal at arm's length for his men.

When union bosses conspire with employers to cheat members or monopolize a territory, members can't be permitted to have a voice in the union's affairs, or to mount a successful rebellion.

So, less than half of the Engineers' members are allowed to vote under a rigged constitution that sets up a variety of second-class, non-voting union memberships. Or locals are put under a form of union martial law known as "supervision" or "trusteeship."[3]

Two Chicago locals of the Engineers were under "supervision" for twenty-nine years. There were no elections for officers; members had no voice over pay or working conditions.

The Philadelphia local, still under trusteeship, has had self-rule for only four years out of the last twenty.

In the Long Island local, the union boss, never elected, dropped out for a year after pleading guilty to extortion, then returned to office—still without benefit of an election. Eventually he was confirmed in office in uncontested voting—from which rank-and-file rebel leaders were barred.[4]

So deeply intrenched are the evils in the Operating Engineers that great corrective forces in society have not availed against some of its practices. Neither Senate Committees, nor the NLRB—nor the courts, nor crusading lawyers and journalists, nor the AFL-CIO. Most frustrated are the members, themselves, who rebel. I've watched with distress as good union men in Philadelphia and on Long Island broke their hearts in agonizing struggles against their union tormentors that went on year after year. All that a band of rebels in the Long Island local can show for six bitter years of battle against their union boss, a convicted racketeer—is hunger. "You blankety-blank rebels will never get a job out of this office [hiring

---

[3] Most international union constitutions permit the president to suspend self-rule in a local and name a trustee or supervisor to run it with dictatorial powers. In honest unions, this device is used only to meet a local emergency, say the theft of local funds. In racket unions, locals remain under trusteeship or supervision indefinitely.

[4] This is William De Koning, Jr., who inherited the local from his father, also a convicted racketeer.

184

hall] as long as we are here in power." This is what a union official told him, a rebel testified before the McClellan Committee.

Only through the ordeal of a union member who gets in the way of the Operating Engineers' collusion with employers can the depth of this destructive unionism be told and understood. Roy Underwood, a Philadelphia crane operator, is one such man who got in the way.

Unsung Hero in a Silent War

Had Roy Underwood been a printer, or a rubber worker, or a pants presser, he would undoubtedly have been one of America's important union leaders. For he is a dedicated union man, self-educated—and the sort of a man other men follow. But Roy Underwood was fated to be a member of the Operating Engineers. Here the qualities that would have made a leader of him elsewhere marked him for destruction.

Underwood is a spectacled, solid man in his early fifties, full-faced and amply girthed, who proves the point that heroes and rebels come in all shapes and sizes. For Underwood is an unsung hero in an unsung war—the struggle against union power that's turned upside down and used *against* instead of for *its* members.

Underwood became a union man in 1937, when he took out a card in Local 542, of the Engineers in Philadelphia.

On the job, he found he had two bosses. One was his employer, the contractor. The other was the union business agent who, as the men put it, was "God on the job."

To this worthy, Underwood and fellow workers had to kick back 5 per cent of their weekly pay—over and above dues. None of the local's eighteen hundred members knew where the money went.

Nor could they find out. For their local was under "supervision," i.e., union martial law, and the supervisor-dictator was Joe Fay, Engineers' fourth vice-president, later jailed for extortion.

Fay was a barrel-chested, iron-jawed rogue of such picturesqueness that newspaper headline writers had trouble titling him properly. Although only one of a number of vice-presidents, he was the Engineers' dominant figure, having direct control over locals in New York, New Jersey and Pennsylvania. He was also czar of all the building trades unions east of the Mississippi, the man to see to straighten out labor troubles. He was, in addition, the underworld's back door to Labor.

Fay sold "soft contracts" to employers, and went into the contracting business himself—where as labor leader Fay he granted concessions to businessman Fay. Naturally, Fay wouldn't tolerate interference by members who had notions that they should know what was going on inside their union.

When Underwood asked questions at the infrequent meetings called by Fay, the union boss would bellow, "When I get through, I'll answer questions." But Underwood and the members never got their answers. For when Fay was through, the meeting was over.

Members never got financial reports. When Underwood rose to ask how dues money was being spent, Fay's huskies up front would start a heated and noisy discussion among themselves that would drown out what Fay was mumbling.

"He'd wave a union dues book like he was waving a club over our heads," Roy Underwood later recalled. "And he'd say, 'Anyone don't like the way this union is run can get out. And if he don't get out, I'll throw him out.'" So thrown out, a union member could starve. For, without his union dues book, he couldn't get work.

If members spoke up anyway, they risked a beating on the spot.

Policing the union hall aisles were a squad of bully boys headed by Fay's crony, the six-and-one-half-foot Pete Weber or Moszcaski.

"Shut up, you troublemakers," the goons would shout at Underwood and his friends. Once when a rank and filer failed to shut up, Fay's hoodlums broke the man's jaw and kicked him until he lost consciousness.

Underwood formed a union "Committee of Liberation." It was in 1945, and, like the freedom fighters who resisted the Nazis, Underwood had to work underground. He visited rank and filers' homes secretly at night to get signatures to petitions asking the International Union to end union martial law over the local and permit a free election.

Although the Operating Engineers' constitution permits members to petition against supervision, supervisor Fay's men fought such petitions as treason. They roughed up rebel leaders and sent some to the hospital. Others they bought off with juicy business agents' jobs.

Underwood and his rebels could get no work through the union hiring hall. Although qualified to do master mechanics work, some —after months of idleness—had to take jobs as apprentices. Others had to scratch for work with contractors who dared defy Fay. It took Underwood three years to mount a rebellion, and, when petitions to the International failed, to go into court to win self-rule.

By the time the suit was filed in 1946, Fay was on his way to jail for extortion, and the International president, William Maloney, unexpectedly sought peace soon after. Underwood and his followers could have their union back. The man who had succeeded Joe Fay as supervisor-dictator would leave. The court would hold an election for officers. In return, President Maloney of the International wanted a promise. The members wouldn't sue to recover looted union funds.

This was prudent, for, when the members took back their union, they found the treasury was a shambles. Books and vouchers that would have told where the money had gone were destroyed.

Underwood was elected president and business manager. The hoodlum business agents and foremen vanished; Underwood wiped out the "permit fee" racket, the practice of barring qualified men from membership and charging them two dollars or more weekly for "temporary work permits." With rank-and-file support, Underwood showed what honest, grass-roots government in unions can do. In four years, the treasury was built from $20,000 to $120,000. The membership—kept purposely low under supervision so as to increase the haul from permit fees from non-members—rose from fifteen hundred to four thousand.

But Fay, in prison, cast his shadow over Underwood's local. The evil Fay did lived after him. This was the evil of the under-the-table deal with some of the contractors.

When Underwood sought to enforce the written contracts Fay had left behind him for the area, he ran into bitter disputes with the contractors who refused to abide by them. One contractor was the giant S. A. Healy Company, then working on a large government project. When Underwood's business agents tried to make this construction company live up to area agreements, Underwood got a telephone call from the International president of the Engineers, William E. Maloney.

"Keep your business agents away from Healy," Maloney ordered. Then he added, "He is a friend of mine, and that is all I should have to tell you."

187

A distinguished arbitrator, Professor Nathan Feinsinger of the University of Wisconsin, found to his amazement that the contractors had verbal side agreements with the business agents. The contractors argued that these agreements—which softened the terms of the written area contract—had the force of the contract itself.

"Why, if the written contracts were enforced," one contractor protested, "we'd be working under completely different arrangements."

As Underwood struggled to institute honest, arm's length bargaining with the contractors, the lieutenants whom Fay had left behind him, taking orders from Fay in prison, conducted a harassing action. Fay's man in Newark, New Jersey, who held no office in the International, kept secret tabs on Underwood's Philadelphia local and sent alarming reports to the Operating Engineers' general president, William E. Maloney.

When Underwood's dispute with some of the contractors flared into a 110-day strike in 1952, the contractors knew what to do. A spokesman went to President Maloney. With him was John J. McGrath, who had just stepped down as Attorney General of the United States. For McGrath's services, the contractors paid $25,000, from which McGrath paid another lawyer a referral fee that court testimony showed was $10,000. A federal judge ruled these services were not rendered by McGrath in his capacity as lawyer.

McGrath, who waited outside while the contractor talked to Maloney at his Chicago office, testified, "I certainly do not think that he (the contractor) could have committed any bribery in the length of time that he had to get acquainted with a man of Mr. Maloney's character."

To Underwood and other members of the Operating Engineers McGrath's reference to "Maloney's character" had a bitter, ironic ring. For, the McClellan Committee found, Maloney "entered into collusive agreements with employers and misused hundreds of thousands of dollars of union funds."

Maloney was, in fact, the despair of Underwood and other union members. It wasn't only that Maloney—investigators found—had waxed fat off the union, owning two mansions, one at Miami Beach and another, a wooded 240-acre suburban estate with stables for blooded horses, outside Chicago—and using a yacht bought by

188

the union for his exclusive use. But it was also because Maloney ran a union that more often resembled a conspiracy of silence than it did a nationwide labor organization.

Maloney never did talk before the McClellan Committee. He went to a hospital instead. One week after the McClellan Committee completed its picture of conditions inside the Operating Engineers, Maloney, then seventy-one, quit his office. As the president of a local, trying to make contact with the president of the International, Underwood found that Maloney accepted no registered letters. These might contain troublesome queries from members—or a court summons. Although Maloney was in office for seventeen years, he remained studiously ignorant, or professed to be ignorant, of what went on in his organization. When Underwood—and later his lawyers—questioned Maloney, they would get bogged down in a morass of tortuous, cunning and unlettered English from which they'd emerge exhausted but with little or no information.

Underwood and other members also had to contend with the heritage of violence that Maloney had brought with him from the underworld.

"In all the stories of Chicago unions seized, looted and run by gangsters, there is none to match the strange story of William E. Maloney and the case of the International Union of Operating Engineers." So wrote the Chicago *Tribune* in 1943. Blood flows as freely as printers' ink in the six-column story that follows—including the murder of a rank-and-file protestor against Maloney.

When Maloney was president of the International Union, the violence was still there.

Once, a rank-and-filer, appealing a grievance before the Engineers' executive board, was pummeled for his pains at the hearing, pushed under a table and there kicked and scuffed about.

Asked about this later, Maloney said, "That's nothing unusual at union meetings."

This then was the "man of character" to whom the contractors went—and who had the fate of Underwood's local in his hands.

Soon after the contractors' spokesman met with Maloney in Chicago, Maloney intervened in Underwood's Philadelphia strike.

"You got to get along with the contractors," he told Underwood, ordering him to make peace virtually on the employers' terms.

189

When Underwood balked, Maloney plunged the Philadelphia local back into "supervision." Maloney could do this, so the Operating Engineers' constitution states, "Whenever in his opinion the best interests of the organization require it"—a broad grant of power.

The job of suppressing Underwood's local fell to former aides of the jailed Joe Fay.

A squad of toughs from Fay's old Newark, New Jersey, local came up to Philadelphia and seized the union office for Maloney. It consisted of the usual occupying troops of toughs—some with guns. Joe Fay's crony, Pete Weber, plumped himself into Roy Underwood's chair. The ousted Underwood tried to telephone his lawyer, but was waved away by a gunman. A Fay lieutenant headed the union judges who tried Underwood on charges of publishing defamatory material about the International president, Maloney— the union's interpretation of Underwood's appeal to the courts for help. The union fined Underwood thirty-five hundred dollars and expelled him from the union for six years.

After only four years of self-rule, the long night of union martial law under a dictator-supervisor closed in on the Philadelphia local again.

An acting supervisor, one Harry Lavery, took over. This trusted one wasn't in the job long, so a federal indictment charges, when he took bribes from employers. The old evil of soft contracts returned. Members complained they had to work for a dollar less per hour than the written agreements stipulated. Ex-felons and killers replaced Underwood's business agents. One, Frank Lentino, had served an armed robbery stretch. (He testified later he was pardoned.) Another, Pete Bozelli, later murdered his own daughter and died in jail. It was the Joe Fay days all over again. The ex-felons beat up rank-and-filers on the job, and at meetings patrolled the aisles to intimidate the men.

Once, at a turbulent meeting, the supervisor's men hustled a rank and filer into an elevator, gouged his eyes, butted him in the groin and knocked out his teeth. Hurled bleeding from the elevator, the indomitable union man, one Ted McCarty, dragged himself back to the meeting hall where some members still lingered.

"Look at me, boys," he gasped through swollen and bloodied lips. "This is what you get from the International."

The supervisor was Hunter P. Wharton, now the secretary-treasurer of the Operating Engineers. The McClellan Committee accused Wharton of responsibility in the brutal beating, and took testimony that Wharton used union money to defend the goons, and, when they were convicted, paid their fines with the local's money. The McClellan Committee also found that Wharton "participated in a questionable contract signed with the Standard Bitulithic Company, which called for lower wages than those other contractors in the same area were forced to pay."

Roy Underwood turned to the courts again. Faced with a lawsuit before, Maloney had promptly retreated. Perhaps he would do so again. But this time when Underwood and fellow rank and filers filed suit, Maloney and the International chose to fight. Maloney threw the full weight of his union's $15,000,000 treasury into the struggle against the rebels. Four law firms, using ten lawyers, defended Maloney and his representatives in Philadelphia.

The lawyers had the assignment of defeating Underwood's suit to free the local from Maloney's "supervision" and to permit the members to choose their own officers. One lawyer was an ex-U.S. Senator. Another was the AFL-CIO's general counsel, Albert Woll. Attorney Woll had also been the lawyer for Dave Beck and for the Teamsters, and so had found himself in the strange position of representing Beck before the AFL-CIO of which he, Woll, was counsel. George Meany solved that one by telling Woll to choose between the Teamsters and the AFL-CIO. Woll dropped the Teamsters. But he didn't drop the Operating Engineers. When the Federation's Ethical Practices Committee was probing the Operating Engineers, and lawyer Woll sought to enter the hearing room, one member of the committee, George Harrison of the Railway Clerks, barred his way.

"Whom do you represent? The Operating Engineers or the Federation?" Harrison wanted to know. Woll continues as Lawyer for the Engineers (under investigation by the AFL-CIO) and for the AFL-CIO.

Against the massed legal brains that Maloney and the Engineers' treasury could buy, Underwood and the rank and filers could muster one lone lawyer, Abraham E. Freedman of Philadelphia. This lawyer not only served without fee, but occasionally dug into his own pocket to help pay stenographic and other court bills.

The classic union defense against members who sue is to drag out the litigation, wear down the members' will to fight, exhaust their money and break their hearts. The Operating Engineers' lawyers so prolonged the suit that the judge admonished them, "Gentlemen, I do not intend to make a career of this case."

But in May, 1957, after four years of motions and counter-motions, pretrial depositions and testimony by witnesses, proceedings that filled four thousand pages of court records—Underwood and other members crowded into a Philadelphia federal court to hear the judge's decision.

"I'm not good on dates," says Underwood. "But I'll never forget May 23, 1957, as long as I live."

This was the rank and filers' day in court, and, as the judge started to speak, the men listened hungrily for every word.

The members nodded as the judge went into their local's history, citing the racket-ridden days under Joe Fay. The judge warmly praised the administration of the local under Underwood from 1948 to 1952. Then, just as warmly condemned the current supervisor.

"The tenure . . . [of the supervisor] has been marked by violence at meetings; people have been denied the right to talk . . . [and] have been discriminated against in job selection," said the judge.

"It is apparent to the court," the judge continued, "that under Hunter Wharton and Harry Lavery [the supervisor and his indicted acting assistant] there will never be a chance for decent operation. . . . As far as the Frank Lentinos are concerned . . ." here the judge named the supervisor's muscle men, "the quicker they are put out of the trade union movement, the better the trade union movement will be."

Then, as the members listened in bewilderment, the judge ordered that the union dictatorship be continued. His reason: the local had pressed a strike in defiance of the International (i.e., Maloney) five years before.

The five-year struggle for freedom had been lost. The risks of limb and livelihood had been in vain.

The supervisor's men had chided Underwood, "You can't fight

the International. You can't fight $15,000,000."

Perhaps they were right.

Still, when the first shock and despair wore off, Underwood and the rank-and-file rebels called a meeting.

"As far as I'm concerned, I'll never give up the fight. I'll never admit it's right to live under hoodlums," a Delaware rebel, Homer Dawson, said.

Underwood and his followers appealed to the higher courts. To pay the costs—printing the record alone, cost five thousand dollars— some union members mortgaged their homes. But the appeal was in vain. The Circuit Court of Appeals refused to pass on the merits of the case on the limited technical ground that the rebels and the union were citizens of the same state and so didn't have the "diversity of citizenship" for access to the federal courts. The Supreme Court refused to review the case.

The members' lawsuit against the Operating Engineers had dragged for seven weary years. Many men who had battled at Underwood's side to get their union back can't get work. Although the Taft-Hartley Act bars the closed shop, contractors hire chiefly through the union hiring hall. There the rebels are either barred, or somehow never reach the head of the list from which men are sent out on jobs.

Where can Roy Underwood and his men turn? The McClellan Committee pieced together a shocking Philadelphia Story and thundered against the Engineers in its interim report. But nothing happened. The AFL-CIO Ethical Practices Committee investigated too. Nothing happened. Philadelphia local members have pleaded for relief with national officials of the union. Nothing happens.

An Underwood rebel tried to introduce an anti-racketeering resolution at the Engineers' convention in Chicago in 1956. He was accused of being a Communist, questioned as to his citizenship and booed. His resolution, the rebel was told, "shocked the signs of decency," and so wild was the disorder that the resolution never reached the floor for a vote. Booing and yelling that the rebel was "a Communist" was Joseph J. Delaney, then secretary-treasurer of the International, whom we've already met as being involved in a welfare fund scandal. Two years after the convention in which he fought the anti-racketeering resolution, Delaney was named president of the Engineers on a "clean-up slate."

Hunter P. Wharton, branded as a condoner of violence, and accused in McClellan Committee testimony of "questionable" deals with an employer, was elected secretary-treasurer—also on a clean-up slate.

Naturally, when the rebels' lawyer, Abraham Freedman, sought a settlement looking toward the end of the Philadelphia local dictatorship—and a court-supervised election in which Underwood could run for office—Wharton sent back word: No.

How long will the Labor movement, the courts and the American people permit this sort of thing to go on?

*   *   *

As this goes to press, I've just learned that Roy Underwood was found dead in his garage—killed by a bullet. The police called it suicide. But I think it was murder—murder by public apathy.

CHAPTER 13

Cruel Sweetheart

At times, grocery clerk Jim Ross (that's not his name) felt as tied, sealed and delivered as the packages he handled. Jim's boss, it was testified before the McClellan Committee, delivered him to a union he didn't want, tied him to a contract he had no say in, and sealed him into a trap from which no outside help—not even that of government—had been able to free him.

Bob Kennedy of the McClellan Committee had workers like clerk Ross in mind when he said of one situation: "The [boss] coerced the employes into the union . . . the contract that was signed was illegal . . . and finally they made a secret agreement. . . ."

What Bob Kennedy was describing was a "sweetheart contract." Employers and union leaders involved in one are known in the union trade as "sweethearts."

The evil reaches into many industries (although not in the mass production fields), and an underground network of middlemen,

194

fixers and "labor relations" lawyers has sprung up to bring the union-employer bedfellows together and to service and defend their deals. The McClellan Committee first glimpsed the extent of the sweetheart contract problem when it looked into the affairs of Nathan Shefferman, the friend of ex-Teamster Dave Beck, who was in the business of busting unions.

In New York City a curious breed of union men conspire with employers to lock thousands of industrial workers into wage agreements so meager that the city has to supplement their earnings with relief. And in New York City and in New Jersey, the McClellan Committee reported the world's biggest grocery chain handed over ten thousand clerks to union bosses of dubious repute, then signed a secret deal that locked them into a forty-five-hour week for five years. One chain store executive admitted the secret deal; others denied any wrongdoing.

To see what happens when union and boss gang up on a man, let's get back to grocery clerk Jim Ross.

Ross worked in a New York store of the Great Atlantic & Pacific Tea Company, which does some four billion dollars' worth of business yearly in forty-five hundred stores in forty states and in Canada. For years, it was testified before the McClellan Committee, when union organizers set foot in A & P stores, the store managers would call the cops.

"Why join the union and pay dues to union bosses who are crooks and ride around in fancy cars?" Jim Ross's superiors would ask him.

So determined was the A & P's stand that, despite many unfair labor practice charges to the National Labor Relations Board and despite several union elections (in which the union also cried Foul!), the store clerks remained unorganized. (The butchers, a fraction of the work force, were already organized in the Meat Cutters' Union.)

Then one day the Great Atlantic & Pacific Tea Company had a change of heart as grand as its title.

Clerks' affidavits to the National Labor Relations Board stated that when union organizers showed up, store managers invited the amazed clerks to go into the backroom and see the union organizer about signing up. Some store managers went even further. The affidavits stated they handed out application cards themselves and told the bewildered clerks that unless they signed and paid a $2

195

initiation fee, they'd have to pay a $50 fee later. Store executives said that representatives of the Meat Cutters, already in the store, did the recruiting.

Then, Senator McClellan summed it up, the clerks "were dragooned into the union."

Earlier, the A & P had resisted two clerks' unions. The outfit they signed up with was the Meat Cutters' and Butcher Workmen's Union, dominated in the East by Max Block, whose brand of unionism gave the McClellan Committee one of its more lurid hearings. Max and his brother Louis Block, it was testified in a New York union looting trial, launched their New York Butchers' local with a financial assist from racketeer George Scalise and his underworld sidekick Little Augie Pisano. (Brother Louis denied this.) Their Meat Cutter Union locals were a private family preserve which the McClellan Committee found had yielded some $350,000 of pay and perquisites to the Blocks in three years and were used by the Blocks to promote an exclusive country club. Louis Block had admitted to the New York Insurance Department that he shared commissions on his local's insurance. Soon after the New York County District Attorney started looking into Meat Cutter Union's affairs, Brother Max stepped down as president.

When the Blocks' organizers started handing out cards in the A & P stores, a curious tableau was enacted in the offices of Local 342 of the Meat Cutters—Max Block, boss. As one participant described it to the McClellan Committee, seven business agents and office girls leaned intently over their desks, absorbed in an exercise of penmanship: before each penman was a list of A & P employee names obtained by the union from time-clock cards, plus stacks of union application cards; the business agents and girls were creating union members by the simple process of forging clerks' names to union applications.

One participant spilled the beans to the McClellan Committee. Let's listen:

Bob Kennedy: Did you personally participate in writing these cards transferring the names?

Ex-Meat Cutter Business Agent Fred Cornelius: Yes, sir. Everyone in the office participated.

Bob Kennedy: What office was this?

196

Cornelius: In the Union office.

Bob Kennedy: Who instructed you to do this?

Cornelius: Local 342 is a two-man organization. Max Block is the big boss, and Billy Casale is the second in command. Casale was the one who directly told us.

Senator McClellan: You said that all those in the office participated. Was that so the signatures would be different?

Cornelius: Yes, sir. The signatures were written backhand and lefthand and every other which way so that they would appear different.

The union team also changed off from pen to pencils, ex-business agent Cornelius explained, and made up phony addresses and social security numbers as they went along.

When an employer is confronted with application cards by a union in quest of recognition, he usually makes sure that the signatures are bona fide. Then, if 30 per cent of the employees have signed up as required by law, employer and union ask the NLRB to hold a union election to see whether a majority want the union. But the A & P and the Meat Cutters held no election. If the cards accounted for 51 per cent of the eligible employees, the union would be recognized as representing all.

So, together, boss and union hired themselves a card counter. This was lawyer Joseph E. O'Grady, once New York City's labor mediator and member of the city's Transit Authority.

Would Lawyer O'Grady count the application cards?

Lawyer O'Grady would and did. Later, he drew a barrage of critical questions from the McClellan Committee.

O'Grady testified he checked the cards at the rate of two hundred an hour, verifying no addresses and only "very infrequently" confirming Social Security numbers.

Others had testified that the union not only forged the names of full-time employees, but also those of part-time workers ineligible to apply. Although tabulator O'Grady spotted many of these ineligible names because they didn't appear on the payroll sheets supplied by the A & P, this didn't stir his suspicions enough to check all of the cards more carefully.

At this point the transcript reads:

197

Mr. Kennedy: And you found 270 [out of 1,411 cards] in that unit alone that had no company slips?

Mr. O'Grady: That is right, sir.

Mr. Kennedy: Didn't that arouse your curiosity and interest to determine that a more thorough check should be made of the other situation as far as checking the signatures?

Mr. O'Grady: It did not suggest it to me, sir.

O'Grady was paid $2,800 for fifty hours' work, giving $100 of it to an assistant counter.

When the ten thousand A & P clerks in New Jersey and metropolitan New York learned they were Butchers and Meat Cutters, many refused to pay dues. So many A & P employees bombarded the New York NLRB with protesting phone calls that the agency had to issue special instructions to handle them. When the NLRB held a "de-authorization" election (to give clerks a chance to withdraw) in one unit, the result was six to one against the union. Many clerks didn't vote, perhaps for fear of company reprisals. This so reduced the turnout to below the necessary majority of employees, that this protest failed too.

An open contract between the A & P and Meat Cutters signed, however, without the knowledge of the employees, tied the employees to a forty-five-hour week for twenty-two months. Then a secret deal had the effect of extending this to five years.

According to an estimate by counsel Bob Kennedy, the forty-five-hour-week agreement saved the company some $23,000,000 that it might have paid in added wages had it had to go on a forty-hour week. One Senator estimated that the Max Block Meat Cutter locals in New York gained some $500,000 of additional yearly dues.

Although company spokesman differed, one executive made no bones about the secrecy of the deal. Asked by counsel Bob Kennedy, "Why weren't the employees notified?" an A & P labor relations expert answered, "I was asked by Mr. Max Block to keep it quiet."

Bob Kennedy observed, "It adds up to one of the worst situations we have had before the committee as far as management is concerned."

Senator McClellan added, "I don't know any milder word than reprehensible for management and labor leaders to enter into these secret agreements; when it is a secret, it is bound to be of some advantage to one or the other or both."

"Reprehensible secret agreements" between employers and union leaders force New York City to spend $25,000,000 welfare money yearly to supplement the depressed wages of captive union members, a witness testified before the McClellan Committee.

The victims are chiefly newly arrived Puerto Ricans and Negroes from the South who have spilled into several hundred plants that make quilting, plastic gadgets, metal parts and hire from twenty to three hundred workers.

Here, with the sweetheart contract, some employers use a union to bust a union. It works this way:

A manufacturer has "union trouble," i.e., his unorganized workers have been approached by a legitimate union that seeks to sign them up, then bargain with the manufacturer for higher pay and welfare benefits. Once the union-fearing manufacturer would have taken this "union trouble" to a gangster who would have knocked the union idea out of the workers' heads—by cracking a few skulls. Now, the manufacturer seeks out a racketeer in the union business. He can do this directly, or through lawyers, or through a middleman who calls himself an "industrial relations consultant" but makes commissions by finding a union racketeer for customers, or customers for a union racketeer.

Alone, and in secret, employer and union racketeer sign a contract that herds the workers into the racketeer's local. The racketeer is now the workers' representative, who alone—under the law—can negotiate wages and working conditions with the boss. And the contract brings to bear the full weight of government—including the courts—to protect the boss and racketeer's plot against the worker. It automatically bars another union, an honest one, say, for two years. If the employees try to withdraw from the racket local, they must go through a "decertification" election—which can be snarled and delayed in the NLRB by the racketeer's lawyer. If, in desperation, the workers strike against boss and racketeer, both will show up in court with the contract; charge that the workers are staging a "wildcat strike" and invoke the sanctity of contract. The court, concerned only with the signatures on the contract, and not with the oppressive conditions in it, will grant an injunction to bar picketing and so break the strike.

One trapped wage earner spelled it out for the McClellan Committee.

Bertha Nunez, a bright, slight Latin girl, had left a Honduras farm at twenty-four to improve her lot in rich America. Three years later, in 1957, she was working in an electrical manufacturing factory that employed 150-odd wage earners, 90 per cent of them Puerto Ricans—lured to New York by employment agency ads that promised good jobs. Most had come off the plane at Idlewild with all their worldly possessions in a paper bag. Only 4 per cent could speak English. Bertha, a born leader and fighter, had worked hard at her English and could give the Senate Committee a fluent account of employer and union racketeer conspiracy:

The weekly pay in 1955 was $36—the bare minimum under the then law. Then one day the boss told all employees to remain after work. "The union is coming to talk to you."

In the presence of the boss and the foreman two men, who identified themselves as "union delegates," told Bertha Nunez and her shopmates to join the union.

"Or you'll get fired," said one delegate. The boss and foreman nodded their agreement.

Bertha and others had paid $12 to $17 to employment agencies to "buy their jobs," as Bertha put it. If they were fired, they'd have to borrow money to "buy another job." So Bertha and her friends signed up with the union. The foreman passed out the union cards and helped the Spanish-speaking workers fill them out. Neither Bertha nor the others could know, of course, that their boss was forcing them into a local that had been founded by Johnny Dio, convicted extortionist and lifelong labor protection racketeer.

But Bertha found soon enough that no union she had ever heard of behaved like this one.

First, there was the initiation fee, $15. But "union members" didn't pay it once—and get it done with. When they were laid off—even for a few weeks—they had to pay another initiation fee all over again.

Then there were the dues: $1 weekly. But since most of the employees got no more than the bare minimum per forty-hour week, enforced by law, Bertha couldn't see what they needed the union for. In fact, union dues depressed their earnings below the level they would have gotten anyway, without a union.

The Taft-Hartley Act defines a union as an organization "in which employees participate" for the "purpose" of dealing with employers concerning "grievances, labor disputes, wages, rate of pay, hours of employment, or conditions of work."

The union in Bertha's shop held few meetings, processed no grievances. When the boss refused to heat the factory during the winter, there was no union representative to argue the point with him. One pregnant woman contracted pneumonia and lost her baby, Bertha testified.

The union's agents showed up at the shop only to collect the dues check-off. When Bertha and others asked to see the contract the agents had signed with the boss, they refused to show it. One worker, braver than the others, grabbed the contract from the organizers' hands. It was then that the "union members" found that many of the usual standard clauses in union contracts had been inked out. The contract provided for no welfare benefits, no paid holidays. Although the contract called for a week's vacation, the employer—with an assist from the union—could get around that too. He simply fired the employees on the eve of the vacation, calling it a layoff. And the union turned its back.

Of the $42 to $50 a week that a Puerto Rican family man earns under a sweetheart contract, almost half or $20 weekly goes for rent—for one room in a tenement flat. Even so, these are so scarce that the tenant often must pay a "bonus" of $50 to the landlord to win one. Here, to make ends meet, three or four families will huddle in one room. Food has to be filling and cheap. So the worker and his family subsist on an unvaried diet of Spanish rice and beans. The dues and initiation fees the union racketeer exacts from the worker, then, are a tax on milk for babies.

Rackets may come, and rackets may go. But they can't live without an assist from men in high places. In this case, high union places.

When an employer signs a sweetheart contract with a racketeer, he wants to know: Will this give me labor peace—i.e., prevent strikes? Will this keep legitimate unions out? To both of these questions, if the racketeer has friends in the Teamsters, he can say

201

yes. No workers' strike against a sweetheart contract can succeed, if teamsters cross the picket lines to bring in supplies or take out deliveries. Similarly, few legitimate unions can organize a shop and make the legitimate contract stick, if the teamsters ignore organizing strike picket lines.

As crucial to the sweetheart contract purveyor as Teamster connections are those friends in other international unions who will provide him with local union charters which he needs to break into the racket. One of the most generous of these friends was the secretary-treasurer of an International Union in good standing with the AFL-CIO. This was Hyman Powell, who was ousted as secretary-treasurer of the Jewelry Workers Union. A slight, fidgety man, Powell was the human bridge between the cruder labor extortion racket of several decades ago and the present sweetheart contract industry.

In the old days, Powell—then known as Palatnik—was indicted on charges that he used his business agent's job with a Building Service Employees' local as a tollgate for exacting tribute from building owners. Because he peached on more important figures, Powell was never tried and went right on in the union business, finding a haven in the Jewelry Workers.

With Powell in it, the Jewelry Workers—a trade union of watchmakers, diamond cutters and other fine craftsmen—branched out, into shoe-polish factories and into shops making quilting, plastic baby shoes, zippers. Five of these locals have been cited before the McClellan Committee as "co-operating with companies to exploit workers." One local set some sort of record by having seven ex-felons on its payroll; and another was a party to forty-three sweetheart contracts out of a total of sixty, the Committee heard. In another local the dealings with the employer were so cozy that workers "represented" by the local didn't even know they belonged to a union.

Neither the old AF of L nor the newly merged AFL-CIO paid any attention to the sweetheart contract racketeer and his underworld allies until a handful of kids, some barely out of their teens, took him on.

The foolhardy band, some studying law at Fordham University, others beginning careers as labor lawyers, heard in 1956 about a type of unionism they'd never read of in their law journals when captive union members brought their plight to the New York office of the Association of Catholic Trade Unionists. Made up chiefly of union men and drawing on professional help from outside, the ACTU lends a hand to embattled workingmen in whatever struggle is going at the time. In the late 1930's, the ACTU pitched in to help the big organizing drives in the mass industries. Later it fought Communist infiltrators in the unions, then the racketeer.

The ACTU chapter in New York, run on a shoestring, is housed in two bare rooms of a onetime brownstone flat. The office can't afford a stenographer and is innocent of any furnishings except a table, chairs, two typewriters and a mimeographing machine. This became the headquarters of a gallant labor struggle.

Two young generals who, of necessity, also doubled as foot soldiers, led the fight. These were law school roommates Norman De Weaver and John McNiff, both twenty-two when they took on the sweetheart contract racket, both of slight build and razor-sharp minds.

The youthful racket busters soon found they had two major enemies. One was a coterie of some twenty lawyers working closely with the employers and racketeers. The other was the lethargy of the Labor movement.

The lawyers served as middlemen who brought employers and racketeers together. Then, when the employer-racketeer deals against workers were challenged before the National Labor Relations Board or in the courts, the lawyers used every trick in their specialist's book to snarl the proceedings in endless delays. So open was the lawyers' role in aiding and abetting the racket that some appeared both for the employer *and* for the racket union.

Snatching scarce hours from their law studies and doing their own laborious typing, young DeWeaver and McNiff sent appeals for financial help to each of the five hundred-odd legitimate union locals and parent labor bodies in New York City. There was only one response. The New York Machinists sent $25.

McNiff and DeWeaver organized strikes against the racket unions and pleaded with legitimate labor leaders to raid the racket unions—i.e., make a fight for their captive members.

"We can't raid," most labor men replied. "The AFL-CIO would

203

object, because we have no-raiding pacts with the Internationals to which the racket locals belong."

In desperation, the young men appealed directly to the conscience of the AFL-CIO. DeWeaver took a group of striking racket victims to the 1957 Atlantic City convention of the AFL-CIO.

These picketed the Convention Hall and asked help of the big unions.

But the "big, strong" AFL-CIO had other troubles.

DeWeaver and McNiff lost this battle. But they won some thirty others and so freed about 10 per cent of the workers caught in the sweetheart contract trap. Young McNiff appeared before the Mc-Clellan Committee and turned the local New York racket into a national scandal. On the following day, George Meany named a special committee to look into the union-employer collusion in the small New York manufacturing plants.

Eighteen months later, the twenty-four-year-old McNiff, a little older but much wiser in the world's ways, reported to the AFL-CIO:

"It is a sad truth that today after all the exposures and all the promises of reform and assistance—after all the committees and banquets—the exploited worker is still very much in the same position that he was in long before his cause became popular."

True, two chief officers of the Jewelry Workers had been forced out. But some of the most evil of the union's locals had seceded from the parent organization and gone independent—so that the AFL-CIO could not get at them. One had moved under the sheltering wing of the Teamsters. And what was more startling still, racketeers were forming a flock of new independent locals to get in on the racket.

The exposures were having the unexpected effect of teaching racketeers that here was a good thing they had missed.

Since it takes two to make a sweetheart deal—the union racketeer and the employer—it would seem that some unscrupulous businessmen were learning a new wrinkle too.

CHAPTER 14

Black Record

The unions have been both the hope and the despair of the Negro. The Negro, in turn, is the human hinge on which—through a curious historic irony—the unions' future must turn.

The Labor movement is founded on the principle that the strong help the weak. It is equalitarian: all toilers are brothers. No one speaks up more bravely for liberty, equality, fraternity than the union constitutions. Yet, in the Negro's long, steep climb toward an equal chance at a job, few American institutions have frustrated him more cruelly than the unions. As recently as 1944, twenty-two national unions barred Negroes from membership, and from jobs in great industries. All but three of these have now dropped the bars officially. But great areas of job opportunity and training are still closed to Negroes by union practices.

A Negro boy who sets his heart on being a plumber, electrician, sheet-metal worker or a printer might as well forget about it unless he's prepared to pick up the trade himself, then scratch for jobs in competition with the white man's hiring hall. Unions that rule these trades—with few exceptions—keep the Negro out.

Many unions that do accept Negro members relegate them to a second-class union citizenship. They are segregated into "auxiliary locals," a euphemistic phrase for "Jim Crow." These give the Negro no voice over his pay or working conditions. The white local supplies the voice.

Some unions conspire with employers or turn their backs as the employer pays Negroes less for equal work or bars him from training and promotions open to white workers. In fact, unions have fought promotions for Negroes with "hate strikes." In this, the unions, as American institutions, reflect the prejudices of the American people.

This, for the Negro, is the despair side.

Now, the hope side. The unions' high command, the men who lead the AFL-CIO, recognize that racial bias menaces the unions' future. So race discrimination is outlawed in the AFL-CIO constitution, just as corruption is.[1] Public pressure has forced the unions to grapple with racketeering first, but at least a beginning has been made against union race hate. Two unions affiliated with the Federation still bar Negroes but have promised to drop the color bars at their next conventions.

Only two decades ago, there were some 300,000 Negro members all told in the old American Federation of Labor. Today, close to 2,000,000 Negroes are trade unionists.

The better part of the struggle for job opportunity still remains to be won. But the unions do lead the fight.[2]

In fact, it was through a union and a union leader that the Negroes achieved more gains in the last seventeen years than in all the years since the Civil War. They won Fair Employment Practice acts in thirteen states, and a chance at jobs on assembly lines, on streetcars, buses and in stores. Jim Crowism was abolished in the Armed Forces. And, as already noted, unions began to drop their color bars. For all this, one man—an unsung Booker T. Washington—is largely responsible. He is A. Philip Randolph, president of the Brotherhood of Sleeping Car Porters.

*　　*　　*

Philip Randolph, at sixty-nine, holds his tall figure with such dignity, wears so serene a look and talks in such rumbling basso-robusto accents that he brings to mind the image of "De Lawd" in the play *Green Pastures*—patient oval face, grizzly gray hair and all.

The comparison goes beyond physical appearances alone. The Negro problem of winning first-class economic citizenship is a moral dilemma for the white man. Randolph is a leader of great moral force, partly Gandhi-like, to jog the white man's conscience—partly

---

[1] The AFL-CIO constitution states: "All workers must share equally in the benefits of unionism . . . without regard to race, creed or color."

[2] With an AFL-CIO Civil Rights Committee headed by Charles Zimmerman of the Garment Workers.

a direct action man and pressure politician.

As a direct action man he waged the longest organizing drive in union annals, and from seemingly unpromising menial, frightened human beings—the humble porters he leads—he fashioned a disciplined union, which he used as a wedge to pry gains from two Presidents of the United States and from the Labor movement itself.

Today, although Randolph runs one of the AFL-CIO's smallest affiliated unions—the Porters have about eight thousand members with "international offices" in three modest rooms in an ancient Harlem building—he is regarded in stature as one of the half dozen top labor leaders in the country. Randolph is a vice-president of the AFL-CIO and a member of its governing Executive Council, a place denied to many union leaders with more members and power. Here, among Labor's elders, who pride themselves on their ability to make a rousing speech, Randolph is respected as the most eloquent orator with a melodious voice capable of stirring large audiences.

For years, delegates to labor conventions would come running from their bars and poker games to hear Randolph denounce racial intolerance. Randolph talks with a rounded elegance, a South of England broad "a" diction and a deep conviction.

Erect and commanding, Randolph would boom out in his great rumbling voice, "Why should a Negro worker be penalized for being black? We don't want charity; we don't want philanthropy. We want equality with other workers." Since the old AF of L was dominated by the building trades unions which discriminated against Negroes, Randolph's audience would always vote against him. But, first, they'd give him an ovation.

Once, in debate, an opponent threw up his hands. "How can we cope with this man?" he complained. "This highly cultured individual [Randolph] is the only one here who has had the full advantage of an education in Harvard University. He studied logic; he studied philosophy; he studied ethics; he studied the humanities and human nature!"

Randolph never went to Harvard. He attended night college classes, and is the product chiefly of his own vast reading. He is also the product of a faith that has moved social mountains: faith in man's ability to overcome his environment and faith in men.

Overcoming his own environment was a challenge to Randolph.

As an inquisitive Negro boy in Jacksonville, Florida, he couldn't browse in the public library, or borrow books; he was restricted to the meager "colored section." When he went downtown with his brother, James, to pick up newspapers to sell, the white boys would keep them at the end of the line, unless they battled their way out. And, once, young Randolph spent the night, terror-stricken, watching his mother, a fine-featured mulatto with long, flowing hair, stand guard at the door with a shotgun. Young Randolph's father had rounded up Negroes in the neighborhood and had gone off to the county jail to stop a lynching.

Randolph's father had his own inspired way of dealing with the problem of rearing children in the world they lived in. He was an impoverished, dark-skinned minister in the African Methodist Episcopal Church, who eked out a living as a tailor.

The Randolph's lived in a shack—two rooms upstairs, two below, with the "living room" largely taken over by the father's mending work. As a minister with share-croppers for a flock, young Randolph's father was paid chiefly in kind—with a shoulder of pig, a bag of sweet potatoes, a cabbage or two. Cash was so scarce the Randolph boys sometimes remained home from school because they lacked shoes. Yet the colored minister hammered pride into young Randolph and his brother.

The father taught the boys that color has nothing to do with intellectual capacity, or with character. What they'd be in the world depended solely on themselves. Whenever he took the boys into the white section to deliver clothes, he'd say to the customer, "Aren't these fine boys? They'll be great men some day."

Instead of good clothes—as a morale builder—the little minister clothed his boys in fine English speech. Although he had no formal education, Randolph's father had read hungrily, and with a sensitive ear had picked up from visiting troupes of Shakespearean actors a clear diction and a South of England accent—the broad "a" of "Hahvahd" and the long "e" as in "bean." These the minister drilled into young Randolph and his brother. And, as a further shield, the minister gave his boys his own eager interest in books.

One book, Du Bois's *Souls of Black Folk,* gave Randolph the driving idea of his life—the idea of the Talented Tenth. One of every ten Negroes must be educated for leadership.

208

Booker T. Washington had taught that Negroes were best off in manual training and manual work. Du Bois taught that Negroes have among them persons of superior intellect like other races, and these should supply the leaders to help fellow Negroes rise to whatever jobs their talents and education fitted them. The fourteen-year-old Randolph tossed at night with the excitement of this idea. He would be one of the Talented Tenth—and a leader for his people.

Young Randolph had the good fortune to live in a community where the American Missionary Association had established, during Reconstruction days, a high school for Negroes staffed with white teachers from New England. A dedicated lot, the teachers—called Marms—not only taught their colored students book learning, but also to have faith in themselves, serve as examples to other Negroes and to fight for equal economic opportunity.

When Philip Randolph graduated from high school, his brother was valedictorian, but Philip was asked to give the class oration. A Negro insurance man was so taken with Philip's ability to sway people that he offered him a job of swaying people to buy insurance. While he worked briefly at selling insurance, Randolph sent away for college catalogues, and with his brother pored nights over manuals from Harvard, Princeton, Oberlin and elsewhere—savoring the sound of the printed courses such as "Greek Civilization from Plato to Pericles." College, to the impoverished Randolphs, was but a dream, however, and Philip drifted north to make his living at Negro jobs—as elevator boy, waiter—and to get an education nights at the City College of New York.

Here Randolph studied political science, economics, philosophy and polished up on his English. He acquired a lifelong friend, the late philosopher, Morris R. Cohen, who gave Randolph scientific tracts which showed that, while individuals differed greatly, the Negro was just another member of the human family, neither inferior nor superior to other races.

Randolph had turned himself into one of the educated, "Talented Tenth." Now, to give himself an operating base and to create a symbol of Negro achievement and stamina, Randolph undertook one of the toughest organizing jobs in union annals: the twelve-year fight to form the Brotherhood of Sleeping Car Porters.

In 1925, the Pullman porter worked about seventy hours a week at an $18 wage or 25 cents an hour. Tips brought his gross monthly income to $100—from which the porter bought his own uniform and shoe polish, paid for his own meals in dining cars, and so used up about one-third of his earnings. And, sometimes, he'd wait all day at the Pullman office for a job assignment—at no pay. All this was set down in a "labor contract" negotiated with the Pullman Company by a company union formed and financed by the employer.

Still there were more applicants than jobs; the porters stood in constant fear of idleness and hunger and were afraid to organize.

So when Randolph started to rouse public opinion against the Pullman Company, he succeeded at first in arousing everybody except the sleeping car porters themselves. Their wives wouldn't let them join, out of fear for their jobs.

Pullman Company inspectors rode the sleeping cars, ferreted out information about new members and fired them. The Negro press, stimulated by company advertisements, either refused to print news of Randolph's organizing progress or attacked him with the bitterness to be found only in family rows.

The porters' meager dollar-a-month dues could barely support a headquarters, and often Randolph and his helpers worked without telephones or lights. Randolph was dispossessed from his meager Harlem flat and often didn't have a nickel for a subway ride.

Yet Randolph visited the Pullman porters secretly in their homes, met trains, held meetings at railroad yards when railroad police weren't watching. In three years, he painfully put together locals with a membership of five thousand porters.

Nine years of organizing rolled by. It was 1934—a depression year—and Randolph's Brotherhood of Sleeping Car Porters still had no contract and no improved conditions. The Porters' treasury was bare. Randolph's wife, Lucille—a graduate of Howard University—had lost her social worker's job, and there was nothing with which to feed four mouths: that of Randolph, his wife, mother and sister.

It was Randolph's darkest hour. And to his ordeal a friend now added temptation. The late Fiorello H. La Guardia, "the Little Flower," then Mayor of New York, offered Randolph a $12,000-a-year job on the city payroll.

"You'll never organize the porters," La Guardia said.

How could La Guardia understand that the fight to organize the

210

Negro porters was more than a union drive alone? It was an ordeal that tested the stamina of the Negro; if he could hold out, he could show that he could achieve a goal under the most adverse conditions. The whole Negro community was involved.

Randolph, neat and carefully mended, borrowed subway fare to go down to City Hall and say no to La Guardia.

Three years later, Randolph won a National Labor Relations Board employee election and, with it, a contract from the Pullman Company. It called for a forty-hour week, a base $250 monthly salary, machinery for settling grievances.

To the Negro in 1937, the "Brotherhood" with its eighteen thousand members was a more significant organization than the United Automobile Workers with its then 400,000 members. Randolph had triumphed under conditions that gave the Negro pride and faith in himself.

In his classic *An American Dilemma,* Gunnar Myrdal points out that a Negro professional man, a writer, a singer, doesn't merely write or sing. He's locked into the Negro problem and so writes about Negro life or sings Negro songs. As a Negro labor leader, Randolph became a champion of Negro rights everywhere. Now, he had a base from which to operate. The Sleeping Car Porters became a launching platform for Negro equality drives.

Wherein a Porter Says No to a President

Before Randolph, the Negro had sought to stir the conscience of the country—by complaining to the white man. Randolph called this "the propaganda of the word." Now, with the Brotherhood as a rallying center, money raiser and leader, Randolph turned to "the propaganda of the deed."

The first "deed" was a drive to open war plants to Negro workers. Here, Randolph, the man who once said no to a Mayor, now had to say no to a President of the United States, Franklin D. Roosevelt.

It happened this way:

Shortly after Pearl Harbor in 1941, Randolph eased his weary six-foot frame into a Pullman car seat of a Washington-New York express. Loyal to the Pullman car to the last, Randolph had yet to

211

travel inside America by airplane. (He flew to Ghana, Africa, last year, but only because trains don't cross oceans.) Now, he settled down for a relaxing ride.

With him was the three-hundred-odd-pound Milton Webster, vice-president of the Sleeping Car Porters. In the first war, Randolph mused in his chocolatey, deep voice, he had been a pacifist and gone to jail. Now, although Jim Crowism still persisted in the Armed Services, Randolph could not oppose a war against an arch-racist, Hitler. Still, there was another problem. Although the war plants cried for workers, Negroes were largely barred from all except janitor's work.

"We've got to stop pleading with white officials; this conference technique doesn't work," Randolph said. "We don't impress the government until we impress the Negro himself." He mulled this over as the train picked up speed out of Washington and said, "We're talking a lot about being the Arsenal of Democracy. Suppose we dramatize the fact that in this Arsenal of Democracy of ours there is no democracy for the Negro citizen. Suppose we put the Negro in motion—get him to march 100,000-strong in protest on Washington."

Back in New York, Randolph and his aides scoured Harlem's grocery shops, churches, beauty parlors to recruit marchers. Randolph had worked with white leaders on prior projects. But this, he decided, was to be an exclusively Negro affair. Only Negroes would be allowed to organize, give money and march. ("You take ten thousand dollars from a white man; you have his ten thousand dollars, but he's got your movement. You take ten cents from a Negro; you've got his ten cents, and you also have the Negro.") The idea of a vast demonstration caught fire, and from Chicago, Detroit and faraway Los Angeles, Negroes began to organize marchers and arrange transportation to Washington.

Randolph and the late Walter White, then head of the National Association for the Advancement of Colored People, issued an ultimatum.

"Unless the government intervenes against prejudice in war plants, 100,000 Negroes will march on Washington."

Alarmed, President Franklin D. Roosevelt dispatched Mrs. Roosevelt—a friend of Randolph's—to talk him out of the idea.

"Where will you put up 100,000 people in Washington?" Mrs. Roosevelt asked. "Where will you get the police protection? There might be rioting. You might be killed."

"No earthly price can stop us," Randolph replied. Mayor La Guardia joined the plea, and when he failed, Mrs. Roosevelt telephoned her husband. "Ask Mr. Randolph to come to the White House," said Roosevelt.

The President brought in Cabinet ministers, War Production Board executives and other dignitaries to underline the solemnity of the White House meeting. He turned on his most dazzling charm. Randolph, as solemn as anybody—but unimpressed by the charm—sat in quiet dignity and merely rumbled in his basso's voice, "The plants must be opened to Negroes, Mr. President. Or I must let my people march."

Roosevelt yielded and issued the historic executive order which commanded war producers to drop color barriers. An enforcement committee was created to police the order. On Randolph's suggestion, it was named the Fair Employment Practices Committee, so giving birth to the conception of FEPC and to the now familiar initials. From it, later, flowed FEPC's in thirteen states and forty cities.

Randolph's "propaganda of the deed" wrested a second landmark victory in 1948, this time from President Harry Truman.

When returning Negro war veterans beat a path to the Porter Brotherhood's door to protest discrimination in the Jim Crow Armed Services, Randolph dispatched a Brotherhood organizer to Negro colleges and other campuses to sample opinion among young Negroes about to be drafted. The opinion sampler was Ted Brown, a Northwestern University graduate and one of the new generation of Randolph's Talented Tenth.

Young Brown's report was simple. "They're disinclined to shoulder a gun in a Jim Crow Army," he said. With some leadership, many would go to jail rather than serve, he reported.

Randolph sought a White House interview and told President Truman, "I haven't found one Negro interested in serving his country, if Jim Crow continues."

Truman was shocked and angry. Unperturbed, the deliberate Randolph went on to make him even angrier.

213

"I may break the law by urging my people to refuse to serve," he said, "but, Mr. President, I'll be serving a higher moral law by opposing discrimination."

The specter of Negro civil disobedience and jails filled wtih thousands of protesting Negroes posed the same political dilemma to Truman that Randolph's threatened March on Washington posed to Franklin D. Roosevelt. Truman capitulated with an executive order that wiped out segregation in the Armed Forces.

But Randolph was only partially successful in the area where victory could mean most: the unions which control jobs.

When Randolph organized the Sleeping Car Porters, his chief foe was an employer. When he tried to help other Negro railroad workers, the chief enemy was the white union. These unions not only barred Negroes from membership, but forced the railroads to fire them, if they already held jobs. When the Negroes sought justice in the courts, the unions used the full might of their treasuries to fight them. And when all else failed, white union members resorted to murder.

Randolph's first rescue expedition was to save the jobs of the Negro locomotive firemen. And this meant war with the powerful all-white Brotherhood of Locomotive Firemen.

Since shoveling coal into an engine used to be hot, backbreaking and foul work, Negroes were welcome to it. So, in the South, virtually every other locomotive fireman once was a Negro, forming a mixed color team with the white engineer. When automatic devices such as the stoker arrived, making the job easier, and when the Diesel followed, making the job a sinecure, the white unions started to drive Negro firemen from the locomotive cabs.

The unions organized "hate strikes" to force the railroads to fire the Negroes; then members turned to violence. Negro firemen were called "Zulus" and were shot out of their cabs. Between 1931 and 1934 ten Negro firemen were killed and twenty-one wounded in the Lower Mississippi Valley alone. Next, the white unions coerced twenty-one Southern railroads in 1940 to stop hiring Negroes altogether and to fire Negroes who had as much as twenty years of seniority.

Randolph couldn't organize the Negro locomotive firemen into a union of their own. The white union had the jurisdiction. So Randolph—turning again to the "propaganda of the deed"—formed a "provisional Committee" of Negro firemen. With Porters Union money, the Negro firemen took to suing the white man's union for damages: loss of pay due to loss of jobs. Soon, the Negro firemen were winning suits and draining the white union's treasury. Randolph and the Negro firemen battled their way to the Supreme Court which in 1944 outlawed the anti-Negro union deal with the railroads. The white union paid off pending Negro suits in a lump sum and, tired of writing checks, ended that phase of its war against Negro firemen.

But in the building trades unions, Randolph met a stone wall.

Here, in construction, the union—rather than the employer—does the hiring. The contractor who needs a dozen carpenters or a couple of plumbers for several days' casual work, calls the union hall. The Negro who can't get into the union can't get into the job-dispensing hiring hall either.

Strait Is the Gate

The building trades union color line was revealed by the Urban League which checked thirty-two cities—North and South—in 1957.

In Columbus, Ohio, the Plumbers and Electricians Unions barred Negroes as a matter of unwritten practice. If a qualified Negro electrician, plumber or painter came into the city with a "transfer card" from an out-of-town local, his white union brothers probably wouldn't honor his card. He was still a non-union man as far as they were concerned.

In Denver, Colorado, the Operating Engineers would take in Negroes "if employers agree to hire them"—but had not taken in any as yet. In the Denver Electricians Union, Local 68, there were no Negroes. In the local union of five thousand carpenters, five were Negroes—$\frac{1}{10}$ of 1 per cent.

It took almost a decade of campaigning to open Local 38 of the Electricians Union in Cleveland to a token number of Negro members. Discrimination by this union so aroused public opinion that the city's Community Relations Board made a public plea to the union to let down the color bar. The city FEPC—which has no enforcement powers—failed too. The union wouldn't budge despite

215

the fact that this barred Negroes from government construction and so violated the President's executive order[3] against discrimination on government work. The local relented only after George Meany ordered the International to intercede. The local was told to drop its color bar or face the loss of its charter.

Lack of vocational facilities is a major barrier. In all of the South —wherever there is segregation—there are no schools to train young Negro mechanics. Training in domestic service, in cooking, sewing, beauty culture, yes. But not in blueprint reading, or electronics or in the use of machine tools.

The federal government's Office of Education in the Department of Health, Education and Welfare helps pay for training programs in many states. Insofar as the unions exclude Negro apprentices, the United States government is, in effect, subsidizing discrimination. So do the towns in which public buildings and public school teachers are part of training work from which Negroes are barred.

Not only does lack of training keep Negroes out of the building trades crafts, but it also presents a terrifying problem to the industrial worker. When an auto manufacturer introduced automatic machinery for turning out a whole motor block, men who had drilled holes into the block were replaced by fewer skilled operators. Those displaced were chiefly Negroes. Recently, a Southern aircraft plant introduced mechanical sweepers. Thirty-one Negro janitors were thus displaced by nine white machine operators. The jobs were no longer Negro jobs; they had become white jobs.

Two great forces are working for the Negro: the triumph of the industrial union idea (the idea of taking in everybody in a plant or industry into one union) and the decline of autonomy—the idea that a union is a private lodge and can handle its internal affairs as it pleases.

When the great industrial unions came along in 1937 in the steel, rubber, auto and other industries, they invited the Negroes in. They had to in self-protection. If Negroes were barred, they would hire themselves out as strike breakers. That is how one of the great early organizing strikes in the steel industry—the one in 1919—was

---

[3] Order No. 10479, issued by President Dwight D. Eisenhower in 1953.

broken. Negroes—barred by the white Amalgamated Iron and Steel Workers Association—were brought in to man the plants when the white men walked out. When Philip Murray founded the United Steelworkers, he remembered this lesson so well that he joined the board of directors of the National Association for the Advancement of Colored People—to encourage Negro steel workers to join his union. Today, one of every four United Steelworkers' members is a Negro, and the union fights its Southern members who want to hold segregated meetings.

Now for the second force: the decline of autonomy in unions. Since the merger of the old American Federation of Labor craft unions with the industrial unions of the CIO, the new Federation has cracked down on color-conscious affiliates.

When Philip Randolph rose in 1935 to ask, "Why should a Negro worker be penalized for being black?" William Green, then presiding at the annual convention, could only wring his hands. "Do we give International Unions autonomous rights?" he asked the convention. "Can we suspend the charter of the International Union because it does not provide for the admission of colored members? Can we do that? Are you ready to do that?"

Twenty-two years later, President Meany didn't ask this question. Corruption among affiliates had forced the Federation to take a strong hand in member unions' affairs. If Meany could throw out a union for being corrupt, he could also throw it out for violating another section of the AFL-CIO constitution—the one against race bias.

Like a rocket to the moon, the Negro's progress toward equal economic citizenship has been a several stage affair. In the first stage he was allowed into industrial plants. The second stage requires that he break through the promotion and training barrier, and reach up into skilled and higher paid jobs.

That's where the color war is being fought today and that's where the union is the Negro's chief champion.

When the Oil, Chemical and Atomic Workers International, an industrial union, organized white and Negro workers in the Southwest, the union found that Negro workers were getting less pay than white employees on the same job. The union went to court and won equal pay for equal work. Next, O. A. Knight, president of the union, did something about white jobs and Negro jobs. (In the "white job," the worker could be promoted to skilled, higher paid work. The "Negro job" was a dead end.)

The NAACP had complained to the President's Committee on Government Contracts that eight refineries were treating Negroes unfairly by locking them into Negro jobs. When action on the NAACP's complaint against one employer lagged, Knight of the Oil Workers ordered his locals there to negotiate with the employer to end the system of Negro jobs.

"Boys, we'll just have to end segregation," he said, "or the government will." White members in the oil worker locals refused to sit in the same room with Negroes at first. But under pressure from their International, they teamed up with Negro members to negotiate away the system of Negro jobs. In 1957, some forty Negroes had won jobs that until then had been reserved for whites only.

A big job still remains to be done. In virtually all Southern factories, most production jobs are held by whites. To the Negroes fall the sweepers', janitors' and maintenance jobs. In the few factories where Negroes do hold assembly-line jobs, they are rarely employed on an unsegregated basis and in jobs comparable to those of whites.

Among the 400,000 textile workers of Virginia, North and South Carolina, virtually no Negro is employed as weaver, spinner or loom fixer.

Dark Man in the Union's Future

For the unions, the Negro problem, long swept under the rug, has become a menace to the union's ability to grow and survive.

Much of the country's growth is taking place in the South and Southwest. But union organizing efforts there have made little headway. This is because the unions of necessity have to be for integration, and some Southern employers use this as a stick to beat the union organizer.

When the International Union of Electrical Workers tried to

organize a Bay Springs, Mississippi, company, its owners—two Chi-cagoans—circulated a picture of the union's president, James Carey, dancing with a Negro woman. Carey's dancing partner was the wife of the Nigerian delegate to a labor conference at Geneva, Switzer-land. But the picture cost the union the employee election.

Everything's fair, seemingly, in love and union wars. When the Textile Workers Union tried to organize a mill in Wilmington, North Carolina, the company circulated a letter to employees warning, "the unions are working day and night and are pouring out the money which they collect in dues . . . to eliminate segregation. . . ." While the company was stirring up this witch's brew in the South, a top executive was receiving an award for "humanitarian services to the community" in the North. The donor, ironically, was the Anti-Defamation League which fights discrimination against minorities.

In the fall of 1957, George Meany admitted at a New York Urban League dinner that racism has sanded the gears of the union's drive in the South. For better or for worse, the unions were wedded to the Negro problem.

Crucible

The union gives the Negro his only chance in American life to belong to and identify with an institution which is not basically racial such as a Negro lodge or a Negro church. In the union he's just an-other member. In the North he sits beside white members at local union meetings. He is called "brother" by fellow unionists, goes to conventions where he sits down to a drink or a meal with white dele-gates. His grievances are processed by the union without regard to his color.

In the South, too, prior to the integration turmoil, unions had done a quiet job—the only job, in fact—of integration. The Negro bricklayer in New Orleans works side by side with white bricklayers, attends a local meeting in which the *minority* of members are whites. On the dais sits a Negro business agent, Arthur Paulette who has been elected seventeen years running by white and black votes alike, and with him is a white secretary-treasurer.

I asked a New Orleans newspaper reporter to witness a meeting of the Seafarers International Union for me.

219

"Integration is no problem," he reported. "A half dozen Negroes sat tightly packed between whites at a meeting of about 250 Seafarers. During the meeting, a white member turned to engage one Negro in discussion. When they left, the white man was hanging on to the Negro member's right arm and talking to him animatedly. One Negro who came into the hall just before the meeting began walked up to a white man, shook his hand and they stood together throughout the session."

Integrated locals of Negro and white auto workers, steel workers, packinghouse workers, construction laborers can be found in Memphis, Atlanta, Birmingham. And there are others.

The unions remain the only lines of direct communication between white and Negro in the South. They are the crucible in which understanding between men of different color is being tested and from which new understanding may come.

VI

What the unions do, and
things you didn't suspect they do.

Can it be true that our triumphs are dreaded?

PIERRE VERGNIAUD, President of the French Assembly, 1792

CHAPTER 15

How to Get
a $100,000,000 Raise

Early in 1958, a jaunty redhead walked confidently in to the boss and asked for a $404,000,000 raise. The boss, of course, thought the request high, but he was willing to talk. After eight months of talk, the red-haired fellow walked out with somewhat less than one-fourth of the demand: an estimated $75,000,000 to $100,000,-000.[1]

The boss was the world's biggest corporation, General Motors; the raise seeker was Walter P. Reuther, head of the world's biggest industrial union, the United Auto Workers. The raise would be spread for three years among 365,000 UAW members who work for G.M.

Some 17,500,000 Americans use union negotiators like Reuther to ask for pay boosts. They practice a species of diplomacy that has its own psychological warfare, meetings at the summit, going to the brink—and, when all else fails, limited wars, more commonly known as strikes.

When Sam Gompers, father of American unions, was a boy— before the turn of the century—an aggrieved worker simply got up at his bench and shouted, "I'm going on strike. Who's with me?"

Boss and workers then fought it out, sometimes bloodily, until one or the other gave in.

That was because there was no orderly method for asking the boss for a raise. The growth of the unions has brought a businesslike

---

[1] This consisted largely of automatic, cost-of-living and productivity pay rises.

relationship between worker and boss. There is a bargaining table to negotiate wages and a business instrument—the union contract—to seal the deal.

The bargaining table is a free society's safety valve against class struggle explosions, providing a place where the free worker may battle for what he regards as justice. But the table's magic works only if both sides have equal strength. If not, one side can bully the other. This can mean, for all of us, price raises without end—or the desperate strikes and riots of preunion days.

What goes on behind the closed doors? What is the secret of getting the boss to say yes—or getting the worker to accept a no? What makes a champion bargainer? And is the conference table the only place where bargaining is done?

Strategy

When the giant Auto Workers Union asks for a raise from the giant General Motors Corporation, nationwide interest is so great that the opening day of the bargaining is charged with the electricity of the day of the big game.

Television cameramen and several score reporters strain to catch every facial expression and every word as Walter Reuther, cocky, with hands on hips like a wrestler strutting in the ring, and G.M. vice-president Louis G. Seaton, sober with the burden of dealing with the most dramatic figure in Labor since John L. Lewis, shake hands before the big debate.

With an eye to the gallery—i.e., the whole country—both sides are alert to say something bright, yet make a shrewd bargaining thrust.

"Have you brought a big knife to carve up the goose?" an auto executive once thrust at Reuther.

"It's the only goose I know that the more you slice it, the fatter it grows," Reuther parried.

Yet, although the actual bargaining sessions get the big headlines, the moves that may bring victory begin months and sometimes years before.

As in power struggles between nations, victory depends both on general strategy, or the master plan of action, and on tactics—the

224

specific moves to carry out the plan. So the bargaining sessions sometimes become only a part of the over-all campaign.

Here is the strategy with which Walter Reuther won a historic victory; company payments to idle workers.

In 1952—fully three years before the next bargaining round—Reuther unveiled his next grand demand: the famous Guaranteed Annual Wage proposal. He gave no details as to how this radical plan could work—indeed his thinkers hadn't yet figured any out. Reuther said merely—in the press and on the radio—that employers should pay blue-collar workers a year-around wage whether they worked or not. Reuther asked a panel of leading economists to air their views on the Guaranteed Annual Wage (let's call it GAW), and soon had virtually every magazine, newspaper and luncheon club in America taking sides on it.

Reuther's strategy was matched by the employers' counterstrategy. There were two ways to resist Reuther's scheme. One was to seek to convince public opinion that the plan was unworkable, then take a strike, if necessary, to fight it. General Motors, deciding on this strategy, announced it would not yield and spent $100,000 secretly on an anti-GAW movie (which it decided at the last minute not to show). The Ford Company took a different strategic course. As matters stood, the company had two choices—both bad. One was to fight it out in a crippling strike; the other was to accept Reuther's GAW, which might be equally crippling. So the company took a third way out. Behind closed doors, the Ford Company set a task force to work to develop a practical plan of its own for paying workers during layoffs.

At bargaining time, the Ford Company surprised Reuther with its own, closely guarded plan: to supplement an idle worker's state unemployment insurance with company payments and so build up his income to 65 per cent of his regular pay. Reuther leads a double life as a bargainer. Outside, before the public, he's a terror, scaring the daylights out of the other side with extreme demands; or he infuriates his adversaries by sounding off on matters that aren't properly a matter for collective bargaining: car prices, for instance. But inside the conference room, Reuther, courteous although loquacious, drops the radical demands and concentrates on the possible. So, although the Ford plan was not a guaranteed annual wage in any sense

225

of the term, Reuther grabbed it up. He said it was his guaranteed wage in principle.

Reuther's strategy in whooping it up for an extreme demand, and Ford's counterstrategy of developing a workable scheme, achieved an ideal bargaining result: both sides were happy.[2]

To counter Reuther's strategic fight for public opinion in advance of bargaining, General Motors has abandoned its orthodox policy of confining the bargaining to the conference table and slugs it out in the press with Reuther.

"If Walter throws a rock, we'll throw it right back," a company man vowed.

So one year G.M. manned the corporate ramparts with a lookout task force whose mission was to anticipate and retaliate.

Researchers went back over eighteen years of life with Walter, following his well-marked trail through millions of words of newsprint, magazine articles, Congressional testimony, UAW convention reports. From this was boiled down a fifty-two-page manual of excerpts which, added up, gave a blueprint of Reuther bargaining strategy and tactics.

G.M.'s anticipators knew that Reuther would invite a committee of influential citizens—clergymen, probably—to hear him argue his demands; that he would appeal to the company's dealers, to the president of the corporation, to the President of the United States— and even, possibly, to the heads of other governments. That's what Reuther once did when he appealed to the British government to intervene in his negotiations with G.M. Clement Attlee, then His Majesty's Prime Minister, although a solid "Labour" party man, politely declined.

G.M.'s counterstrategic fight for public opinion paid off. Reuther dropped his two chief demands—a short work week and a cut of profits.

Tactics

Some sixty days before a contract expires, both sides meet at the bargaining table, and strategy gives way to tactics. Here the adversaries are no longer trying to convince the public; they're trying to

---

[2] General Motors went along with the Ford plan reluctantly. In the automobile industry, what one company gives all give, or suffer costly quickie strikes.

226

convince each other. The responsibility is sobering. For giant General Motors, for instance, a penny saved at the bargaining table is $7,000,000 earned, that year.

A quick brain and a ready tongue are weapons. Here, the union leaders—used to the rough and tumble of union hall debates—sometimes have the edge.

Once, during bargaining, a Ladies' Garment Worker leader demanded that employers be more efficient. Even with high piece rates, the ILG man argued, a worker could starve if his boss didn't keep the machines in order or slowed production with slovenly methods. When the employers, fearing a trap, wouldn't promise to be efficient, the union negotiator—a veteran of forty years of bargaining—whirled on the employer spokesman.

"What do you know about fatigue?" the union man bellowed. "Have you ever read a book on fatigue?"

The employers' man didn't even know there was such a book. Crushed, the poor fellow subsided into silence. The union got its efficiency promise.

Cyrus S. Ching who negotiated for U.S. Rubber Corporation for twenty-eight years, then headed the last War Mediation Board, says two assets are more prized than all others at the bargaining table. One is to be prepared: to know the other fellow's problem as well or better than he does. The other is to be so honest the other side trusts you implicitly.

As the all-time bargaining table great, expert Cy Ching nominates John L. Lewis of the United Mine Workers. First, he has the force of personality. An autocrat at the bargaining table, Lewis will say, "Gentlemen, I have the miners in the palm of my hand. What am I bid?" Then he'll sit still and imponderable until the fretting and talking coal operators come around to his way. Equally important, according to expert Ching, is that "Lewis knows as much or more about the economics of coal than anybody in the industry. He knows what the industry can pay without hurt." Because he knew the industry, Lewis departed radically from the usual labor practice of several decades ago and let the coal operators mechanize. Half of Lewis' miners lost their jobs, but those who remained got twice as much pay and the finest medical and pension protection of any workers.

227

"Today's best union negotiator," in the opinion of mediator Ching, "is the man who bargains for the United Steelworkers and is special counsel to the AFL-CIO, Arthur J. Goldberg. Lawyer Goldberg, who drafted the Ethical Practices Code for the AFL-CIO, brings integrity to the bargaining table. When Goldberg reports on a condition among workers or a situation in a plant, executives believe him. Goldberg bones up on industry conditions with great care and presses the union's demands with the courteous decorum of the courtroom and with a gifted lawyer's disciplined skill.

Courtesy goes a long way in asking for more pay—or in convincing the other side to take a no.

Louis G. Seaton of General Motors talks in a deliberately low voice to the UAW bargainers three feet across the table. Soft speech, he finds, keeps tempers down and makes the other side listen more attentively. In the Niagara of talk that pours over the participants, it's sometimes hard to keep awake—let alone attentive. So Seaton introduced the coffee break. G.M. provided the coffee for both sides until Reuther, objecting to the fraternization, insisted that the union men pay for their own and have it by themselves.

So eager are both sides of the rubber industry to avoid bad blood that might delay an agreement that union leaders and company executives, alike, "mister" each other decorously—and weeks of talk go by without anyone ever raising his voice in anger. This gentle dealing comes easy to the rubber company bargaining, because the United Rubber Workers' president, Leland Stanford Buckmaster, is a former schoolteacher—and tends to turn the conference room into a classroom. "He's always trying to teach you something," a company man said.

Yet the bargaining sessions can get rough. A bitter strike against the Westinghouse Electric Corporation by the International Union of Electrical Workers was prolonged because personal feelings between union leaders and executives became so strained that negotiations were broken off and weren't resumed for weeks. At General Electric negotiations, when tempers flared, General Electric's chief bargainer, urbane Virgil Day, would say, "We'll take a ten-minute recess, gentlemen, so that you can compose yourselves."

Since the modern union contract is as big as a fat, pocket-sized book—and spells out hundreds of items ranging from management rights to toilet facilities—the bargaining moves forward in several stages. In the first or "once over lightly" stage the union makes its demands, and both sides look for words, facial expressions and signals which will telegraph what the other side will fight for. In the second stage, the bargainers talk out technical details: how the contract will be administered, how to settle "beefs" under the contract. Then comes the sticky stage: the argument over money.

Here, the poker game really begins. Because boss and union men have dealt with each other for many years, the executives may know whether a union man is bluffing or means business by familiar personal mannerisms. One union man pounds the table when he's not sure of his ground. Another rises and walks nervously about the room, because the talks have gotten down to the cents-per-hour line on which the union man will fight—all summer if necessary. Union men, knowing that their mannerisms telegraph their intentions, sometimes try to change them or to show no emotions at all. The ultimate in this kind of poker-face negotiation was reached not long ago in a session between the International Typographical Union (the printers) and employers in New York. Both sides just sat there for days—with arms crossed, without uttering one word. They feared that such a word would give away their true bargaining position.

When tongues and attitudes get knotted this way, the union makes its power play. The leader takes a strike vote and sets a deadline. "Collective bargaining gets down to this," a veteran mediator said. "How much will a company pay to avoid a strike? How much will a union take without having to strike?" Often, then, the bargaining doesn't enter its final stages until the union unsheathes the sword.

"Why don't you fellows set a strike date, so that we can get down to business?" an auto company negotiator asked an Auto Union man in the 1958 bargaining.

Secret Diplomacy

Once the strike date is set, the official bargaining sessions may become mere shadow play for public consumption, while the real bargaining goes on elsewhere. Often bargainers can't reach an agreement at the bargaining table, because the union spokesman must always remember his audience—the rank-and-file members back home; the company spokesman, on the other hand, can't reveal his innermost, candid thoughts, because he has executive brass above him to consider. So two or three men from company and union get together at the summit—away from the bargaining table—for closely guarded exploratory talks.

"You don't have the boys in the bleachers," a company man will say to a union leader. "What do you really want?" Talks like these the public rarely hears about.

Confidential soundings at the summit require long friendship and absolute trust between participants. Once, after a U.S. Steel vice-president and the late Phil Murray of the United Steelworkers, had secretly explored each other's bargaining demands, the two men met for a further talk a week later. At this discussion—during luncheon at the swank Duquesne Club in Pittsburgh—the steel executive protested to Murray, "But you agreed to this last week."

"How do you remember what I said last week?" Phil Murray wanted to know.

"I wrote it down," the executive replied.

Murray was so incensed at the idea that the executive had recorded their confidential, off-the-record conversations that he rose in anger and stalked from the club. The executive in turn, was so dismayed at innocently risking a valuable, lifetime relationship that he followed Murray outdoors. It was raining, and the steel executive presented an odd appearance, running along beside the stalking union leader, holding an umbrella solicitously over him and calling, "Mr. Murray! Mr. Murray!"

A similar friendship between Phil Murray and a Bethlehem Steel executive led to negotiations at the summit that paved the way for one of the Steelworkers' most important gains. When Murray asked for pensions for steel workers, and the companies balked, Murray made a tour of the steel towns to arouse the workers to fighting pitch. Arriving in Bethlehem, Pennsylvania, Murray asked for a suite at the town's only hotel. He found that the hotel's only suite was permanently reserved for a vice-president of Bethlehem Steel.

But, said the hotel clerk, the steel executive had left orders that that suite be made available to Mr. Murray, who had come to town to denounce the executive's company. It was the first tipoff to Murray that the executive was willing to talk. Soon after, the two men reached the understanding that broke the industry-wide front against worker pensions.

When union leader and management man reach a secret understanding in an off-the-record talk, a famous New York mediator told me, "They may even write the script"—agree on the way they'll "bargain out" the already agreed-on result. The "script" may call for a fake break in negotiations or belligerent statements or even an all-night final bargaining session to make believe that hard bargaining is going on. With this kind of shadow play, bargainers convince the people they represent that they've fought as hard as they could for the best possible bargain.

"Unless you write about the off-the-record deal," one veteran negotiator said, "you won't give a true picture of collective bargaining."

Perhaps the most curious secret summit role played in any bargaining, anywhere, was that of David Dubinsky of the International Ladies' Garment Workers (ILG).

Since the dress business is probably the most competitive in America, and a penny an hour may break an employer's back, getting a raise in the New York Garment Center involves the wily trading of an Oriental bazaar—plus every trick in the book, besides.

One year, as usual, the dress industry's periodic asking and resisting match opened with a public show. Some three hundred union people, representing locals in New York, New Jersey and Pennsylvania, met in a hotel ballroom with two-hundred-odd representatives from the five trade associations that bargain for twenty-five hundred employers in the region. For the benefit of television cameras and reporters, a union man solemnly read the union's demand. An employer's man just as solemnly said, "We'll think it over."

Then the several armies of union and trade association committeemen dispersed to their home towns, and two teams of ten key spokesmen each squared off across a table in New York City. At neither of these two bargaining places—the hotel ballroom or the small conference room—did Dave Dubinsky appear. He sat back in his office on upper Broadway and awaited events.

Within a week or so, the bargainers disposed of most of the contract details and got down to cases: the wage demand. Here the union asked for a 15 per cent boost and held its ground; the dress men offered 4 per cent and wouldn't budge. When the adversaries couldn't stand the ordeal of hearing each other's arguments repeated any more, both sides started sending emissaries quietly to Dubinsky.

Union boss Dubinsky commands respect in the Garment Center because he's the biggest man in it—and because he scrupulously observes a basic bargaining rule: know what the other side can afford. Although a word from him can shut down the dress factories, his union had asked for no pay increase since 1953.

Now, in 1958, when his own bargainers came to him, Dubinsky wanted to know, "What do you fellas really need? What are you ready to trade away?" Some of the union men, facing members' revolts in their locals, told Dubinsky heatedly they couldn't trade anything—and the bargaining between Dubinsky and his own aides became as excited as any with "the bosses."

To the emissaries from the employers, Dubinsky said, "How far do you think your people will go? Look, you don't have to give me a commitment. I'm not holding you to anything. I'm just sounding you out." With this sort of maneuvering, Dubinsky narrowed down the bargaining. His own people went down to an 11 per cent demand. The employers went up to an 8 per cent offer. At this point they wouldn't budge unless the union showed it meant business by calling a strike, something the Garment Workers had not done since 1933.

With the dress factories shut down and both sides standing firm, only mediation could break the deadlock. But here came a problem. If Dubinsky asked for mediation, it meant his union was willing to come down. If the employers asked for mediation, it meant they were ready to go up. Secretly, Dubinsky sent a message to New York City's Mayor Robert Wagner, which said in effect, "This is your own idea, but don't you think that a man like ex-Senator Herbert Lehman would be a fine mediator for this strike crisis?"

Soon, with the eighty-year-old Lehman mediating the dispute, and with a bargaining session that began early one day and lasted until 4:30 A.M. the next morning, an agreement was reached. It gave Gar-

232

ment Workers an 11 per cent pay increase plus benefits including severance pay for discharged workers.

Buildup

Union leaders and management men know that theirs is a marriage—for better or for worse. They know that there will always be another bargaining table, just as in marriage there's always a breakfast table in the cold light of the next morning. So union man and executive try to do nothing during bargaining that will humiliate or embitter the other. If the marriage is a happy one, one partner will even try to build up the other.

When Phil Murray died, some steel industry executives believed that his successor, David McDonald, would be a force for stability —a man who could hold a disciplined work force together and give the boss a full day's work for a full day's pay. So the steel industry gave McDonald concessions to build him up with his followers. As a result (and thanks to the skill of McDonald's lawyer, Arthur J. Goldberg), the steel worker is the highest paid wage earner in industry, getting some twenty-four cents per hour more than Walter Reuther's auto workers.

The relationship between rubber industry executives and union leader L. S. Buckmaster is so friendly that formal bargaining has sometimes been preceded by informal talks in which one or two top rubber executives on one side, and Buckmaster and a chief aide on the other, sounded each other out concerning basic demands and counteroffers. Veteran negotiators know that a union leader justifies himself chiefly to his people by winning "more." So, some years ago, when pensions and other fringe benefits were first coming in, rubber manufacturers would let union leader Buckmaster get the credit— even if the company had initiated the offer. They'd take him aside. "If you'll ask for a Pension Plan this year," they might say, "we think you'll have a good chance of getting it."

When Charles E. Wilson was president of General Motors, he liked to exchange ideas with Walter Reuther. There'd be small meetings between the two men and their top aides. Wilson would get on the telephone and chat with Reuther—sometimes for a half

233

hour. From this warm relationship came General Motors' historic voluntary offer of automatic wage increases to cover rising living costs—and give workers a share in improved productivity.

Bernard Goldfine, the New England textile producer and friend of Sherman Adams, ex-Presidential Assistant, has an original way of establishing a friendly atmosphere before bargaining.

The following Goldfine vignette is from John Herling's informative labor letter: "Mr. Goldfine always likes to put on a party for all the negotiators. He generally hires a series of interconnecting suites in the Parker House in Boston. One wing is reserved for the union representatives [Textile Workers Union], another for the company men, and in a large center room a buffet is spread, and Mr. Goldfine presides at the summit.

"In the presence of union officials, Goldfine asks his own highly trained counsel, 'How much do I pay you?' The lawyer mentions his hefty fee, and Mr. Goldfine mutters, 'That's a lot of money.' He puts the same question to his other executives. Then he says, 'All right, you high-priced expensively educated fellows. With all that dough I'm paying you, you don't know as much about the textile industry as [pointing to the union leader] Johnny Chupka—who didn't go beyond grammar school. Go ahead, Johnny, tell them what the facts of life are.' "[3]

Goldfine is known as a hard and fair bargainer, and this bantering—a periodic ritual—helps ease prebargaining tensions.

Even when executives don't get along openly with the union leader they respect his position as spokesman for their employees. They seek to avoid acts that will hurt him with his people and so drive him to irresponsible retaliatory acts.

When General Electric developed a savings and security plan for its employees, the company kept the plan under wraps until executives had a chance to explain it to union leader Jim Carey and his aides. Even during the most heated bargaining table tiffs, G.E. bargainers respect Carey's good faith and integrity. After such sessions Carey would sometimes go off to a social dinner with G.E. executive Virgil Day, where Carey—the Mr. Hyde of the bargaining table—would become the witty and engaging Dr. Jekyll of the dinner table.

[3] John Herling's *Labor Letter,* Washington, D. C., June, 28, 1958.

234

Company people have long been restive about the dog-in-the-manger role that the bargaining process imposes on them. An employer who wants to give his people a ten-cent raise won't dare to make this his first offer, for fear he'll be bargained up to, say, fifteen cents, by the union. So he starts with two cents, makes a shadow fight and yields the ten cents he wanted to give in the first place—under the seeming pressure of the union. The union gets the credit, and the employer emerges as a churlish fellow who must be forced to do the right thing.

Actually, many historic wage innovations and security plans have been devised by the company side and offered voluntarily.

To shift from the employer's traditional defensive role and to change the workers' concept of his boss as a reluctant dragon, General Electric has pioneered in a type of bargaining which has aroused interest—and controversy. It is called "Boulwarism," after its vice-president Lemuel R. Boulware. As company spokesmen describe it, General Electric goes to great research lengths to dig out the truth about just wages and workers' needs. If the truth is that a G.E. worker should get several additional cents per hour—because that is the market value for his skill, or for other reasons—G.E. makes a firm offer of the raise at the outset of the negotiations.

"What we're trying to do," said a G.E. man "is to get away from the haggling school of bargaining, and, with the help of the union fellows, turn the negotiations into a search for the truth."

Union negotiators, of course, take a dim view of General Electric's strategy. They describe it as a "take it or leave it, Papa Knows Best" technique that leaves little or no room for the give-and-take of bargaining.

One observer and consultant to management has criticized "Boulwarism" in the *Harvard Business Review* as "an example of business cynicism." The critic, Professor Benjamin Selekman of the Harvard School of Business Administration, argues that General Electric's strategy ("management knows best what should be done for its employees") "denies workers adequate and competent representation."[4]

---

[4] "Cynicism and Managerial Morality," *Harvard Business Review,* September-October, 1958.

The controversy over "Boulwarism" points up a union-management problem that goes beyond bargaining table strategy. This is the seeming hardening of attitudes between unions and employers —and a growing antagonism akin to a cold war.

This rises in part from managers' fears that unions are using bargaining table power to whittle away the manager's rights to manage; it stems, too, from some businessmen's fears that labor leaders aim at a Socialist America. (Actually, as we've seen in these pages, no unions anywhere are more devoted to the private property principle.)

Since labor leaders need look back only twenty years to remember how hard employers fought unionism, some fear that employers still want to "bust unions." These fears are nourished by corporations who enter state political campaigns to support laws that unions feel will hamstring them.

Bargaining in key industries, then, is conducted in an atmosphere of suspicion and ill-will that makes it difficult for responsible men on both sides to avoid strikes.

CHAPTER 16

Labor U.S.A. vs. the Kremlin

Of all the unions' wide-ranging activities, their war against U.S.S.R. aims makes one of their most glorious chapters.

American union men and dues payers' money prevented the Communists from seizing Western Germany's unions at the war's end—which would have created chaos and blocked recovery. America's unions dug up the evidence on Russia's slave labor camps and fashioned it into a major international scandal.

Union researchers in New York ferreted out the ammunition that blasted open the deadlock truce negotiations at Panmunjom in Korea. American unions provided an estimated $1,000,000 and leg men to smash a Communist monopoly over the unions of Italy, France and Japan. And today, the AFL-CIO pours some $1,000,-000 yearly of American unionists' dues money into a world fight against the Soviet drive for world domination. The unions are one of the major unofficial forces in American life waging war on World Communism.

The late Sam Gompers first turned Labor's eyes overseas in 1910 by taking the old AF of L into the International Federation of Trade Unions. Housed in London, it had two modest aims: to collect union membership figures and to press for laws to bar the importing of strike breakers.

Until World War I, international affairs were the concern almost exclusively of the striped-pants set. But the rise, after the war, of a nation that called itself a "workers state" yet introduced a new type of state slavery turned American union leaders' eyes abroad. As leaders of a pragmatic union movement, free from dogma, American union men were the first—among the Western labor leaders—to awaken to the challenge of Communism.

Today, the AFL-CIO has its own "State Department," the Department on International Relations and a staff headed by Michael Ross. It has a "Secretary of State," George Meany, who counsels on foreign policy with a cabinet committee (The Executive Council's committee on foreign relations). And there is even a union "Voice of America," that is beamed to foreign readers: the *Free Trade Union News,* published monthly in English, German, French and Italian.

Behind Meany, who was a member of the American Delegation to the United Nations in 1957 and is a foreign affairs authority in his own right, is a little-known figure who has sparked ideas and often spearheaded major union campaigns against Communist intrigue abroad.

He is Jay Lovestone. Inside the Federation he holds two modest jobs: assistant director of the International Department and director of international publications. But as we shall see he's much more— and at one time was so controversial a figure that explosions over him rocked the Federation.

Until 1957, Lovestone played an independent role, working outside the Federation with a Free Trade Union Committee financed voluntarily by half a dozen unions. He directed the anti-Communist cloak-and-dagger activities of field workers in Western Europe and North Africa, had his own anti-red intelligence network, published an anti-Communist paper for foreign consumption and lobbied mightily before the United Nations.

All this stirred varying emotions in high union places. Walter Reuther demanded that Lovestone's free-wheeling, lone wolf work abroad be curbed; that he be brought into and supervised by the Federation—and that the AFL-CIO, itself, stop going it alone abroad and channel its work through the international trade association of national labor movements—The International Confederation of Free Trade Unions (the ICFTU).

George Meany insisted that the AFL-CIO, as the biggest workers' federation in the world, couldn't simply content itself with paying dues to the ICFTU, but could make the most of its great influence abroad through independent projects. Reuther won the battle; Lovestone was brought into the Federation as a staff man. But Meany seems to have won the war. As months passed, and tempers cooled, the AFL-CIO worked more closely with the ICFTU, to be sure. But American unions, sparked by Lovestone ideas and the Lovestone information-gathering-network, continued to push their own independent fight against Kremlin activity abroad.

To Catch a Red

George Meany regards Lovestone as the "most effective anti-Communist in America." He has lectured before the U.S. and Canadian War Colleges. For all that, only a handful of men inside the labor movement—and hardly anyone outside it—know the dimensions of the job that Lovestone, backed by union funds, has done.

This is a tribute to Lovestone's self-effacement which borders on invisibility. He even has a phrase to describe it: "Technological anonymity." Lovestone has worked out a science or technique for remaining in the shadows.

One reason for the withdrawal is that it is no easy matter to bear the burden of having once been a Communist; even if it was long ago and one has atoned with a quarter century of zealous fighting against Communism.

238

A reporter's first meeting with Lovestone takes on a sparring and cloak and daggerish quality. After an initial interview in Lovestone's book- and pamphlet-cluttered office in the Garment Workers building—which yielded little information—I left him and walked down the corridor to the elevator. He dashed after me.

"You have violated the first rule in undercover work," he said. "You have left telltale documents behind." He handed me my notebook.

At nineteen, Lovestone was already secretary of the American Communist party. This was in 1917, when it was underground. He journeyed often to Moscow (he made eighteen pilgrimages in all) to meet with the bigwigs of the Communist world. An unregenerate name-dropper, Lovestone engages in the sport with a subtlety that goes beyond the mere mention of the mighty. Lovestone drops only the first name of the great man, leaving the listener to infer the depth of the intimacy.

"Joe would send for me, most every time I was in Moscow," Lovestone will say casually. "Joe had a wicked sense of humor," Lovestone will go on, "but mostly at other people's expense."

"Joe," of course, was Joseph Stalin. And the most exasperating part of the business is that Lovestone seems to have earned the right to drop "Joe's" name. He not only saw him at the Kremlin but chatted with him over a glass of tea at Stalin's home.

Conversation with Lovestone is likely to be a fascinating business. Out come stories of the time that "Tito stood up in a meeting of the Comintern and defended me and shouted everybody down, and yelled, 'Let the comrade from America speak!' "

Or Lovestone tells of his last talk with the old Bolshevik Nikolai Bukharin in Paris, who, facing certain death at the hands of his old partner, Stalin, nevertheless chose "to return to my homeland and die."

Lovestone even knew the mightiest Bolshevik of them all, V. I. Lenin, the architect of the Russian Communist revolution.

"He was a master of dirty politics," Lovestone will recall.

Lovestone's palship with the Russian Communists ended in 1929 when he came to Moscow to resist Stalin's efforts to take over the American Communist party. No less a figure than Vyacheslav Molotov was named by Stalin to look into Lovestone's "deviationism," and to boot him from the Party.

The disgraced Lovestone—to his former Comrades he was now a leper—lingered long enough in Moscow to get an audience with his onetime pal, Joe, and complain about the rough treatment.

"A Bolshevik must know how to take a horse brush through his hair," Joe said.

Lovestone, penniless in Moscow, sold his underwear and his typewriter to get fare home. Back in America, he tried for a while to create an "American Communist party" free of Kremlin control, (the Lovestonites), then broke with Communism altogether in the mid-thirties. Today, he forms a unique human bridge to the minds, the methods and the drives of the conspiratorial Communist world. To this savvy, he adds further attributes.

Jay Lovestone is a medium-sized man with the look of an owl and the telltale facial pallor and softish body lines of the intellectual who spends too much time in libraries.

The birdlike cast of features is heightened by a strong, nose, surmounted by heavy-lensed glasses.

These are honestly come by, for Lovestone has condemned his eyes to hard labor all his life. None of the usual adjectives that describe excessive reading can convey what goes on between Lovestone and the written word. In his modest two-room flat in midtown Manhattan, the four walls of the living room are lined with books from floor to ceiling. Additional thousands of volumes have spilled over into a warehouse nearby. These contain, Lovestone says, virtually everything published on the Russian revolution, on the early Nazi movement and much on American history.

To his bookish aerie, Lovestone nightly lugs a briefcase or two plus a supplemental manila envelope crammed with periodicals, newspapers, field reports and monitored radio programs. Some forty-seven newspapers and magazines flow to Lovestone's office weekly from the four corners of the earth. About fifty correspondents—scattered from Reykjavik in Iceland to Delhi in India and from Warsaw in Poland to Melbourne in Australia—add periodic field reports to the flood of political and economic information.

Pencil and notebook in hand, Lovestone curls up for a night's study with a *Far Eastern Economic Review* (published in Hong Kong) or the *China News Analysis,* a compilation of news from

Communist Chinese newspapers, or the *Manchester Guardian,* or the *Armenian Review.*

Even Russian novels—relaxation for others—are read with pencil and notebook.

"Novels are a social force," says Lovestone. "Very important. Give me a Russian novel and I'll give you a rundown on what the Russian people are told to like, what they hate, what they are doing."

The information gathering and monumental sifting and ingestion of counter-Communist intelligence are part of his own private war with the Communist enemy. This occupies almost every waking hour of his day.

He takes no vacations, and, until friends presented him with a television set, he didn't have one. Unencumbered by family—he never married—Lovestone battles Communism with the zeal of one who has seen the enemy up close. His influence is felt in the most unlikely places.

Lovestone is listened to in the State Department. And on occasion he would canvass the world Communist situation in a talk with the then Secretary of State John Foster Dulles.

He helped convince the Eisenhower administration to name a labor man permanently to the United States delegation to the UN. The delegate as this is written is George Harrison of the Railway Clerks.

To understand Lovestone's influence, it is necessary to go for a moment to Lovestone's shield and power source, George Meany.

Back in 1933, when George Meany was president of the New York State Federation of Labor, he attended a meeting at which labor men discussed Hitler's rise to power and formed the Anti-Nazi Non-Sectarian League.

"I learned there," Meany says, "that under any dictatorship, whether Fascist or Communist, no unions can survive. Nor can any other kind of voluntary organizations where people can meet and express themselves.

"For the first time, I realized how the impact of events in other areas of the world could affect the unions."

241

When Meany became secretary-treasurer of the old AF of L in 1934, there was virtually nothing for him to do because William Green, then president, jealously tended to everything. So, with the encouragement of his friend, David Dubinsky—already head over heels in foreign relief work—Meany turned to international affairs.

As is his tenacious custom, Meany read widely, boning up on events abroad, and so became the logical choice for delegate to the UN when Secretary of State Dulles looked around for a labor man for the job. Meany was assigned to the Third or "Human Rights" Committee. Long dominated by the Russians, it was known as the Lullaby Committee, because Soviet filibusters there put other delegates to sleep.

Meany changed this. As the voice of the American toilers, Meany became something of a puzzle to the Russians who had been in the habit of assaulting American UN delegates as spokesmen for the "capitalist exploiters." Meany's resourcefulness in debate, particularly his boundless erudition and information, confounded the Soviet delegates even more. And this brings us back to Jay Lovestone.

Once Meany found himself up against a woman Soviet delegate who thundered—with glares at Meany—that "American unions belong to the ruling classes."

After the recess, Meany showed up with a copy of the Soviet Constitution (in English) and read that part of it that declares that the unions in the Soviet belong to and must take their guidance from the Communist party that rules Russia. It was a stopper.

None in the committee knew that Meany had hastened to the phone during the recess and posed his debating problem to Lovestone, a human Univac for storing information.

"You can murder them with their own constitution," said Lovestone, and from his memory dredged up chapter and verse.

One non-admirer has described Lovestone as "Meany's intellectual valet," implying that Lovestone helps lay out Meany's pronouncements. Meany, as everyone in Labor knows, has a tough mind of his own. Still it is Lovestone who digs up ammunition for the policy decisions that Meany threshes out with his Executive Council.

242

for regulating the unions. Union "experts" arriving with the Russian troops had these rules ready.

The Russians proposed as a chief regulation that no man could hold union office unless he was a worker in a plant.

Fair enough? Yet, had this rule been imposed, the West German unions would have been lost to the West.

Western labor leaders had had a cruel time. The Nazis in Germany and the Fascists in Italy had herded them into concentration camps or simply slaughtered them. A similar fate awaited labor leaders under the Nazi occupation. Even those union men who evaded the Nazis and joined the underground resistance movements couldn't be sure of their lives: Communists fighting at their side, their own countrymen, murdered key democratic unionists to remove opposition to postwar Communist control.

Now, liberated from concentration camps and returning to rebuild their old unions, the union freedom fighters found themselves barred from union office by Russian regulations.

It was as if George Meany and Walter Reuther, having been jailed by an occupying power, could not return to their union offices because they weren't plant workers.

Nevertheless, the Russian union blueprint had the support of American Communists within the military government—including one who later renounced his American citizenship to live in Czechoslovakia.

At this point, from the trade unions of the new world came help to the unions of the old.

The AF of L sent Irving Brown, a onetime associate of Lovestone in his youthful radical political adventures (but never a Communist)—and later a union organizer and then advisor to the War Production Board. Brown, at 48, is an intense, darkish, bespectacled man with fierce energy—and a mission.

Brown bombarded our military government with public harangue. And, at the risk of life and limb, he started to help reorganize free West German unions. Back home, the AF of L raised a clamor before the War and State Departments against the American Communists in the military government. These were cleared out, and the West German unions were rebuilt as anti-Communist labor organizations.

245

Split Is a Beautiful Word

During the era of good feeling in 1944, toward "our gallant allies, the Russians," the powerful British Trades Union Congress and our CIO joined hands with the Soviet's labor organizations to form the new World Federation of Trade Unions (WFTU).

The CIO had been blocked out of world affairs, because the older AF of L would threaten to withdraw if the rival CIO were invited into any world federation of which the AF of L was a member. Now, with the AF of L refusing to have anything to do with the Russians, the way was clear for the CIO. Sparked by the ambitious Sidney Hillman, head of the Amalgamated Clothing Workers, the CIO was eager to play a world role and to make a go of the partnership with the Russians. As for Britain's unions, they had joined up reluctantly, largely under pressure from the British Foreign Office.

The new World Federation had noble aims—on paper: to improve the conditions of working people everywhere; to help build unions everywhere; to oppose war.

But to the AF of L, and to Lovestone, in the wings, the new federation was a classic Communist united front—behind which the Communists would pursue Kremlin policy. But how do you wage war on a worldwide federation claiming 70,000,000 members in fifty-three countries?

American politics teaches: if you can't lick 'em, join 'em. But Communist politics teaches: if you can't lick 'em, split 'em. Lovestone had learned how. You raised questions and issues—on which those inside the enemy camp could not agree. To be specific, you raised questions which would make it impossible for the CIO and Britain's unions to remain in the Communist-dominated world federation.

The AF of L's top command gave the green light to Lovestone to polish up two wedges.

One wedge: the Soviet union is using slave labor. Hundreds of thousands, perhaps millions, of workers are herded into forced labor camps, both in the Soviet union and in the satellite countries.

From outposts behind the Iron Curtain, there was dug up the slave labor evidence, the first to be gathered. A pamphleteer with a dagger for a pen, Lovestone broadcast the evidence as far as the printed word could reach. Before AF of L conventions and the United Nations, and through Irving Brown in Europe, the slave labor disclosures were turned into an international issue and into prickly thorns for the free unions inside the Communist-controlled World Federation. Unable to convince the Communist majority to take a stand against slave labor, the CIO and the British unions began to wonder what they were doing inside the Red-controlled World Federation.

Another wedge was available: The Marshall Plan for economic recovery abroad. To West Europe's unions, the Marshall Plan meant jobs and food. The AF of L needled these unions to force their world federation to support the Marshall Plan. This brought out the World Federation's true color—Red. In its *Information Bulletin* the World Federation branded AF of L field man Irving Brown as a "propagandist of American Capitalist Monopolies." It published the captive Iron Curtain unions' attacks on the Marshall Plan—but permitted *no* space *for* the plan.

In vain, the CIO sent its secretary-treasurer, James Carey, to Europe to demand that the World Federation support the Marshall Plan. When Carey failed, the West's unions withdrew. The World Federation was split. Only the Communist unions remained. The World Federation's potential for mischief was blunted, for it could no longer pose as anything but a Kremlin puppet.

This big split was followed by lesser splitting operations of Red-controlled unions in France, Italy and Japan.[2]

Soon after, the AF of L and the CIO buried the hatchet to help form a new world labor organization, the International Confederation of Free Trade Unions, limited to the bona fide unions of the free world.

Now, in 1950, there was in the field the largest federation of unions in history. The International Confederation of Free Trade Unions could draw on the resources of 53,000,000 members in

---

[2] In Italy, with American help, dissidents were split away from the Communist Italian General Confederation of Labor to form the democratic Italian Confederation of Workers Unions (CISL—pronounced Chisel). In France, the Red Confédération Général du Travail was pried open to let out anti-Communists who formed the Force Ouvrière.

eighty-three countries to pursue its chief aims: to build unions, particularly in underdeveloped countries, and to fight Communism on all fronts.[3]

Lovestone is much in evidence around the United Nations and is probably the most zealous lobbyist there. His acquaintance among delegates, like his researches, is impressive.

These UN friendships and lobbying bore dramatic fruit during the Hungarian revolt. Lovestone's aim, as an instrument of AFL-CIO policy, was to hang the Hungarian revolt and suppression like a bloody albatross around the Soviet's neck. Here is how it was done:

A distinguished Hungarian refugee, Anna Kethly, minister of state in the democratic Nagy government, who had started to America as her country's representative to the UN, arrived to find her government suppressed and herself without friends or funds. The AFL-CIO supplied both, and won friends for her among the United Nations delegates.

Lovestone worked for the idea of a "watchdog committee" to investigate and report on the Hungarian revolt. The watchdog committee evolved into the Special United Nations Committee that unearthed and reported the now famous UN findings on Hungary.

In the fall of 1957, Lovestone had a quiet dinner in New York with a friend whose occupation is as secret as his own: the "king's taster" and security chief for King Sidi Mohammed Ben Youssef of Morocco. The King, himself, by his own royal request to our State Department, had met—on arriving in America—with George Meany. The King visited the AFL-CIO's headquarters, a stone's throw from the White House. There the King passed the time of day with high and low labor bureaucrats.

It was the first time that visiting royalty had paid this homage to the American Labor movement.

It was the King's way of thanking the unions for a significant piece of dungaree diplomacy: the role the unions had played in

---

[3] One example: The International Confederation of Free Trade Unions raised $854,000 among its 117 affiliates to provide Hungarian relief and help labor leaders flee during the revolt of 1956.

making Moroccan independence an international issue.

Capitalism with a Union Label

Dungaree diplomacy is yielding an unexpected dividend. Contact with American unions, plus agitation by visiting American firemen, is causing foreign unions to break with dogmas of the past. Before Mussolini, Italian unions, for instance, were organized on religious and political lines. There were the Christian Unions (Catholic), the Socialist unions and the Anarcho-Syndicalist unions. Today the Italians are beginning to take a leaf from the book of the American workers who organize simply on economic lines—and shun domestic political and religious entanglements.

The American union example of bargaining for more now rather than waiting for a worker-government millennium is even having an influence in England, where the unions have long been the backbone of the Labour party. English unions are having second thoughts about nationalization of industries—as a cure-all—and are turning to more aggressive bargaining instead. There is a diminishing faith in the concept of the state as a hander-outer.

The American union label, it turns out, is doing a giant job of selling the idea of a free economy abroad.

CHAPTER 17

Will the Unions Elect Our Next President?

The unions, potentially, are the most powerful single political force in the country—and they can prove it.

In 1944, the famous PAC (Political Action Committee) of the CIO, mobilized such armies of union voters that it helped re-elect Franklin D. Roosevelt to a fourth term.

249

Again, in the fall of 1958, political machines built overnight with union labor helped the Democrats sweep the country and to swamp "Right to Work" proposals in five of six states.

How do the unions do it?

When do they do it?

After all, union members and their families muster one-third of the country's eligible voters. If these voted as a bloc, they could elect our next President.

Wherein Labor Leaders See an Analyst

To the reporter in search of answers, California is a state where political wonders never cease. Here, the late Senator Hiram Johnson banished party bossism with a non-partisan ballot. But reformer Hiram Johnson would have goggled at the new political force that emerged, overnight, to sweep the state in 1958.

One morning in June of that year a group of long-faced labor leaders told their troubles to a San Francisco market research analyst and political pollster, studious and graying Hal Dunleavy.

Some 354,000 Californians had just signed petitions to put a referendum on the November ballot on a "Right to Work" proposal that would outlaw the union shop.[1] The labor men were worried, because they didn't know how their own members would vote on the issue. They had also begun to ask members for a "buck a man" to build a defense fund against the Right to Work proposal, and the members weren't responding.

Researcher Dunleavy asked, "How many of your members are registered voters?"

The union leaders had no idea. They had never thought of finding out, since their politicking in the past had been limited largely to endorsing candidates they favored. Now, when the union leaders hired analysts to compare their membership lists with registration rolls, they had something more to worry about.

Union members, it turned out, were apathetic citizens. Registrations ranged from a low of 30 per cent in some unions to about 50

---

[1] A union shop provision in a bargaining contract requires workers to join the union, usually thirty to sixty days after hire. Under a closed shop, the employer agrees to hire only persons who are already union members. Taft-Hartley bars the closed shop.

per cent in others. This was at least 25 per cent lower than the registration for the rest of the voting population.

There are 1,500,000 union members in California, about 20 per cent of the voting population. How could the union leaders rouse this slumbering giant? Where could they get additional votes for their point of view?

First, the union men called in a San Francisco advertising agency. Because California voters can pass their own laws by voting yes or no on many proposals, there has developed there an institution peculiar to the state's politics. This is the political advertising and promotion agency which is used by "clients" to sell or unsell voters on a referendum proposal. When the American Medical Association sought promotion experts to fight national medical insurance laws, it could find such experts only in California.

Now, copying the American Medical Association, the California Federation of Labor retained advertising men Leonard B. Gross and Curtis Roberts. Both are registered Republicans; one had managed the successful election campaign of Republican Senator Thomas H. Kuchel.

Partners Gross and Roberts had a simple idea.

If customers bought soap because a famous movie star endorsed it, couldn't the reverse method—the *non-endorsement*—by famous persons be used to unsell customers, i.e., voters?

The advertising men framed a brief campaign message:

"These leaders say no to 'Right to Work' "—and an impressive array of names followed: Eisenhower-Stevenson-Nixon-Truman. (Eisenhower actually took no stand for or against the California measure—holding that Right to Work laws were matters for the states to decide.)

Next step was to test the message, just as a manufacturer tests a new product. Market researcher Hal Dunleavy drafted a test postcard and mailed copies to eight thousand sample voters.

"If you were to vote today, how would you vote on 'Right to Work'?" the postcard asked.

Of those who replied, 42 per cent said they'd vote yes; 46 per cent said they'd vote no. The remainder were undecided.

Then, to the same sample of eight thousand voters went a second card.

251

"How would you vote on 'Right to Work' if these were the arguments? the card asked:

"Those who are *for* 'Right to Work' say it will cure union corruption, bar compulsory unionism.

"Those who are *against* say: 'These leaders—Eisenhower, Stevenson, Nixon, Governor Knight—say no to "Right to Work."' "

Now 56 per cent voted against Right to Work—a switch of 10 per cent to the union point of view.

Gross and Roberts suggested a $500,000 advertising budget. Unions downstate added a similar amount. Soon, throughout the state, there blossomed on billboards, in newspapers, on car stickers, the news that Eisenhower, Stevenson, Nixon, etc., were saying no to "So-Called Right to Work."

Senator William Knowland, who had staked his political life on the anti-union shop issue, protested that President Eisenhower had never said no to California's Right to Work proposal—and produced a "Dear Bill" letter from the President, in support.

The unions replied that Labor Secretary James Mitchell had attacked state Right to Work laws up and down the country, saying that he spoke for the administration. The billboard message stayed up.

To these were added radio singing commercials, beamed primarily at the wage earner.

> *Old McDonald had a farm*
> *dum-de-dum-dum-dum,*
> *And on this farm he felt secure*
> *dum-de-dum-dum-dum.*
> *With a holiday here, and overtime there,*
> *And a pension he could share*
> *dum-de-dum-dum-dum.*
> *Then came along old Right to Work,*
> *And drove McDonald quite berserk.*
> *Etc.*

There were other jingles. One described Right to Work as the right to work for less and less. Another boomed that Eisenhower is against it, "and Nixon and Truman—and everyone human."

There was no escape on television. Here in twenty-second "spots," costing $500 each in San Francisco and $800 in Los Angeles, viewers soon became familiar with a beaming President Eisenhower who was flashed on the screen while the announcer boomed, "Ike agrees with Adlai Stevenson [flashed next on the screen]," who agreed with a smiling Vice-President Nixon. All agreed on no on "So-Called Right to Work."

To the advertising drive the union men now added something that money alone couldn't buy: statewide organization of manpower, precinct by precinct, and block by block—to get out the Democratic vote.

Old-line party political machines, built around job patronage and handouts in time of need, have largely vanished—destroyed by unemployment insurance, old-age pensions and other government assists with which the old ward boss couldn't compete.

In California, the Democrats had started to fill this vacuum with a network of Democratic Clubs. These now joined forces with the unions.

Union men have a word for the leg work that goes into the distribution of leaflets at plant gates, the calls on workers in their homes. It is known as "Jimmie Higgins work."[2]

Dedicated union organizers once did "Jimmie Higgins work" to build unions. If union members could be convinced that their unions—and their collective bargaining gains—were in danger, they could be turned into zealous political "Jimmie Higginses."

The unions were already beaming bread-and-butter advertising arguments against Right to Work at their members. To this was added face-to-face persuasion. The unions put on "Family Night" to bring members to meetings. They promised "refreshments and personal appearances by radio and television stars."

The personal appearances were by fellow unionists, members of the American Federation of Television and Radio Artists (AF-TRA), who put on professional skits lampooning the foes of the union shop.

The union member no longer regards himself as a part of the "protest movement" that Labor was several decades ago. He is likely to own his own home, fully gadgeted, and a car and tele-

---

[2] After a fictional organizer created by Upton Sinclair in his novel *Jimmie Higgins*.

vision set. Union leaders may have trouble stirring him up to fight for more—but it isn't difficult to arouse him to fight for what he has. Convinced by their leaders that the attack on the union shop was an attack on their gains, the union members and their wives turned themselves into a fanatic band of political Jimmie Higgins workers.

To harness this manpower, some three hundred union leaders—presidents of locals, business agents—met in San Francisco and divided themselves into Assembly District committees. These set up neighborhood registration offices and recruited rank and filers to do the leg work. California permits its citizens to serve as voluntary deputy-registrars who, sworn in, can register voters wherever they can find them.

Guided by Democratic Club officers, union leg men went into heavily Democratic neighborhoods and registered voters from house to house. They went into supermarkets, and even stationed themselves on street corners to sign up passers-by. And in factories, union shop stewards went from man to man.

The union political organizers overlooked nothing.

For instance: The California ballot, never simple, lists dozens of state and local candidates and propositions. This creates a California phenomenon known as the "drop off," the voters' tendency to give up before reaching the bottom of the ballot. To make sure that voters wouldn't "drop off" before voting no on Right to Work, union men brought voters to district headquarters where, on borrowed voting machines and on paper ballots, they taught voters to attend first to the No on Right to Work. Some 15 per cent of the state's voters usually "drop off." This time all but 4 per cent voted on Right to Work. According to analysts, this meant some 300,000 additional votes.

To this organized political effort, many unions added their own gimmicks.

The Teamsters offered $10,000 in prizes—first prize $5,000—to the voter who could guess the "margin of votes by which so-called 'Right to Work' will be defeated." Printed up in hundreds of thousands, the contest's entry blank also urged the contestant to "Follow Your Guess; Vote No on 18."

In Los Angeles a union group printed up bales of miniature greenbacks. Soon, whenever a union man or his wife went to the grocer or butcher, they handed over, along with real dollars, a picture green-back which read:

> This purchase was made with Union Dollars . . .
> I spend Union Wages. . . .
> Proposal 18 would cripple my purchasing power
> as your customer. . . .
> *Vote No—Proposition 18!*

On the eve of the election, members of the Television and Radio Artists union put on a two-hour statewide television show. Eddie Cantor, Sammy Davis, Jr., and other stars donated an estimated $60,000 of talent services to urge votes against Right to Work. The television time and promotion cost $40,000.

To sum up: The unions raised and spent some $2,500,000, most of it raised from members' contributions. (About $100,000 came from outstate: this included $25,000 from the Brotherhood of Carpenters at Indianapolis; $20,000 from AFL-CIO in Washington, D.C., and $10,000 from the Western Conference of Teamsters.)

The unions helped increase Democratic registration by 330,000 voters. With professional help, they convinced two of every three voters to vote against Right to Work and so defeated the measure by almost 1,000,000 votes.

"Without the unions, this would have been a completely different election," one political observer said. "Pat Brown thinks he defeated Bill Knowland by a landslide. Actually, he was swept in by the no vote on 'Right to Work'!"

As against the union effort, business groups who relied heavily on contributions from oil, lumbering and manufacturing interests reported they raised and spent an estimated $1,000,000.

Manpower Plus Soft Money Equals Victory

In Ohio, where union leaders tried vainly to defeat the late Senator Robert Taft in 1950, they managed this time to turn their 1,200,000 members into the most potent political force the state has ever known.

255

"They can't match our manpower," union campaign literature said. Which meant that "they"—the advocates of Right to Work—couldn't match actual union campaign costs either. For the services performed voluntarily by members and their wives would have cost millions if the unions had had to pay for them.

There is, in union political lingo, "hard money" and "soft money." Hard money has to be raised by soliciting the members. Soft money simply comes by writing a check on the union treasury. In Ohio, the unions took the soft money route, tapping their treasuries a "buck per man." Additional sums came from outstate.

With these resources of money and manpower, Ohio's unions printed and distributed 30,000,000 pieces of literature with special words for special groups.

For Negroes: "Don't Bring Little Rock's Bigotry and Shame to Ohio" (Arkansas is a Right to Work state).

For housewives: "Don't let them shrink your shopping bag."

For Republicans: "Labor Secretary James Mitchell says 'Right to Work' is wrong."

For unemployed: "Special interests back of Right to Work are costing you $20 a week."

Union members distributed 8,000,000 sample ballots. And members' wives organized pro-union shop coffee klatches. "The goal," said one union "blueprint for victory" was to have 4,000,000 cups of coffee used in neighborhood klatches. A handy "Coffee Klatch Kit with answers for the ladies" could be had at union headquarters.

As in California, much of the psychological warfare offensive was beamed at union members themselves. In Cleveland, three movie projectors were busy night and day grinding out a twenty-minute pro-union shop movie before workers in plants and union halls. The movie, produced in Hollywood, cost the AFL-CIO thirty-five thousand dollars.

And, as in California, the unions won important allies. The Ohio Council of Churches, whose national organization is headed by Charles Taft, the late Senator's brother, took a stand against curbing the union shop. So did Ohio's six Catholic archbishops.

Ohio's best vote getter and shrewdest politician, Senator John Bricker—three-term Governor and two-term U.S. Senator—pleaded with Ohio Republican leaders not to take on the union giant. But no one believed him when he predicted that the unions would defeat even him, Bricker.

The 829,000-vote plurality against Right to Work swept into office in a traditionally conservative state—a Democratic Senator and Governor, three new Democratic Congressmen—and a Democratic State Legislature.

The most significant fact about Labor's explosive political role was its local, grass-roots character. If you had your eye on the big labor leaders—George Meany or Walter Reuther—you should have been watching some other fellows. George Meany made but one speech during the campaign. Reuther made none. As for the AFL-CIO's political arm, COPE (Committee on Political Education), it remained largely in the background too. COPE reported spending $570,000 on favored candidates, raising the money in a "buck a man" campaign among members of the AFL-CIO's affiliated unions. Only one in seven union members contributed. (Taft-Hartley prohibits unions from contributing treasury money to candidates in national campaigns. So separate agencies like COPE solicit individual gifts.)

The money raised and spent by the unions in '58 had to be pieced together from sources other than the AFL-CIO. The Teamsters alone spent $800,000. The *New York Times* estimated that total union spending on favored candidates was $3,500,000. Preliminary reports to state officials indicate that another $4,500,000 was spent in the fight for the union shop. As a yardstick for this estimated $8,000,000 expenditure, the Republicans spent a total of about $13,000,000 during the presidential campaign of 1956.

The unions learned valuable political lessons. One was that money alone doesn't win elections. At least, not in states where the unions muster less than 8 per cent of the voting population, as in Arizona. Here, some $14,000 sent by members of the Garment Workers in New York, the Steelworkers in Pittsburgh and COPE in Washington, D.C., to defeat Senator Barry Goldwater backfired against his opponent. Goldwater successfully raised the issue of outside interference and got a helping hand from COPE which sent into Arizona a field worker once convicted of "malicious mischief" during a strike.

But, in Wisconsin, union money, coupled with union manpower,

257

helped re-elect Democratic Senator William Proxmire, the candidate who seems to have been most favored with union money. The Wisconsin Senator received $25,500 from members of a group of unions that included the Steelworkers, the Communications Workers, the Textile Workers and others. This helped him put on a dramatic "get out the vote" campaign.

In Milwaukee County alone, a brigade of union volunteers manned ninety-three telephones, while six hundred others went from house to house in a highly selective get-out-the-vote effort. First they tackled precincts that had gone 80 to 88 per cent Democratic in the past—then followed up with a second group that had voted 76 to 79 per cent Democratic.

On Election Day, in twenty-seven cities, some six hundred volunteers manned telephones, while another 2,600 workers went from house to house. The volunteers were paid five dollars each from contributions collected from union members. The old party machines whose canvassers were paid with political jobs and handouts had been replaced by union members and their wives.

Professional political technicians with years of successful campaigning behind them lent a hand.

One such pro, working anonymously, performed miracles of public relations which, among other things, helped defeat the Right to Work proposal in agricultural Idaho. This was John M. Redding, a lieutenant colonel during the war and former public relations director of the National Democratic Committee.

Redding was hired by the newly created National Council for Industrial Peace whose prime movers were Mrs. Eleanor Roosevelt and former New York Senator Herbert Lehman.

With some $370,000 to spend, half of it raised from unions, Redding hit the road for the six states that voted on the Right to Work issue.

A master builder of broad-based, organized group support for causes or candidates, Redding soon had the Fraternal Order of Eagles, Policemen's Benevolent Associations, Disabled Veterans resolving against the Right to Work proposals. These in turn set up their own committees to work for the union shop.

But it was in Idaho that Redding pulled his most impressive coup. The state has but twenty-five thousand union members, and

258

union leaders there had little hope of convincing farmers to vote against a law to restrict unions. But Redding had $30,000 to spend on a radio and newspaper advertising campaign, ($10,000 of it donated by the Western Teamsters Conference). He selected as his chief target the farmwife.

"Mrs. Housewife," the campaign messages urged, "don't let them lower Idaho's living standards to Alabama's—the Right to Work state whose housewives have $1,000 a year less to spend than you have." Idaho rejected the union shop ban by five thousand votes.

What does the proved union political heft of 1958 mean to the future of the two-party system?

I put this question to Senator William Knowland in his office at the Oakland *Tribune,* one of the three newspapers that have long dominated California Republican politics. Knowland, a powerful man of fifty-one, still showed the ordeal of the recent campaign. His deep voice was throaty, and his eyes heavy and tired. He had based his fight on the union shop issue and—as one time Senate majority leader—was the most distinguished casualty of the union political storm.

"I think we've seen a complete change in the pattern of American political life," Knowland said. "Unless steps are taken to offset Labor, no party can stand up against it. By 1964, Labor may swallow the Democratic party."

At the state capitol in Sacramento, Governor Goodwin Knight, another union casualty, answered questions about the future of union political power, by lifting the veil on what had happened inside the California Republican party in the recent past.

Handsome and vigorous at sixty-one, the Governor was philosophical about his retirement to private life and quoted from Shakespeare:

> Sweet are the uses of adversity;
> Which, like the toad, ugly and venomous,
> Wears yet a precious jewel in his head. . . .

He was no victor, the Governor said, but he *was* a prophet. For a full year before the California primary, the Governor had stumped the state with a speech, "Blueprint for Disaster." Knight had opposed Right to Work proposals for years. Now, he pleaded that in a state with 1,000,000 more registered Democrats than Republicans, it was folly to alienate the unions and their members.

Knight had just about convinced key Republicans to let him run for Governor again (instead of Senator) and to keep the Right to Work issue off the ballot—when Vice-President Richard Nixon intervened. Nixon sided with the party's chief financial backers who wanted two things: to put a Right to Work referendum on the ballot and to put a Conservative, William Knowland, into the governorship.

So Knight was overruled. And by taking on Labor, the California Republicans turned Knight's "Blueprint for Disaster" into an actuality.

No, the Governor didn't think that Labor would continue to vote as a bloc. If you take away Labor's reason for ganging up, union members will vote like other Americans with varied interests, the Governor said.

The Governor was right in New York—where there was no reason for ganging up.

Here, union leaders worked hard, too, to get out the vote. They went into factories to electioneer for Governor Averell Harriman. They organized workers' rallies for him.

I heard union president David Dubinsky orate in the Garment Center area where candidates Averell Harriman and Nelson Rockefeller had sampled Jewish delicacies along with the usual baby kissing and handshaking.

Dubinsky hammered his hand into his fist.

"You've given him [Harriman] your herring.

"You've given him your knishes and blintzes;

"Now give him your votes!"

But union voters won't be pushed where they don't want to go. Knishes and herring were all that many of them would give Harriman.

Short, Short History with a Moral

The curious thing about unions and politics is that the unions couldn't get a foothold until they got *out* of politics.

The early workers' movements—the Knights of Labor, for instance—were reform parties as well as collective bargainers. So energy and brainpower were dissipated on wrangles over political formulas for achieving workers' utopias.

Sam Gompers' "pure and simple unionism" narrowed union efforts to the bargaining table and the contract.

All Gompers wanted from government was to keep hands off as workers organized and stood up to the boss. When government threw its great weight to the boss—when judges crippled strikes with injunctions and lawmakers curbed unions with restrictive laws—Gompers went into politics to survive.

Gompers shrewdly feared that if the unions built a minority voting bloc, they'd stir resentment, and reaction. So he preached a non-partisan political gospel: "Reward your friends and punish your enemies." To punish one enemy—a Republican Congressman —Gompers once stumped Maine, and did such a job on the fellow that he lost about 80 per cent of his prior plurality and squeaked through by less than a thousand votes. This so scared the man that he didn't seek re-election the next time around.

Another time, Gompers and his aides hired a trolley car and campaigned up and down Ohio against another union target, the late Uncle Joe Cannon, for many years the Speaker of the House. Uncle Joe survived. But Ohioans didn't soon forget that trolley car.

Gompers' politicking helped save the unions, for it ultimately brought "Labor's Magna Carta," the Clayton Act which barred the use of the anti-trust laws against Labor.

When New Deal social reforms were threatened by a conservative Congress in 1942, the unions went into politics again. The breezy, brawling and dedicated young unionists who built the new CIO (Congress of Industrial Organizations) now formed PAC—Political Action Committee. Scholarly Sidney Hillman of the Amalgamated Clothing Workers took the helm.

Instead of making speeches, PAC did something new. PAC's men swarmed into the home areas of target Congressmen and turned virtually every union man, his cousins, his uncles and his aunts into registered voters.

Facing certain defeat, one union target—Texan Martin Dies, then head of the powerful Un-American Activities Committee—didn't

261

even run again. Two other Congressmen on PAC's "hate list" (both on the Dies Committee) were retired from public life by the newly registered voters.

Such was the political heft of the CIO's PAC that Sidney Hillman was a key figure in the Democratic convention of 1944. Franklin D. Roosevelt told aspirants for Vice-President to "Clear it with Sidney." The PAC marshaled so many votes in California, Illinois and New York that F.D.R. won his fourth term.

When the CIO merged with the AF of L, a new union political arm was born. Called the Committee of Political Education, its job was to stir union men to political action. It had a skeleton staff of some twenty persons—at AFL-CIO headquarters in Washington, D.C., and in the field. It raised about $500,000 yearly in union members' contributions, which it shared with local COPEs. It distributed literature. And it caused very little stir. So little stir that some voices started to urge Labor to drop its "political education" and get out of politics.

Then, in 1958, Republican candidates and industrialists raised the "labor boss" issue, supported Right to Work state laws to ban the union shop—and so brought the unions back into politics again in a big way.

Is there a moral to this story?

Yes. We've learned that when union leaders can convince their members that their unions and their gains are in danger, they can help elect a President (as in 1944) and defeat a party (as in 1958).

But will there be a fighting issue around which labor leaders can rally their dues payers in the next presidential election?

Maybe not. But if there is, the unions may elect our next President.

VII

How can we return stolen unions to their members?
And turn labor leaders into quasi-public
servants? And what of the future?

New laws are followed by new tricks.

GERMAN PROVERB

CHAPTER 18

How to Steal a Union—
And How to Get It Back

Behind every piece of union skulduggery lies a "how done it" story. Yet while the "who-done-its"—the Dave Becks and Jim Hoffas—are now household words, the "how" of their operations remains a mystery to most of us. "How could Hoffa be elected Teamster president after all the scandals?" people ask. A Hoffa can do it, because a union is just about the least protected piece of valuable property lying around.

While a union is really a private government, to be run by and for its tax (dues) payers, any resemblance between union government and public government is purely impossible. The union is protected by few of the safeguards that check and balance our public government. There's no two-party system,[1] no free press, no independent judiciary, no bill of rights. The union boss must face the voters at periodic elections, of course, and there's the scrutiny of the regular meeting. But once in, the "ins" have the tools to cope with both.

What follows should not be taken as an indictment of unions generally. Most are honestly run despite inadequate democratic safeguards. But where members are deprived of a voice over their affairs there's an ever-present danger of corruption.

---

[1] The exception is the Typographers' Union which has two parties.

Who steals a union may, in turn, transform it into a burglar's tool for big-time looting. He can make deals with employers to cheat the union man of overtime, or turn his back as the employer pays below scale or conspire with the employer to shortchange the worker through sweetheart contracts. Or hold up a whole community by policing a milk delivery monopoly, or laundry service, or jukebox racket, for a closed ring of businessmen.

A potent implement, the union. Yet there are as many ways to walk off with a union as there are imaginative and brassy men to dream them up.

Here is how to do it. Let's start with the voting.

How to Keep Them Off the Ballot

To get elected, the rank and filer must first be nominated. In the Teamsters, the member confronts a method we'll call the "bum's rush."

You're a rank and filer; your friends put you up for secretary-treasurer, and you campaign for votes. But the day before the election you get a letter from a regional vice-president. You're disqualified, it says here in the letter, because your dues haven't been paid on time.

"How can this be?" you protest. Your employer checked off your dues during the middle of the month and had two full weeks to send them to the union hall. Sure he did. But he doesn't send the dues in until the first of the month, because the Teamster local doesn't provide him with a list of members until then. So rank and filers' dues in many Teamster locals *never* get to the union hall by the first of the month. Only the dues of those already in office, paid by the union, arrive on time. And if the office seeker tries to beat this rap—by taking his dues personally to the union hall—they won't be accepted.

So the only members who are qualified to run for office are those already in office. Or those whom the Teamster powers permit to pay their dues on time.

Then there's the "obstacle course" method used by the United Steelworkers.

To be nominated for president of the Steelworkers, a dues payer must first win nominating elections in at least forty locals. This

266

means that he must mount forty separate local campaigns and push them in the face of opposition by local officers, usually allied with the top boss of the International Union, the incumbent president.

Some union bosses use the "hire a hall" method. When, as it must to every union boss, nomination time comes around, the leader hires a hall above a saloon. If there are several thousand members in the local, the leader has prudently taken a hall that can hold only a small fraction. Just as prudently, he sets the meeting time at 6 P.M. when most of the members are on their way home from work or having dinner.

Long before the meeting time, the boss's business agents—beholden to him for their jobs—and other pals jam the hall. When rank-and-file members show up, they can't get in—but the boss has thought of that too. He has strung loud-speakers outside, so that the men milling in the street—there may be as many as a thousand—can hear that everything's democratic, fair and square, on the inside. So the men on the outside hear the men on the inside nominate the incumbents "by acclamation," then shut off further nominations.

Helpful Hints for Election Time

Should some persistent fellow negotiate the nominating obstacle course and achieve a place on the ballot, there are procedures galore to keep him in his place—out of office—at election time.

Consider the "caste" method developed in the Operating Engineers.

In the Long Island local (138) run by convicted racketeer William De Koning, Jr., less than half of the thirteen hundred dues payers may vote. These are the 500-odd members who are called "engineers," pay $8 monthly dues and belong to the "parent local." Another 300 members pay $6 dues and drive the same caterpillar tractors and cranes as the "engineers"—but work in sand pits and brickyards instead of road construction—are called "branch men." They *can't* vote. The Operating Engineers' constitution says so. Another 450 are called "apprentices." They pay $8 dues. Some have been apprentices for ten or more years. They *can't* vote either.

Since not all of the five hundred-odd voting members show up at meetings, the local's boss needs only 250 votes to control thirteen hundred dues payers. The Pittsburgh local of the Operating Engineers had three hundred-odd members in its "parent local" and so its former boss controlled a union of four thousand men with a handful of votes.[2]

If you know the ropes, you can perform feats of election larceny equal to the caper of extracting cash from the vaults of a Federal Reserve Bank. Not long ago, a New York local union voted for president. The members used voting machines. They identified themselves with IBM cards showing their last dues payment. A driver's license or some other identification was shown too. And an outside, neutral labor expert "watchdogged" the balloting. Fair enough?

Yet the opposition claimed the incumbent stole the election. He had armed hundreds of "ringers" (non-members) with fake dues slips, the opposition said. Sure, the dues ledgers were there, and the names of the voters were checked off against them. But nobody knew whether the names in the ledgers were those of current members or not. The boss wouldn't let anybody near the books before the election—nor after it.

There are more direct methods. Your business agents and other porkchoppers (pay rollers) can howl down the opposition at election meeting time, or beat up "them troublemakers." You can lift the bums' cards and so boot them out of the union and out of a livelihood.

But there's a simpler way, even than this. Don't hold elections.

When election meeting time came around at Joplin, Missouri, rank-and-file Teamster members would find the union hall in darkness and the door bolted. The "ins"—to stay in—simply didn't show up, and there was no election. Some New Jersey Teamster locals haven't had elections for years.

How to Make Delegates and Influence Conventions

If you're the president of an International (the parent union) and play your cards right, you should be as safe from those below as Khrushchev.

---

[2] More than half of the Operating Engineers' 283,000 members aren't allowed to vote, according to McClellan Committee testimony.

There are methods to fit all types of International Union elections. If the election is by delegates at a convention, you can get useful tips from the "how done it" story of the re-election of James G. Cross, president of the Bakers and Confectioners (now ousted from the AFL-CIO).

First, Cross tied most of the fifteen vice-presidents on his executive boards to himself with bonds of gold, giving them salaried jobs as "International representatives." These and other "International reps" whose jobs Cross controlled were powers in the locals back home and could handpick pro-Cross delegates from seventy-five local unions.

So armed with a docile board and delegates, Cross next changed the union constitution so that members had no direct voice in the presidential election. He abolished the members' plebiscite and substituted an election by convention delegates. Outflanking the dues payers this way, he won hands down.[3]

Jimmy Hoffa, an artist in the uses of union power, can teach us much too. While the Senate of the United States, federal prosecutors and courts, and the massed press of the land were closing in on him in the fall of 1957, the cold-eyed Jimmy was taking steps to assure his further rise. Through his own sizable control of locals and the control exercised by his immediate aides, Hoffa was gathering delegates. The methods were informal but effective.

"Are you a delegate to the coming Teamster convention?" Senator John McClellan asked a business agent from Hoffa's Detroit local.

"Yes," said the Hoffa man.

"When were you elected?" asked McClellan.

"I'm going to be elected tonight," was the reply. It was a tiresome formality in which no members, only Hoffa and his officers, participated—in unblushing violation of the union constitution.

Some ABC's of Ballot Counting

We've learned about election by delegates. Now let's look at an election by ballots.

---

[3] Rank and filers pulled out and formed their own rival American Bakery and Confectionery Workers (AFL-CIO), so indicating that the only way you can get out from under an unwanted regime is to secede, break up the union.

One international union is so highly centralized that it collects dues for the locals and buys their paper and pencils for them. At election time, headquarters sends out the printed ballots to the locals.

To a local of two thousand members, say, the parent union sends two thousand ballots—one for each member. These ballots are not numbered, and there's no way of knowing how many members voted. So, if only five hundred members turn out on election night—leaving fifteen hundred ballots unused—a local boss, friendly to the incumbent administration, is free to do one of two things. He can mark the unused ballots for the man of his choice—a simple "x" will do it. Or he can simply make up his own election returns and send them in on a tally sheet to the International headquarters. The counters there see only the tally sheets—the ballots remain with the local. The temptations this poses to incumbents are obvious.

Tips on Troublemakers

As the winner of a union election, you take all. You take the union paper, and nobody but you and your friends can sound off in it. For a year after he'd been discredited Dave Beck, as president of the Teamsters, beamed happily from the inside of the *Teamster Journal,* assuring readers, as editor, that all was well in the best of all possible unions. No doubters could get space to reply, of course.

As winner, you get control of union meetings and the union trial machinery, and can use both to deal with troublemakers.

For members who want to stick their noses into union business, the Teamsters have developed a meeting procedure we'll call the "splinter session." You divide a local of five thousand men, say, into subdivisions. The hearse drivers, about fifty of them, meet once a month by themselves, on a Monday. The haulers of beer, the men who deliver for the butchers and bakers and cement-mix makers all meet on separate days too.

Since only 10 per cent of members show up for meetings (they know they're wasting their time, anyway), your stooges, the old reliable business agents, are holding cozy confabs with them. That way the splintered membership can't get together in one place, at a prearranged time, to compare notes as to what's going on in the union—or gang up on you.

If the boys below form an opposition to belt you at the next election, you have the union trial machinery, remember, and so can bring them up on charges.

When the New York local of the Masters, Mates and Pilots (AFL-CIO) elected officers in 1952, rank and filers challenged the union's boss, Tommy Atkins, and lost.

Two of the defeated members, Bernard C. Madden and Robert Liddy, decided to keep the opposition alive. "We believe," they announced, "that two parties within the union will be a good and healthy thing for our local." So they formed a minority party inside the local.

The local's president, Captain Tommy Atkins, charged the two members with setting up a "dual" or rival union, and found them guilty via a trial committee he, himself, named. When rank and filers Liddy and Madden appealed to the International Union, the ruling came down upholding the "findings of the trial committee." So Liddy and Madden, tried by the man who had accused them, were expelled from the union. Without their cards, they could get no work at their trade.[4]

It took Liddy and Madden four long years in the civil courts to win a reinstatement verdict. Even then, Boss Atkins refused to take them back, and they had to push a further court fight for an order enforcing the earlier reinstatement decision. Atkins has since been convicted on charges of taking bribes. But the conviction was reversed on appeal, and a new trial ordered. The system which permits union leaders to try the members they accuse still persists.

Some Booby Traps for the Union Constitution

As an American citizen, the wage earner is protected against tyranny by the federal Constitution with its Bill of Rights—that guarantees his rights to free speech, to assembly and so on. But as a union member, he can become a second-class citizen, because no union constitution has even a rudimentary bill of rights.

In fact, the union constitution can be studded with all sorts of

---

[4] Mates and Pilots, regarded as supervisory employees, are not covered by the Taft-Hartley Act which protects non-union employees in their right to work.

booby traps to trip up the dissident rank and filers. So, as a union boss, you can purge rebels for "conduct unbecoming a member," or for "creating dissension among the members," or for "destroying the interest and harmony of the local union"—which can mean anything you, as boss, want it to mean.

Instead of curbing the officeholder by spelling out his duties, the union constitution is sometimes a blueprint for tyranny, giving czar's powers to the leader.

The proudly unlettered James Caesar Petrillo when president of the Musicians Union was permitted to ". . . annul and set aside the whole constitution . . . or any of its provisions [except financial], and to submit therefore other and different provisions *of his own making.*" This clause remained as long as Petrillo reigned—until the spring of 1958 when he quit in the face of a revolt by West Coast members.

Most International Union constitutions permit the president to take over a local during an emergency. The Operating Engineers, for instance, allow their head man to "suspend or remove members, officers and charters whenever in his opinion the best interests of the organization require it."

With authority like this, it's a cinch to take the union away from the members altogether. You put the local under trusteeship. Then you name yourself—or a pal—to run the local as trustee-dictator without the benefit of elections or meetings.

A little while back, we asked, "How could Jimmy Hoffa be elected Teamster president after all the scandals?"

Union martial law under a trustee gives part of the answer. By 1957, Dave Beck and Hoffa had taken 108 locals (of 890-odd in the International) out of the hands of their members. From captive locals came delegates who helped elect Hoffa.

The imperious John L. Lewis, who—by temperament—is reluctant to take union members into his confidence, discovered the trustee device when he became president of the Miners back in 1920. It's called "provisional" government in the Miners. With it, Lewis has virtually abolished self-rule and reduced the once proud and brawling coal diggers' union to a cowed dictatorship.

*   *   *

If you steal, you must face the occupational hazard of getting caught. Retribution is catching up with the union stealers, and the punishment falls heavily on honest men in the Labor movement and culprits alike. First, there is the loss of public sympathy which, in the 1930's, backed the laws that made today's unions possible. Worse, there is the loss of the union man's loyalty. The union man who can't speak up with his mouth at a meeting will speak up with his feet. He'll stay away.

The unions are losing the fighting allegiance of the workers that was once their chief shield against hostile employers. In the 1958 NLRB elections for union recognition, 40 per cent of the employees voted for *no* union, preferring to remain unorganized. This is the highest *no* union percentage since 1939.

Union organizing has virtually dried up in some parts of the country. And a union movement that can't get new members is a sterile and declining movement.

How to Get the Unions Back to Their Members

There ought to be a law imposing regular, secret elections on the unions, say well-meaning lawmakers. Will these laws also provide sleuths to check up whether a labor boss has disqualified opponents before an election, through tricks with dues payments, as in the Teamsters? Or whether the union leader has disenfranchised most of the members—as in the Operating Engineers? Unless union elections are policed, they could be meaningless—as we've seen. And how do you police the voting of 17,500,000 union members without creating a vast new army of bureaucrats?

To get the unions back to their members, the unions need some of the checks and balances of public government.

The chief balance wheel that's missing from union government is a court, a place outside the dues payer's own union where he can get a fair hearing, if his union boss pushes him around—or where he can bring a union leader to book for stealing an election or signing a sweetheart contract.

The regular courts have been inadequate. For one thing, judges are reluctant to meddle in internal union affairs in line with the tradition that unions are, after all, voluntary associations, like Elks

273

Lodges. For another, a union member who brings suit against a union leader must be prepared to fight for years against the best lawyers his own union's treasury can buy. Two unions, the United Automobile Workers and the Upholsterers have made a start toward an independent court, with boards of review composed of prominent men who give their time free.

Although the United Auto Workers reputedly run one of the best unions as far as members' rights are concerned, the UAW Review Board has been called on for help in two dozen cases. In one, the watchdogs got right down to an ancient union abuse: the abrogation of a dues payer's personal rights, guaranteed to him as a citizen. Two UAW members from a Buffalo local, quarreling during an election campaign, sued each other for damages in a civil court. They were suspended for committing the cardinal union sin of going outside to settle a beef instead of using union channels first.

The Watchdog Review Board ordered the members reinstated, telling the UAW in effect that a man doesn't sign away his personal rights (such as going to court) when he signs a union card.

None of the other national unions have shown much enthusiasm for the voluntary court idea. And it's obvious that those unions that most need appeals watchdogs are least likely to have them.[5]

So, demands are growing that the AFL-CIO set up an independent union court within the Federation, or that such a court be created by law—outside the AFL-CIO.

Bernard H. Fitzpatrick, a New York lawyer who devotes time free to battle for Operating Engineers members' rights, urges a "Judicial Commission," appointed by the AFL-CIO. He argues, "The great trouble with unions is not the unfairness of union laws, but the fact that the laws are interpreted by the same people whose own acts are being questioned. The judges are judging their own conduct; naturally they find it good."

One trouble with setting up a court inside the AFL-CIO is that it would be available only to members of AFL-CIO affiliates. What about the union members who need it most—those whose unions have been ruled as corrupt by the Federation?

---

[5] The exception, of course, is the Teamsters, now subject to the policing of three outside monitors—accepted reluctantly by Jim Hoffa as a condition of his becoming provisional president.

274

Significantly, many friends of the unions who once abhorred the idea of government intervention in union affairs now urge it.

J. B. S. Hardman, author and lifelong student of Labor, urges a Court of Intra-Union Relations, set up by law "to provide legal redress of grievances" and further self-rule.

Such a court, Mr. Hardman argues, "would in effect be a Public Defender office for the protection of union members."[6]

The job of any democracy is to keep the channels of citizen protest open, so that the governed can influence and restrain those who govern them. The special job of union democracy is to keep the leader powerful enough so that he can deal effectively with the employer, yet not so powerful that he is free from control from those below.

Or so powerful that he can make off with the union with the burglar tools described in this chapter. A court where a member can yell, "Stop, thief!" and apply some of the checks and balances available to him as a citizen would help.

---

[6] "Legislating Union Democracy," J. B. S. Hardman, the *New Leader*, December 2, 1957.

CHAPTER 19

What Shall We Do
with the Labor Leader?

For a third time in twenty-five years, the American people are taking a long, hard look at the labor unions. The first look, in 1933, brought government support to unions via the Wagner Act. When this rocketed the unions to giant size, a second look—a scared one—brought the Taft-Hartley Act to redress the power balance between unions and employers.

Then, we were worried about union rights and employer rights. Now, we're worried about the rights of union members. All eyes are focused on the labor leader.

He has been catapulted to great power almost overnight. Yet, in a democracy which operates on checks and balances, here is a man whose power seems neither checked nor balanced.

The country is facing up to some hard questions about this man. How do we keep him powerful enough to bargain with the boss for his people—yet not so powerful as to make a good thing of the union for himself? Unions exist to give the worker a voice over his working conditions. How do we keep the labor leader from robbing the worker of this voice? How do we save wage earners from an employer-dictator only to have him fall into the hands of a union dictator?

A debate has raged on how to solve these problems by law.

Let's ask some basic questions. From the answers will come the image of a new labor leader.

To begin at the beginning: What is a labor leader?

He is a merchant of labor power—the head of a co-operative society banded together to market a common product, its labor.

He's also a general. If automobile manufacturers refuse to pay Merchant Walter Reuther's price, he'll become the general of a disciplined army of union members ready to march out of the plants and lay siege to an entire industry.

This general is elected by his troops. So the labor leader is also a politician, so skilled at building a union machine to keep him in office that he can give pointers to Tammany Hall.

Some labor leaders are bank presidents. Jacob Potofsky of the Amalgamated Clothing Workers presides over the "Amalgamated Bank" which lends money to members and to outside unions.

But fundamentally, in all his jobs, the labor leader is the assembler and user of power: the power to hold his members in line; the power to wrest higher wages from employers; the power to disrupt an industry or a city. This is so obvious to union leaders that they refer to their unions as their "power base."

Where does the labor leader get his power?

This may come as a surprise to some union leaders, but he gets it largely from the government.

Before the Wagner Act, John L. Lewis' Mine Workers Union was a dispirited, dwindling band of 75,000 men. Employer opposition was grinding the union out of existence. Then came Franklin D. Roosevelt and the laws that forced employers to bargain with unions.

The mighty Teamsters—1,600,000 strong today—had but 100,-000 dues payers in 1935. Many cities that are union bastions today, like Pittsburgh, didn't even have enough members to make up a Teamster local. The story of union growth through government help is much the same for all unions.

How does the labor leader keep his power?

The government again. The government keeps its hand on the scale in favor of the union.

When a union leader can show a pro-union majority in a plant he can bargain for all, including those who voted against the union. If the labor leader cooks up a contract with an employer—without the consent or the approval of the workers—all workers are still bound. The government clothes the labor leader with the power to bind them. When a contract is signed, no individual can bargain with an employer; no employer can bargain with an individual.

The labor leader, then, exercises power with the assistance of the government. This is the critical difference between a union official and, say, a corporation executive. The union is, in effect, a private government with powers lent to it by the public government. And

277

the labor leader is a government-made man. His union job is a position of trust involving the public interest. He is, in many ways, a public servant.

Yet John L. Lewis says, "The union is a voluntary association like a fraternal lodge, or a church. If you pass laws to govern the affairs of unions, where will you stop? You will then go on to pass laws affecting churches and other voluntary associations."

Does it make any difference if labor leaders see unions as Elks Lodges or country clubs?

Yes, the difference, often, between clean and corrupt unionism. Labor leaders who think they head voluntary associations may regard union business as nobody's business but their own—a whimsical way to regard the affairs of 17,500,000 Americans.

But if the labor leader thought of himself as a government-made man and a public servant, many things would follow.

Ex-convicts like Johnny Dio would not be entrusted with union charters any more than men with criminal records are entrusted with public office. Known racketeers—like George Scalise, or Ducks Coralla, who are not bona fide union men but infiltrate the unions for criminal purposes—would have no more chance of holding union office than Frank Costello could hold public office.

Were they clothed with the public service concept, bona fide leaders like David McDonald of the Steelworkers would no more think of spending $122 a day for a hotel suite, plus another $50 daily for a bodyguard, than the postmaster general would think of spending government money in this way.

James Caesar Petrillo of the Musicians would hesitate to reward himself—at union expense—with a plush apartment in New York's Waldorf Astoria Towers. William L. McFetridge, who represents a union of elevator operators and scrubwomen, would think twice about amassing wealth on the side. James Cross of the Bakers and Confectioners would have had second thoughts about competing with businessmen's material rewards—with fine homes in Washington, D.C., and in Florida.

Why doesn't the Labor movement make its leaders behave like public servants?

It has tried. The AFL-CIO has adopted ethical practice codes known as "Labor's Ten Commandments."

278

Listen to Code No. 4: "A union official holds a position comparable to that of a public servant. He has a high fiduciary duty not only to serve the members honestly but also to avoid personal economic interest which may conflict with his responsibility."

Fine. But what has the AFL-CIO done to enforce this?

It has taken heroic steps to police and to punish—but the Federation has achieved only modest results because it has only limited enforcement tools.

To begin with, the Federation has no subpoena powers of its own to dig out corruption among its affiliates. So it has to rely on outsiders like Senate investigators. So far, the Federation has acted chiefly on unions already exposed by Senate Committees and other public agencies. George Meany, the AFL-CIO's president, has forged new powers to police these unions and try to clean them up. But when the McClellan Committee spotlight is turned off, the Federation will be in the dark again about a good deal of union corruption.

Then, too, the Federation has only one weapon: expulsion. At great sacrifice, the AFL-CIO expelled its biggest and most powerful affiliate, the Teamsters. But this only cleaned the Federation's skirts. The Teamsters, strong and saucy under James R. Hoffa, are still a problem to the public and to the union member.

If the Labor movement can't make a public servant out of the labor leader, what can?

The government can. By law. The gist of reform proposals is that the labor leader is a public servant, a trustee. And the new laws will try to nudge him into playing that role.

A public servant has to live in a goldfish bowl; the public has a right to know everything about the way he conducts his office. So, the labor leader, too, should be put into a goldfish bowl. He should be made to bare all of his union's money affairs.

A law fathered by Senator Paul Douglas of Illinois makes all unions and employers reveal their welfare and pension fund activities in detail: the insurance commissions and who gets them, the service fees, the benefits to workers.

Senators John Kennedy and Sam Ervin back a more sweeping proposal. It would make the labor leader disclose what he earns, what he spends on expenses, what he borrows from the union, to whom he lends union money, what's in the treasury. A new Labor

Commissioner would check up on the reports, have the power to call witnesses and dig out fraud. Erring labor leaders could be indicted, and unions that failed to file could lose their tax exemption.

Don't union constitutions already require leaders to make financial statements?

Yes. But there are as many kinds of financial statements as there are unions. The honest unions use the reports to reveal; the dishonest ones, to conceal. Even the McClellan Committee's chief accountant, Carmine Bellino, couldn't make head or tail out of the financial reports of Michigan Teamster locals. "They grouped the cash, investments, loans, furniture, fixtures, in one large item—and showed no liabilities," reported accountant Bellino. How could you tell what was going on inside the union from that?

What would we see if we turned the disclosure law spotlight on the labor leader?

Much. That is, if he filed an honest answer.

I have before me the new questionnaire that labor leaders may have to answer under a proposed law.

Had it been in force during the past few years, it would have revealed some curious spending.

It would have shown that $54,000 of Teamster money was spent to defend—all the way to the Supreme Court—two Minneapolis union bosses who had betrayed members by taking money from an employer to break a strike.

Honest disclosure might have shown what the Senate Committee later found: that James R. Hoffa used union money to hide out and support his ex-convict brother, William, when police hunted him as a fugitive; that when brother William's wife ran away, Jim Hoffa used $5,000 to $7,000 of dues payers' money to send a union organizer to California in a vain effort to find her; and that two top officials of the United Textile Workers[1] bought fine homes with union money and, when exposed, borrowed from employers with whom they dealt and paid the union money back; and that they also spent $11,000 on theater tickets.

Forced disclosure might have prevented shenanigans like these in the first place. If the boys knew they'd have to bare all, they would

[1] This is a former AF of L affiliate, and is not to be confused with the Textile Workers Union of America.

have been less casual with other people's money.

But is the prospective questionnaire enough?

No. It wouldn't touch large areas of possible corrupt conduct: side deals that conflict with the leader's union responsibility; the granting of charters to shady characters.

Take the case of Jim Hoffa.

When the Teamster president-elect had finished four dramatic days as witness before the Senate Rackets Committee, Chairman McClellan summed up with a devastating catalogue of forty-seven violations of union trust by Hoffa. After the Committee heard more witnesses, Senator McClellan listed more breaches of trust for a total of eighty-two. These outraged virtually every precept of union responsibility. Yet only nine of the eighty-two could have been bared by the proposed goldfish bowl law.

Here, as Senator McClellan listed them, are a few:

"James R. Hoffa attempted to put thirty thousand New York cabdrivers under the leadership of Johnny Dio, three times convicted labor extortionist."

"Hoffa played a key role in chartering seven paper locals in New York City, knowing these locals to be racket-controlled."

"Hoffa and his chief aide entered into a highly collusive business arrangement with a [land promoter] for their personal profit and to the detriment of union members."

"Hoffa defended Teamster officials who were selling out the interests of their union members with highly improper business activities and collusive agreements with employers."

Obviously, only investigation with subpoena powers—or lawsuits—could have flushed out these activities.

Should Senate Committees be continued indefinitely then?

No, the Senate's job is to pass laws, not to police labor leaders. Senator McClellan, himself, told this writer he believes his committee should wind up its affairs at the end of 1959.

If a questionnaire is not enough, and a permanent Senate investigation is too much, how can we be sure union bosses are keeping clean?

The British have one answer. New York State has another.

When a scandal requires attention in England, the Prime Minister names a Royal Commission (with the Queen's approval). Headed by respected public figures, these have delved into such matters as betting and lotteries, the justice of the peace courts. When homosexuality in high places stirred public concern, the Prime Minister named three law lords (judges of the highest court) to hold hearings, publish findings. When its specific job is done, the Royal Commission disbands.

New York governors can call up similar commissions under the State's Moreland Act. When owners of horse-trotting tracks were suspected of corrupting politicians in 1953, the then Governor, Thomas E. Dewey, named three Moreland Act commissioners, including a former high state court judge. With the help of investigators and counsel, the Commission laid bare the race-track corruption. Its job finished, the Commission went out of business.

A new federal law could empower the President to call investigating commissions into being as the occasion arose, and so supplement the proposed labor questionnaire disclosure.

Some union leaders would protest that this singles out the Labor movement for special surveillance. But others are convinced that occasional investigations into Labor would be healthy.

David Dubinsky, told this writer, "You know, a good investigation, with subpoena powers, every three years or so would be a fine thing. It would keep the boys on their toes. It would keep them honest."

Why don't union members do their own policing by taking faithless leaders into court?

Excellent idea. Some have tried. One trouble is that courts still hesitate to intervene in unions' internal affairs. Precedents have not been clearly established as they have, say, in stockholders' suits against corporate officers.

But this may be remedied soon. The President wants to spell out and establish by law that "officers who handle union funds be held to the highest degree of responsibility." And that union members "be given an unequivocal right to sue in federal and state courts to enforce this responsibility."

Fine. But will members dare sue?

Probably not. You'll notice that, despite exposure, no union members have hauled Dave Beck into court for an accounting of union money—or to make him restore any profits he may have made from the use of the union's treasury.

Dues payers don't want to stick their necks out. Besides, lots of money is needed to battle the lawyers that the union's treasury —controlled by the labor leader—can buy.

But there is an answer here too. Professor Archibald Cox of Harvard and other labor law experts, among them the former counsel for New York's State Labor Relations Board, Daniel Kornblum, suggest that a government agency do the suing in behalf of the members.

New York Governor Nelson Rockefeller has a proposal before him that writes into law the concept that the labor leader is a quasi-public servant with a fiduciary (trustee) duty.

The unions have grown so swiftly that many labor leaders bridge an earlier era when the unions were underdogs in a minority movement. Now, the leaders have to grow up to a new role that fits Labor's new status and power.

The leaders will be prodded by law into making this transition. Until now, the chief proposals for reform have come from friends like Labor Secretary Mitchell and Senators Paul Douglas and John Kennedy. These men believe the unions perform a vital function in our economy and want to meddle as little as possible in the unions' internal affairs. But the reform proposals could fall into less friendly hands.

The American people have given the unions their power. The American people can take it away unless the labor leader makes the transition to a public servant who balances power with responsibility.

CHAPTER 20

When Machines Don't Need Men–What of Labor U.S.A.?

Not long ago, an automobile executive proudly showed Walter Reuther through a new plant. Pointing to a battery of newly installed self-operating drilling machines, the executive turned to the union leader.

"How are you going to collect dues from those fellows, Walter?"

"How are you going to sell them cars?" Reuther shot back.

This exchange underlines a historic industrial upheaval that is no laughing matter to the unions. Speeded-up mechanization and the harnessing of electronic brains to mechanical muscles have brought a second industrial revolution. It is displacing production workers by the thousands and may ultimately change the face of the Labor movement.

Consider what has already happened.

The United Mine Workers, 750,000 strong in 1923, had shrunk to 200,000 by 1959.[1]

The Textile Workers Union of America, 450,000 strong in 1951, has shrunk to 200,000.

The United Auto Workers, which had 1,500,000 members in 1955, is down to 1,000,000 members and sliding.

The Steelworkers, Electrical Workers, Chemical Workers—and other industrial unions once grouped in the CIO—are losing members too.

To see why, let's watch some of the new machines at work.

The "X-A," let's call it the Wizard of Oxygen, is a mechanical monster, or angel—depending on how you look at it—that produces gases for industry with no human assistance at all.

The Wizard hums along happily twenty-four hours a day, literally living on air which it breathes in and separates out into oxygen—

---

[1] The declining use of coal due to the rise of other fuels played some part in this, but mechanization of the mines was the chief factor.

284

needed in steel making and other industries—and into nitrogen. The Wizard works right at the customer's site—in a self-contained plant all its own: no need to manufacture oxygen in a chemical factory, then haul it in cylinders to the customer. The Wizard takes its own temperature and pressure. When things go wrong, the Wizard of Oxygen automatically telephones a supervisor at a service station in the area, giving its symptoms. If the Wizard just feels low—is operating inefficiently—it will so signal and keep running manfully until the supervisor arrives. If the trouble is more serious, the Wizard will signal it's going to bed—i.e., that it is shutting itself off.

When the Union Carbide Company first developed its "X-A" air-separating plant (the Wizard), the company dubbed it the "Z Unit," the "Z" standing for Zenith. The engineers felt they had achieved the zenith of automation, which indeed they had.

For workers who once produced oxygen, the "Z"—which ends the alphabet—means the end of the line, as far as their working lives are concerned. Some 250 chemical workers—members of the Chemical Workers Union—used to produce oxygen and other industrial gases for the Pittsburgh area and had the power to shut off this needed commodity to enforce bargaining demands. The Chemical Workers Union in Pittsburgh no longer has this power, for the 250 have shrunk to 80 and will continue to dwindle as the new automatic oxygen-producing units are installed elsewhere.

Late in 1958, at the Ford Motor Company's great River Rouge plant, outside Detroit, I watched a steel casting move down an assembly line and—untouched by human hands—turn into a finished engine block. Gone were the assembly-line workers who used to drill cylinder holes into the block and transfer it from one machine to another. "Transfer machines" maneuvered the casting automatically and "positioned it" before automatic drilling machines.[2] No production men remained. Several men played the role of watchmen —policing the line for breakdowns—which were signaled on an electronic panel.

A plant superintendent stressed one reason for the endless drive to be more efficient. The Ford Motor Company, along with other

---

[2] Because the "transfer machines"—grappling devices for handling parts on an assembly line—were first introduced in the automobile industry, they are known as "Detroit automation."

auto manufacturers, gives its workers an automatic 2½ per cent wage increase each year on the assumption that improved machinery and methods permit the worker to produce 2½ per cent more with his hour's work. So obligated, the auto companies must find new ways of making machines more efficient—which is another way of saying: use less men.

The changes at the Rouge reflected the larger changes in all industry.

Scientists, working with our military men during—and after—the war, have pushed industrial progress ahead by decades: first, by developing electronic computer devices to solve gunfire problems, then by creating machines with mechanical brains (like the guided missile) that are set to do a certain job, take note of changing conditions, and automatically correct themselves.

So car makers can produce twice as many automobiles as they did a decade before—with virtually no more workers than were needed then.

The steel companies can also turn out twice as much steel as they did a decade ago—and with 18 per cent fewer production workers. The country's needs will grow as the population grows. Yet, one steel company economist told me the new requirements will be met without adding any more workers.

The textile industry can produce as much as it did in 1951—with one-third less workers. (The work force here has shrunk from 1,300,000 to 850,000.) Chemical manufacture has almost doubled in ten years, but the work force keeps shrinking.

Yet it is the blue-collar wage earner who is the backbone of the Labor movement. In fact, the blue-collar worker accounts for 85 per cent of our unions' 17,000,000-odd members.

As the blue-collar work force shrinks, the unions must find replacements among the white-collar salaried employees—the office worker, the technical man, even the professional—the engineer. These, traditionally, have resisted unionization. Yet unless—as one union analyst put it—the unions "break out of their blue-collar shell" and organize the rising white-collar class, the power they now wield may be short-lived.

Indeed, the tidal shift in the work force—away from the production worker—confronts the unions with their second life-and-death crisis in twenty-five years.

The first came in the mid-1930's. Then, employer resistance and the depression had shrunk union membership by 50 per cent. In steel, autos, rubber, cement, there were no unions at all. Unless the unions broke into the great industries that had kept them out, they were doomed to continue a minority or to be ground out of existence altogether.

Today, just as the great industrial unions (Auto Workers, Electrical Workers, etc.) thought they had it made and could coast along with administrative tasks—they face an organizing problem as difficult as John L. Lewis'. They must mount great new organizing drives. More urgently, they must cope with the tragic problem of unemployment that has struck thousands of their members.

In the past, the introduction of new machinery involved the displacement of small numbers of individual workers who could find work elsewhere. Today, as manufacturers abandon plants in order to build new, more efficient factories elsewhere, the displacement is wholesale.

As this is written, the first large-scale "productivity unemployment" begins to make page-one news. In Detroit, fully one-eighth of the work force—some 300,000 workers—are facing the heartbreaking truth that their jobs are gone forever. The automobile companies stepped up their production, but didn't call back laid-off workers. And so the idle auto workers were suffering in Detroit what textile workers had suffered only several years before in textile towns like Lawrence, Massachusetts. Would Detroit become a distress area—due to technological change—just as the New England textile towns had, or the coal towns of Pennsylvania?

Would Pittsburgh? Here some 200,000 steel workers were idle, in January, 1959, and the *New York Times* reported that the city had twice as many jobless as it had during the recession January of 1957.

Would pools of permanently unemployed develop in other shrinking industrial centers? For January, 1959, the government reported some 4,700,000 unemployed—the highest January figure since before the last war.

The unemployment reflected the violent change that automation is making in the industrial landscape. Plants are being abandoned in the older established areas in the North and Northeast and new ones are being built in a great geographical crescent, beginning at the northern end of the Pacific Coast and extending into the Southwestern and Southern states. The reasons for moving are many. Managers of the new automated plants want to be near centers of learning, where scientific help is available. They also want to go where living conditions will be more congenial for the engineers and other technicians they want to attract.

Whatever the reason, the decline of the older areas with their tradition of unionism—and the shift to areas new to unionism or hostile to it—is a disaster, and a challenge to the unions.

Not only do the unions have to find members among white-collar groups, but they must do this organizing in regions where unions have taken little root.

Who Shall Lead Them?

This is the problem. Where will the leaders come from to cope with it?

Leaders for the big industry breakthrough of the late 1930's came, logically enough, from an industrial union. The United Mine Workers supplied its president, John L. Lewis, and two vice-presidents, Philip Murray and Van Bittner, for the Big Push.

Now, the new faces in Labor may come either from unions that are invulnerable to automation—or will grow and prosper because of it. For, while the new industrial revolution hurts the big industrial unions, it opens up opportunities to others.

What is happening is this: Automation, as we've seen, shrinks the factory work force. But the resulting increased production and greater national wealth can support new service industries. The result is that there are as many adults working today (relative to total population) as there were ten years ago. There are more people at work in retail stores, on trucks that distribute goods, in warehouses that store them; there are more TV repair men, more law clerks, more people in restaurants, in banks, in government.[3]

This means opportunities for some unions.

---

[3] No shrinkage here. Government employment is up 41 per cent in a decade.

The Teamsters—with jurisdiction over the movement and storage of goods, will continue to grow as the country grows. The Teamsters are, indeed, the fastest growing union in America—having gained some 500,000 members since 1953—a 50 per cent rise. Its 1,600,-000 members should make the Teamster president a power inside the Labor movement—just by virtue of his position. The last two presidents, Dave Beck and Jim Hoffa, have forfeited this role by making the Teamsters a pariah among unions. But should the Teamsters clean house, a future president could play a lead role in the coming organizing drives.

The International Association of Machinists is another union from which leadership can be expected. The Machinists have grown swiftly, gaining a quarter-million members since 1953, to become a union of almost a million in 1959. This is the union whose members make Univac and whose slogan is: "Any machine with a brain in its head wears a union label."

The Machinists enter the new industrial age with the solid advantages that spreading one's eggs in many baskets brings. The union is half industrial (members work in plants), and half craft (members do service and maintenance work). The Machinists' industrial members make the new automated machines, including the electronic computer and other office equipment.[4] They work in airplane plants, on guided missiles, on machine tools—the machines that make other machines.

The union's craft members are in a key position to do the maintenance work for the new automated machinery.

With all this the Machinists are blessed with a tradition of honesty and high-grade leadership.

When George Meany looked about for a labor leader to head up the AFL-CIO Ethical Practices Committee, his eye naturally fell on the Machinists. It is one of the country's oldest unions.[5] The union still calls its locals "lodges" and its handsome headquarters building

---

[4] As an indication of the spread of the automatic device, consider the rise of the computer. Developed during World War II to solve gunfire control and other wartime scientific problems, the computer's first civilian use came in 1951 when the government installed one in the Bureau of the Census. By early 1958, eight hundred medium-sized computer systems and two hundred large-sized systems had been installed by business firms, insurance companies and educational institutions.

[5] The Machinists were founded in 1888, the same year as the AF of L.

on Connecticut Avenue in Washington "the Grand Lodge." Although the union deals with little employers where industrial relations are often corrupt, as well as with big employers, the union has a reputation for antiseptic cleanliness. Its president, A. J. Hayes, a onetime machinist in Milwaukee railroad yards, a stolid, quiet man, is little known to the public. Yet inside the Labor movement—where leaders are likely to take a cynical view of each other—he is highly respected. Although most of his own executive board opposed the Federation's expulsion of the Teamsters, Hayes supported the move inside the Executive Council. As chairman of the Ethical Practices Committee, he has had to tangle with the Teamsters, on whom the Machinists have traditionally relied for help in organizing and in strikes. Hayes, born in 1900, must retire as Machinists' president in 1965. Whoever succeeds him should have an important voice in labor councils.

As the economic face of America changes, the pure craft unions —whose members are the skilled aristocrats of labor—will regain their old importance.

Consider the Plumbers Union whose 243,000 members handle everything to do with piping—whether it's for waste and sanitation, air conditioning, chemical manufacture, heating or whatever.

Many chemical and oil-refining operations are largely automatic, requiring human attention only to clean out the piping, a plumber's job. Aware of the coming new golden era for the plumber, Peter T. Schoemann, Plumbers Union president, has opened schools throughout the country to retrain journeymen members for the new skilled maintenance jobs.

The unions most likely to provide key leaders are those already grappling with the problem of organizing white-collar workers. This brings us to James A. Suffridge, president of the International Association of Retail Clerks whose members sell and handle goods in supermarkets, department stores, auto salesrooms and other retail outlets.

Tennessee-born Jim Suffridge is a tall, handsome and carefully groomed man of fifty who looks like what he once was—a store manager. Suffridge's Retail Clerks must recruit union members from the toughest of all union targets—the employee who doesn't relish being called a "clerk" and hopes some day himself to be an

290

executive. The union sales pitch to middle-class oriented people like these must obviously be different from the appeal that the organizer of an industrial union makes to the factory hand. Suffridge has succeeded so well in selling unionism to white-collar people that his union has picked up some 100,000 members in five years and now numbers 350,000. This makes the Retail Clerks tenth in size in the country. Suffridge hopes within the next five to ten years to build a union of 2,000,000 or more.

Suffridge is a vice-president of the AFL-CIO and as such sits on the Executive Council where, until now, he has bided his time, saying little, except to follow the leadership of George Meany. But he obviously has a future. He has impressed fellow labor leaders with the clean-up job he did among some of his locals that were captured by New York racketeers. He has fought it out with the Teamsters, defying and defeating Dave Beck in a Los Angeles organizing drive. And significantly, Suffridge has developed a close friendship with George Meany, who likes to refer to Suffridge as "My Jimmy."

Suffridge and Meany are neighbors in Bethesda, Maryland, outside Washington. They play a good deal of golf together, visit at each other's homes and are together at parties, such as New Year's Eve.

To Meany, Suffridge is obviously one of the new breed of labor leaders on whom will largely fall the task of shifting the Labor movement from its blue-collar, industrial worker base to a new white-collar base of the technically trained, the skilled, and even the professional.

After the End—the Beginning

Can the unions make this difficult transition? If the unions cannot capture the imagination and loyalty of the white-collar man, they may shrink within a decade to a minor place in the country's life. If they do organize the white-collar man, the unions will become a different kind of Labor movement with different kinds of leaders.

In any case, as we come to the end of our story of Labor U.S.A. the unions are beginning a new and crucial chapter.

Sources

This book is largely the product of investigative reporting—digging out the facts about men, or problems, or institutions, the unions in this case, through the questioning of people wherever possible, plus reliance on published material and documents.

Whenever it was possible, then, to witness an event such as the AFL-CIO ouster of the Teamsters, or to talk to a witness of an event, or to gain insight from some wise old head in the Labor movement such as David Dubinsky, or to check with a veteran racket buster such as Al Scotti of the New York District Attorney's office, or to question the subject of the inquiry himself, such as Jim Hoffa—I did it. Hundreds of men and women—many willing, some reluctant—are the primary sources of the facts and many of the insights of this book.

Beyond that, I leaned, as all writers must, on those who have plowed earlier ground: experts, scholars and historians.

I have been gathering material on unions and union people for five years—tucking away virtually everything reported on subjects I was interested in—in the *New York Times,* the *Wall Street Journal, Business Week* and *Fortune.* When I began work on this book, I lined up some twenty-odd cardboard filing cases—each representing a chapter—on a bench behind me in my workroom. Into these went interview notes, records, clippings, magazine pieces, pamphlets, reports. As a chapter was completed, I moved the cardboard filing case from its position behind my work table out in front, ahead of me. The accumulating evidence of work done is a wonderful morale booster on a long project. On the other side of the room, too, was a floor-to-ceiling bookcase which was soon overflowing with books, union convention proceedings, union constitutions, union and management publications.

I hope the following sources will help—and perhaps inspire—some readers to pursue further fascinating bypaths in the field. I've tried to avoid a mere listing of materials, and between the lines of what is put down below (who knows?) some budding journalist may glimpse and gain some small profit from the work methods of what, to me, is the most absorbing profession in the world: investigative reporting.

CHAPTER 1   Six Days That Shook the Union World

This chapter is mainly an eye-witness account of the dramatic AFL-CIO convention at Atlantic City late in 1957—backstopped by the two volumes of published *Proceedings of the AFL-CIO Constitutional Convention, Dec. 5–12, 1957.* (Some of the oratory here is of anthology caliber.)

For historic background that gave significance to the action at the convention, I found Arthur J. Goldberg's *AFL-CIO: Labor United,* McGraw-Hill Book Company, Inc., New York, 1956, of great value. I am indebted to John Brophy of the AFL-CIO, who has attended several decades of Federation conventions, for conversations which gave perspective to the 1957 one. The proceedings of the seventeenth convention of the International Brotherhood of Teamsters, etc., 1957, was required reading.

CHAPTER 2   Plumber with His Finger in the Dike

George Meany's speeches are one of the best sources for understanding him. His address to the rebellious Building Trades Department of the AFL-CIO in December, 1957, is a key speech. Vol. 1, *Proceedings of the AFL-CIO Constitutional Convention, Dec. 5–12, 1957,* contains two others, one on Hoffa, the other on James G. Cross of the Bakers. The *Report of the Proceedings of the 66th Convention of the A.F. of L.,* San Francisco, October 6–16, 1947, contains the speech in which Meany, then secretary of the AF of L, outfaced the mighty John L. Lewis. The turbulent closed meetings of the AFL-CIO Executive Council provide excellent light on George Meany—when the reporter is fortunate enough to learn from insiders what happened.

Beyond that, a study of Meany requires keeping abreast of major developments in Labor. For this, the *New York Times,* John Herling's *Labor Letter from Washington,* plus *Business Week* and the *Wall Street Journal* are "must" reading. In the periodical literature about Meany, I found these provided excellent analyses: "New Task for the Blunt Meany" by A. H. Raskin, *New York Times Magazine,* February 20, 1953; "Crusader for Clean Unionism" by A. H. Raskin, *New York Times Magazine,* October 20, 1957; "Big Labor's Big Boss" by Paul F.

Healy, *Saturday Evening Post,* June 23, 1956; "Where Does Labor Go from Here?" by Daniel Bell, *Fortune,* December, 1957. For background reading on the role of a Federation president and the structure of the Federation I found these books helpful: *The Practice of Unionism* by Jack Barbash, Harper & Brothers, New York, 1956; *The House of Labor,* edited by J. B. S. Hardman and Maurice F. Neufeld, Prentice-Hall, Inc., New York, 1951.

CHAPTERS 3 and 4   The Teamsters

When I first wrote about James R. Hoffa ("Riddle in the Middle of America's Most Powerful Union," *Reader's Digest,* December, 1955), I relied on legwork in Detroit, Chicago, Washington and New York; on the files of the Detroit *Free Press* and the Detroit *News;* on a one-man grand jury report to the Michigan State Circuit Court in Detroit; on court and other records, including a probation report; on the Kefauver (Senate Crime Committee) hearings; and on the 1953 hearings of the special subcommittees of the Committee on Education and Labor and the Committee on Government Operations of the House—popularly known as the Clare Hoffman (Rep., Mich.) hearings. Since then, Hoffa and the Teamsters have become the chief target of the McClellan Committee, and mountains of detail are available, especially in Parts 13, 14, 36, 37 and 40 of the Committee hearings. Senator McClellan lists eighty-two specific items bearing on Hoffa, and there's a summing up of early testimony in the Interim Report of March 24, 1958. Two reports of the Board of Monitors to the U.S. District Court, Washington, D.C., covering the period from January 31 to July 31, 1958, are particularly valuable; so is the list of 203 charges filed with the Monitors by rank and file members—seeking the trial and removal of Hoffa. A book has appeared, *The Teamsters Union,* Robert D. Leiter, Bookman Associates, Inc., New York, 1957, which has some valuable chapters on the union's early history and on the economics of the trucking industry, but glosses over the scandals. A pamphlet, "The Name Is Hoffa," published by the Teamsters Joint Council 13 of St. Louis, April, 1956, is a brief, authorized biography of Hoffa, which contains some interesting Hoffa quotes.

Of the growing volume of periodical literature on Hoffa, I found these valuable: "The World of Jimmy Hoffa," Paul Jacobs, *The Reporter,* January 24 and February 7, 1957; "Reuther vs. Hoffa," A. H. Raskin, *New York Times Magazine,* September 22, 1957. As for the men about Hoffa, *Fortune* published an excellent brief piece on Edward Cheyfitz in April, 1958; the Teamsters News Service has prepared a biography of Harold Gibbons, in April, 1958, and Gibbons' hometown newspaper, the St. Louis *Post Dispatch*, is invaluable as a source on his career.

CHAPTER 5   Why They Hate Walter Reuther

Some excellent books bear directly on Walter Reuther or tell the dramatic events surrounding the birth and rise of the United Automobile Workers. *Labor on the March,* Edward Levinson, Harper & Brothers, New York, 1938, relates with great narrative skill the mass industry organizing drives of the late thirties in which Walter Reuther and his brothers, Victor and Roy, played important roles. *The UAW and Walter Reuther,* Irving Howe and B. J. Widick, Random House, New York, 1949, is a thoughtful study of Reuther and his union. *When Labor Votes,* Arthur Kornhauser, Harold L. Sheppard, Albert J. Mayer, University Books, New York, 1956, is indispensable for understanding the UAW's political power in Wayne County, Michigan.

Part of Our Time, Murray Kempton, Simon and Schuster, New York, 1955, has an engaging chapter (IX) about the Reuther boys. This contains as interesting an analysis of Reuther's youthful visit to the Soviet Union as any I've seen.

We Never Called Him Henry, Harry Bennett, as told to Paul Marcus, Gold Medal Books, New York, 1951, is an absorbing account of Henry Ford and pre-UAW Detroit. What it meant to be a member in the early organizing days of the UAW is told in *Union Guy,* Clayton W. Fountain, The Viking Press, New York, 1949.

There is, of course, a great deal of periodical literature on Reuther. For a critical view, there is: "We're Heading for a Labor Government," *Nation's Business*, December, 1955, and "What Makes Reuther Big?" by Henry Hazlitt, *Newsweek,* September 9, 1957.

I found "Labor's New Men of Power," Daniel Bell, *Fortune,* June, 1953, a thoughtful analysis. Among scores of articles, I found the following the most helpful: "The Union That Grew Up," Mary Heaton Vorse, *Harper's Magazine,* July, 1954; "How Do We Live with Bigness?," an interview with Reuther by Henry Brandon, *The New Republic,* July 21, 1958; "Detroit: Focus of the Basic Duel," A. H. Raskin, *New York Times Magazine,* May 4, 1958; "What Labor Wants Next," Walter P. Reuther, *The American Magazine,* January, 1956, has early autobiographical data; "The Trouble in Detroit," William B. Harris, *Fortune,* March, 1958; "Creeping Capitalism," John C. Cort, *The Commonweal,* February 14, 1958.

296

For Reuther's philosophy, i.e., "for what Reuther wants," his own speeches and testimony before Congressional committees are valuable. A UAW pamphlet, *Price Policy and Public Responsibility,* Walter P. Reuther, gives his statement before the Sub-Committee on Anti-Trust and Monopoly, United States Senate, January 28, 1958. The 1955 and 1957 proceedings of the UAW conventions at Cleveland and Atlantic City, respectively, provide a good look into Reuther and his union. The preamble to the Auto Workers' constitution is probably the longest of any among the unions, but it shows what's troubling Reuther and the UAW. I am greatly indebted to industry executives, whose names obviously can't be revealed, for some aspects of Reuther's character and leadership.

CHAPTER 6 The Man Who Lives with a Ghost

For material on Philip Murray, I relied heavily on conversations with men who knew him intimately: John Brophy of the AFL-CIO; Clinton S. Golden, who helped organize the Steelworkers; and Father Owen Rice of Pittsburgh. The books on the early CIO days, already mentioned, deal peripherally with Murray.

John Chamberlain's study of Murray in *Life,* February 11, 1946, is worth reading. The Steelworkers' own book, prepared by Vincent D. Sweeney, director of the union's public relations, *The United Steelworkers of America,* gives a good chronological account of the rise of the union. I found these articles of value: "Five Hot Days in Gary, Indiana," by Warner Bloomberg, Jr., *The Reporter,* August 11, 1955; "Not Steel But Silk," *New York Times,* April 20, 1957; "Man of Steel," *Time,* July 9, 1956; "Steelworkers at the Polls," Dan Wakefield, *The Nation,* February 23, 1957. The United Steelworkers' convention proceedings from 1954 through 1958 provided valuable backstopping to news reports and interviews. An authorized biography, no longer available, made interesting reading: *Man of Steel,* Kelly and Beacher, North American, New York, 1954.

CHAPTER 7 David Dubinsky: He Bosses 400,000 Women

The trouble with biographies of labor leaders is that they are often written by staff men or otherwise authorized. *The World of David Dubinsky,* Max D. Danish, World Publishing Company, Cleveland, 1957, is a success story seen through the eyes of a former ILGWU press agent, but it has valuable narrative on Dubinsky nevertheless. *David Dubinsky, a Pictorial Biography,* with text by John Dewey, Inter-Allied

Publications, New York, 1951, gives highlights. *Tailor's Progress,* Benjamin Stolberg, Doubleday, Doran & Company, Inc., Garden City, N.Y., 1944 (not authorized), is, as the author puts it, "the story of a famous union and the men who made it."

Dubinsky has been for years one of the most publicized union leaders in America, and the pieces on him are legion. I'll list only a few: "David Dubinsky" by Irwin Ross, in the New York *Post,* May 6–13, 1956; "How I Handled the Reds in My Union" by David Dubinsky, *Saturday Evening Post,* May 9, 1953; "Dubinsky: A Study in Labor Leadership" by A. H. Raskin, *New York Times,* December 12, 1948; "Pacemaker for Labor" by Serrell Hillman, *Life International,* August 18, 1958. "The Schooling of David Dubinsky" in the August, 1949, *Commentary,* by Waclaw Solski, contains excellent material on the young Dubinsky.

The most dramatic part of the Dubinsky story concerns the underworld that has fastened itself on the New York Garment Center. Part of this story was pieced together from corporate records which showed the links between some Garment Center truckers and dress manufacturers and the big eastern gangs. Official records of the New York County District Attorney's office and the files of the old New York City Crime Commission were helpful. Unfortunately, the names of some of the brave men and women who know Garment Center hoodlum terror at first hand cannot be divulged. Nor can other human sources to whom I owe much.

CHAPTER 8   Sam Gompers: Father with Labor Pains

This telescoped history of the unions, focusing on Samuel Gompers, drew on three sources: the generalized accounts of the rise of the unions; accounts of the times in which Gompers lived; and material on Gompers himself.

For a detailed history, there is the classic four-volume *History of Labour in the U.S.,* John R. Commons and Associates, The Macmillan Company, New York, 1946. I found rich material on the lives of workers during Gompers' time in *The Final Report and Testimony of the U.S. Commission on Industrial Relations,* Vol. X, Government Printing Office, Washington, D.C., 1916. A selective reading of testimony in the other volumes of the Commission's investigation proved helpful.

298

For background on Gompers' times, I also used *The Growth of the American Republic*, Morison and Commager, Vol. II, Oxford University Press, New York, 1942—especially Chapters VI, VII and VIII, which deal with the economic revolution, labor and immigration. I also found *Our Times*, Mark Sullivan, Charles Scribner's Sons, New York, 1927, of value. Gompers' own *Seventy Years of Life and Labor*, E. P. Dutton & Company, Inc., New York, 1957 (revised), is a stuffy and dephlogisticated account of Gompers' life—but, of course, valuable. *Samuel Gompers*, Rowland Hill Harvey, Stanford University Press, Stanford, California, 1935, is more sprightly. For a detailed study of the growth of the AF of L, Philip Taft's *The A.F. of L. in the Time of Gompers*, Harper & Brothers, New York, 1957, is invaluable. Historian Taft had access to all of Gompers' papers, as preserved by the AFL-CIO, and proved a generous guide, counselor and invaluable repository of Gompers anecdotes for me.

Florence Calvert Thorne, who worked with Gompers, has produced a small book culled from his speeches, published by the Philosophical Library, New York, 1957, *Samuel Gompers—American Statesman*.

Two books were of special value. One is a little book on theory which, for me, raced along like an adventure story: *A Theory of the Labor Movement*, Selig Perlman, Augustus M. Kelley, New York, 1949. The other is a trenchant and prophetic work which foretold, in 1926, both the great organizing drives that were to come a decade later and the corruption later still. This is *Trade Unionism in the U.S.*, Robert F. Hoxie, D. Appleton & Company, New York, 1926.

"Samuel Gompers As I Remember Him," by John P. Frey, in *The American Federationist*, August, 1949, has some anecdotes on Gompers' conviviality. Two articles on Gompers in *The Antioch Review*, summer, 1953—one, "Gompers and the Irony of Racism"; the other, "Gompers to Hillman: Labor Goes Middle Class"—were helpful. A *Voice of America* interview with Lucy Robbins Lang, social worker who collaborated with Samuel Gompers, yielded interesting material.

CHAPTER 9   John L. Lewis: Labor's Rogue Elephant

Two exciting biographies have been written about John L. Lewis, one critical and one uncritical. *Labor Baron*, James A. Wechsler, William Morrow and Company, New York, 1944, is a study of a man's drive for power. *John L. Lewis*, Saul Alinsky, G. P. Putnam's Sons, New York, 1949, is described by the author as "an unauthorized biography" and by John L. Lewis (in conversation with me) as a "potboiler."

Nevertheless, it is a very sympathetic narrative of Lewis's life, and because Lewis apparently co-operated generously with the author, it is full of valuable and illuminating anecdotes which cannot be found elsewhere. *Sidney Hillman*, Matthew Josephson, Doubleday & Company, Inc., Garden City, N.Y., 1952, deals much with Lewis. So, of course, does *Labor on the March*, Edward Levinson, Harper & Brothers, New York, 1938, already described.

Of the many magazine pieces on Lewis, those by A. H. Raskin in the *New York Times Magazine*—"Secrets of John L. Lewis' Great Power," October 5, 1952, and "John L. Lewis—A Glorious Anachronism," February 13, 1956—are especially good. I also found value in: "Lewis Strikes Steel" by Walter Davenport, *Collier's*, August 21, 1937; "I Am Only As Strong As You Make Me" by C. L. Sulzberger, *Saturday Evening Post*, June 18, 1938; "The Warwick of the House of Labor" by Louis Stark, *New York Times Magazine*, February 10, 1946.

For a feeling of Lewis's magnificent oratory, I read some of the convention proceedings of the old AF of L (particularly 1947 and 1935), and of his own United Mine Workers. Lewis's oration before the AF of L convention of 1935—that presaged his break with the Federation—is stirring stuff. The UMW proceedings give the best testimony of the destruction of democracy inside the Mine Workers.

An unpublished manuscript of memoirs by John Brophy, who battled Lewis inside the UMW, provided a detailed and valuable history of the conflicts inside the Miners, and the later rise of the CIO.

CHAPTER 10   The Corrupters

The files of the National Labor Relations Board, particularly an examiner's report involving Sears, Roebuck stores in Boston, provided the initial clues to the operations of middlemen who help employers take unions, and I first discussed this in a *Reader's Digest* article in July, 1957: "How Influence Peddlers Shortchange the Union Wage Earner." Subsequent testimony (Parts 5, 8, 14, 15, 16, plus the First Interim Report, March 14, 1958) before the McClellan Committee helped fill in the details. For historic background on union busters of the past, I found these books helpful: *I Break Strikes!*, Edward Levinson, Robert M. McBride & Company, New York, 1935; *The Labor Spy Racket*, Leo Huberman, Modern Age Books, Inc., New York, 1937. Testimony before the Subcommittee of the Senate Committee on Education and Labor, known as the La Follette Civil Liberties Committee, published by the Government Printing Office, 1937, contains dramatic case histories. So does the *Report of the U.S. Commission on Industrial Relations,* Washington, D.C., 1916. Periodical discussions of the union middleman evil are scant. *Fortune,* February, 1958, however, published an excellent article by Daniel Bell: "Nathan Shefferman, Union Buster." "Cynicism and Managerial Morality," Professor Benjamin M. Selekman, *Harvard Business Review,* September–October, 1958, was excellent for background.

Two papers prepared by Professor Philip Taft of Brown University contain valuable historic background material. They are "An Overall Look at Racketeering in the Labor Movement" and "Racketeering in Labor Unions: An Attempt at an Explanation."

CHAPTER 11   Journey to the Underworld

Uncovering the links between the underworld and the respectable worlds of politics, business and labor has been a journalistic labor of love for some fifteen years. I drew heavily here on material gathered for prior writing, particularly: "The Capone Mob Muscles into Big Time Politics," *Collier's,* September 30, 1950; "The Man to See in New Jersey," *Collier's,* August 25 and September 1, 1951; "New Menace Over Missouri," *Collier's,* October 29, 1949; "Do the Mobs Write Your State Crime Laws?," *Reader's Digest,* March, 1953; "Joe Fay—He Ruled an Empire from Prison," *Reader's Digest,* December, 1954.

Invaluable help—over the years—has come from the New York District Attorney's office, particularly Rackets Bureau Chief Al Scotti, and his assistant, Harold Birns; and from Virgil W. Peterson, director of the Chicago Crime Commission, who is also author of an excellent book on the Chicago Capone gang: *Barbarians in Our Midst,* Atlantic–Little Brown, Boston, 1952. *The Tax Dodgers,* Elmer L. Irey as told to William J. Slocum, Greenberg, New York, 1948, contains in Chapter 14 the classic Browne-Bioff story of mob infiltration into the movie business—via a union. The McClellan Committee hearings, which have already filled forty volumes as this is written, spell out gangster influence in some unions, and a summary of some of this influence is to be found in the First Interim Report of the Committee, March 14, 1958.

CHAPTER 12   The Union That God Forgot

This is largely a reporting job, supported by the following official documents: the transcript of the trial of Joe Fay on charges of extortion, 1945; depositions and record of the U.S. District Court suit by Roy Underwood and other Philadelphia union members against the Operating Engineers; Vol. 118, *National Labor Relations Board Reports,* page 174, 1957, concerning Local 138 of the Operating Engineers. A courageous article in the Chicago *Daily Tribune,* published on March 26, 1943, shed light on the rise of William Maloney of the Operating Engineers. Lawyers who have taken up the fight of rank and filers—as a crusading cause, at no pay and at great sacrifice—helped me greatly. They include Bernard H. Fitzpatrick and his associate William J. Keating, who represent rebels of Local 138 (the Long Island Local); and Abraham Freedman of Philadelphia. The McClellan Committee hearings (Parts 19 and 20 and the First Interim Report) contain much testimony on the Operating Engineers Union and its leaders.

CHAPTER 13   Cruel Sweetheart

I have relied here to some extent on the brilliant investigative work of a twenty-one-year-old Fordham University law student, John McNiff, who—working with the modest facilities of the Association of Catholic Trade Unions—was one of the first to uncover the use of under-the-table union agreements to exploit Puerto Rican immigrants and other New York City industrial workers. McNiff's thirty-five-page report on some locals of the Jewelry Workers Union was extremely helpful. The McClellan Committee material is from Parts 10, 28, 29 and 30.

CHAPTER 14   Black Record

The required reading of *An American Dilemma,* Gunnar Myrdal, Harper & Brothers, New York, 1944, as part of the preparation for this chapter, was a memorable experience. So was the reading of *Souls of Black Folk,* W. E. B. DuBois, A. C. McClurg & Company, Chicago, 1903. *Organized Labor and the Negro,* Herbert R. Northrup, Harper & Brothers, New York, 1944, was extremely helpful. *A Man Called White,* Walter White, The Viking Press, New York, 1948—particularly Chapters XXIII and XXVII—gave authentic stories of the threatened Negro march on Washington in 1941 and discussed the Negro auto worker in Detroit. For historic background, "Samuel Gompers and the Negro Workers," *Journal of Negro History,* Washington, D.C., January, 1956, was helpful.

Periodical literature on this problem is scant, but these articles were helpful: "Negro's New Economic Life" by Emmet John Hughes, *Fortune,* September, 1956; "How Negroes Are Gaining in the U.S.," *U.S. News & World Report,* January 28, 1957; also, in the same periodical, "Why Unions Can Bar Negroes," April 19, 1957.

I gratefully acknowledge the help of Boris Shishkin and Theodore Brown of the AFL-CIO staff, and Charles Zimmerman, chairman of the AFL-CIO Civil Rights Committee, and of the National Urban League, particularly for its *Report on Negroes in the Building Trades in 32 Cities*, February 13, 1937. The several afternoons of talk with A. Philip Randolph, president of the Sleeping Car Porters, were invaluable—and memorable.

CHAPTER 15 How to Get a $100,000,000 Raise

This is mostly a reporting job with background support from *Review and Reflection*, Cyrus S. Ching, B. C. Forbes and Sons, Inc., New York, 1953—a delightful book of memoirs involving a half century of dealing with unions; *The Dynamics of Industrial Democracy*, Clinton S. Golden and Harold J. Ruttenberg, Harper & Brothers, New York, 1942; *Labor Relations and Human Relations,* Benjamin M. Selekman, McGraw-Hill Book Company, Inc., New York, 1947; *The Practice of Unionism,* Jack Barbash, Harper & Brothers, New York, 1956. I am indebted to Lemuel R. Boulware and Virgil Day of the General Electric Company for making available to me the transcript of the negotiations with the International Union of Electrical, Radio and Machine Workers.

CHAPTER 16 Labor U.S.A. vs. the Kremlin

The developing role of American unions abroad is discussed in *The International Labor Movement*, Lewis L. Lorwin, Harper & Brothers, New York, 1953; *American Labor and the International Labor Movement 1940 to 1953,* John P. Windmuller, Cornell International Industrial and Labor Relations Reports, Ithaca, New York, 1953. Communist activity in America is described in *The Whole of Their Lives,* Benjamin Gitlow, Charles Scribner's Sons, New York, 1948; *Pages from a Worker's Life,* William Z. Foster, International Publishers, New York, 1939. Other materials that proved helpful: "Current Issues in International Labor Relations," *The Annals of the American Academy of Political and Social Science,* Philadelphia, 1957; the International Confederation of Free Trade Unions, *Report on Fifth World Congress,* Tunis, July, 1957; "World Labor's New Weapon," David Dubinsky, *Foreign Affairs,* New York, April, 1950.

The pamphlet series *American Labor Looks at the World,* published by the AF of L, International Labor Relations Committee Reports from October, 1949, through 1953 were helpful, including one by Jay Lovestone, of the AFL-CIO, *American Labor and the World Crisis,* first delivered as a speech before the Industrial Relations Research Association in December, 1956. Conversations with Arnold Beichman, New York representative of the International Confederation of Free Trade Unions were helpful. So were files of the *Free Trade Union News*, published by the Free Trade Union Committee, New York.

World Communism Today, Martin Ebon, McGraw-Hill, New York, 1948, and *Forced Labor in the "People's Democracies,"* Richard Carlton, editor, F. A. Praeger, Publishers, New York, 1955, provide excellent material on international Communism.

CHAPTER 17   Will the Unions Elect Our Next President?

This is largely based on on-the-ground investigation in California, Ohio, Washington, D.C., Michigan and New York, with assists from Robert M. Lewin of the Chicago *Daily News* and John Pomfret of the Milwaukee *Journal*. *When Labor Votes*, Arthur Kornhauser, Albert J. Mayer, Harold L. Sheppard, University Books, Inc., New York, 1956, raises such interesting questions as "Is there a labor vote?" and answers them on the basis of a study of auto worker voting in Detroit. "Organized Labor in Politics," by James B. Carey in the *Annals of the American Academy of Political and Social Science*, Philadelphia, September, 1958, gives labor's point of view.

CHAPTER 18   How to Steal a Union—and How to Get It Back

For my education in union democracy I am indebted chiefly to those members in the Teamsters, the Operating Engineers, the Musicians and other unions who risked their livelihoods—and sometimes their lives—in battles with local and national union tyrants. Their stories are the chief source for this chapter. Background sources (for analyses of union constitutions) include *Handbook of Union Structure and Procedure*, National Industrial Conference Board, New York, 1955, and *Source Book of Union Government Structure and Procedure*, National Industrial Conference Board, 1956, which contain excellent and time-saving studies of union constitutions.

The constitutions themselves, particularly of the unions mentioned above, make enlightening reading. Periodical literature in this field is limited but excellent. I found "Legislating Union Democracy" by J. B. S. Hardman, *New Leader*, December 2, 1957, and "Some Thoughts on Union Democracy" by Jack Barbash, *New Leader*, December 23, 1957, very helpful. A pamphlet published by the Fund for the Republic, New York, *Unions and Union Leaders of Their Choosing* by Clark Kerr, provides a well-written statement of key union democracy problems. For case histories of union abuses, there are the indispensable McClellan Committee hearings, particularly Parts 4, 7, 8, 9, 10, 13 and 14. *Madden v. Atkins,* New York Supreme Court, Appellate Division, 2nd Department, as reported in the *Labor Relations Reporter,* is an absorbing case history of one struggle for democracy, via the courts. For students of union democracy, I also recommend the convention proceedings of the United Mine Workers, October 6 to 14, 1942, Cincinnati, Ohio, particularly pages 232 through 242. Also the *Proceedings of the Teamsters 17th Convention* at Miami Beach, Florida, September 30–October 5, 1957. *The Supplemental Report of AFL-CIO Executive Council on Ethical Practices Cases,* December 5, 1957, has case history material.

CHAPTER 19   What Shall We Do with the Labor Leader?

An ocean of words is pouring forth on laws to regulate unions. There are some thoughtful books about the role of the labor leader in our society. *The New Men of Power,* C. Wright Mills, Harcourt, Brace and Company, New York, 1948, and *The New Society*, Peter F. Drucker, Harper & Brothers, New York, 1950 (particularly Parts III and IX), are extremely interesting. The Labor point of view on union legislation is given in the testimony of George Meany before the Sub-Committee on Labor of the Senate Committee on Labor and Public Welfare, March 27, 1958.

An antithetic point of view is contained in a provocative book, *The Labor Policy of the Free Society,* Sylvester Petro, The Ronald Press, New York, 1957, which, among other things, counsels the abolition of the National Labor Relations Board and the repeal of the Norris-LaGuardia Act.

Changes to Make in Taft-Hartley by Theodore R. Iserman, The Argus Company, Albany, New York, 1953, was helpful. *As Unions Mature,* Richard A. Lester, Princeton University Press, Princeton, New Jersey, 1958, was excellent for background. These pieces were of help: "Labor Leaders and Society," *Harvard Business Review,* January, 1950; "The Capitalism of the Proletariat," Daniel Bell, *Encounter,* February, 1958.

CHAPTER 20   When Machines Don't Need Men—What of Labor U.S.A.?

For the basic theme in this chapter—automation's threat to the industrial unions—I am indebted to Everett M. Kassalow of the AFL-CIO and to Solomon Barkin, research director of the Textile Workers Union of America, for his paper "The Economic Impact of Automation."

I found *New Dimensions in Collective Bargaining,* Harold W. Davey, Howard S. Kaltenborn, Stanley H. Ruttenberg, editors, Harper & Brothers, New York, 1959 (especially Part II, "Collective Bargaining and Technological Change"), helpful. The hearings before the Sub-Committee on Economic Stabilization of the Joint Economic Committee, December 12, 13, 14, 1956, and hearings before the same committee on November 14 and 15, 1957, plus the Committee's Report of January 5, 1956, U.S. Government Printing Office, Washington, D.C., contain valuable testimony and findings on automation and technological change. The U.S. Department of Labor has published some excellent pamphlets, among them: *A Case Study of a Modernized Petroleum Refinery,* Bureau of Labor Statistics Report No. 120; *Case Study of an Automatic Airline Reservation System,* BLS Report No. 137; *The Introduction of an Electronic Computer in a Large Insurance Company,* BLS report, October, 1955; *Automation and Employment Opportunities for Officeworkers,* BLS Bulletin No. 1241. *The Impact of Automation,* a pamphlet published by the United Automobile Workers, is the best of the union material on this problem. Walter Reuther's testimony before the Joint Economic Committee, February 9, 1959, gives Labor's view of "productivity" unemployment.

Index

Accardo, Tony, 167
Adams, Sherman, 234
Adelstein, Bernard, 169–171, 173
Adonis, Joe, 172
advertising agency, use of in Right to Work program, 251, 253
AFL-CIO (American Federation of Labor-Congress of Industrial Organizations), 152, 163, 184, 202–204, 248; Atlantic City Convention, 1957, 3–12; Civil Rights Committee, 206; Committee on Political Education (COPE), 257, 262; Department of Internal Relations, 237; ethical practices codes, 4, 25, 191, 228, 278–279; Ethical Practices Committee, 193, 228, 289–291; Executive Council, 3–8, 15, 18, 35, 67, 80, 98, 135, 237, 291; expulsion of Teamsters from, 46; expulsion power as main weapon against corruption, 279; fight against Soviet world Communism, 237; fights Right to Work bill, 250–256; Free Trade Union Committee, 237–238; headquarters building, Washington, D.C., 14, 135, 255, 262; in Operating Engineers Union fight, 191; Plumbers Union and, in Hoffa case, 56; racial discrimination outlawed by, 206; Reuther as chief vice-president of, 78; total annual per capita dues, 1957, 125 n.; total membership, 1957, 10, 125 n.; union court needed for, 274; votes to expel Teamsters Union at Atlantic City, 9–10; see also AF of L
AF of L (American Federation of Labor prior to merger), 7, 12, 99, 118, 120, 151, 206, 237, 242, 245; battle with Socialists, 130–131; boycott used by, 132; civil war with CIO, 25; Executive Council, 157, 176; founding of, 124; Free Trade Union Committee, 244; Gompers and, 124, 131 (see also Gompers, Samuel L.); Meany as third president of, 24 ff. (see also Meany, George); membership, 1924, 134; World War I, 143; merger with CIO, 14, 19–20, 87; mistrust of Reuther's social unionism, 78; see also AFL-CIO
Alinsky, Saul, 139 n.

Aliquippa, Pa., company domination in, 87 n.
Amalgamated Clothing Workers of America, 15, 24, 41, 246, 261, 277
Amalgamated Iron and Steel Workers Association, 217
American Communist party (Lovestonites), 240
American Communists, penetration of government departments by, 244; see also Communism; Communists
American Dilemma, An, 211
American Dream, the, 129
American Federation of Labor, see AF of L; AFL-CIO
American Federation of Teachers, 41
American Federation of Television and Radio Artists (AFTRA), 253–255
American Hotel, Miami Beach, 85
American Medical Association, 251
American Missionary Association, 209
American Telephone and Telegraph Company, 90
Anarcho-Syndicalist unions, Italy, 249
Anastasia, Albert, 17, 32, 105, 167, 172
Anastasia, Anthony, 17
Anchorage, Alaska, Teamsters local in, 52
annual wage, guaranteed, 65, 225
Anti-Defamation League, 219
anti-Labor laws, 4; see also labor legislation
"anti-membership" unionism, 185 ff.
anti-racketeering resolution, AF of L, 1940, 23; Operating Engineers Union, 193
anti-trust laws, Labor exemption from, 261
Anti-Trust Monopoly Subcommittee, Kefauver's, 75
Armed Forces, segregation in, 213–214
armed guards, management use of, 12
Ashton, James, 92
assembly-line plants, vs. craft unions, 144
Association of Catholic Trade Unionists, 203
Atkins, Tommy, 271
Atlantic City Convention, AFL-CIO, 1957, 3–12
autocracy, Lewis' pattern of, 142
automation, effect of on union membership, 12; fear of among steelworkers, 88; threat

307

earth-moving equipment, 182
Eden Roc Hotel, Miami Beach, 54
"Edge, The," in garment industry, 107–108, 110
Edison, Thomas A., 120
Einstein, Albert, 97
Eisenhower, Dwight D., 216, 251–253
elections, policing of, 273; rigging of, 266–268; *see also* ballots; voting
Electricians Union (International Brotherhood of Electrical Workers), racial discrimination in, 215
electronic brains, threat to labor from, 284, 289
Elks Lodges, unions likened to, 274, 278
Embroidery Local, New York City (ILGWU), 100
Englander Company, 162–163
English, John F., 6–7
Ervin, Sam, 279
ethical practices codes, AFL-CIO, 4, 25, 191, 228, 278–279
Ethical Practices Committee, AFL-CIO, 193, 228, 289–290
Executive Council, AFL-CIO, 3–8, 15, 18, 35, 67, 80, 98, 135, 237, 291
expense accounts, early union leaders', 126
expulsion, as main AFL-CIO weapon against union corruption, 279
extortion, in labor unions, 155, 168, 183, 187; in Operating Engineers Union, 182

Fair Employment Practices Committee, 206, 213
Fairless, Benjamin F., 81
Fascism, unions' fate under, 241, 245
Fascists, 245
Fay, Joe, xiv, 22, 24, 176, 185, 187, 190, 192; Sing Sing labor empire of, 176–177, 182
Federal Bureau of Investigation (FBI), 112
Federation (AFL-CIO), *see* AFL-CIO
Feinsinger, Nathan, 187
Feldman, Samuel (Shorty), 179
Fifth Amendment, refuge in, 26, 56–57, 98, 157–158, 160, 178, 183 n.
Fitzgerald, George, 39, 72
Fitzpatrick, Bernard, 274–275
Followers of Lafayette (trade union), 125
Force Ouvrière, France, 247 n.
Ford, Edsel, 68, 96
Ford, Henry, 101
Ford, Model T, 101
Ford Motor Company, 69, 76, 96, 144; automation at, 285; Guaranteed Annual Wage proposal and, 225
forgery, in Meat Cutters Union, 196
Fortune, 166
France, union-splitting attempts of Communists in, 247
Fraternal Order of Eagles, 258
Freedman, Abraham E., 191, 194
Free Trade Union Committee, AFL-CIO, 237–238, 244
Free Trade Union News, 237
gangsters, in labor unions, 14, 23, 167–181;

gangsters, (*cont.*)
charters given to, 4; as deeply rooted fixture in American city life; Dubinsky's fight against, 95; in Garment Center, 104, 111; Hoffa's refusal to rid Teamsters of, 39, 43; infiltration of, xiv; prosecution of, 180; Teamster aid to, 45; *see also* hoodlums; racketeers and racketeering
garbage rackets, 168–173
Garment Center, New York City, 95, 100, 104–105, 231–232, 260; Dubinsky's role in, 109; gangsterism and racketeering in, 104–105, 180; organization and control in, 106–107; violence against union organizers in, 109–110; *see also* protection
garment industry, non-union shops in, 108
garment trucks, monopoly and racketeering through, 105–107
Garment Workers Building, N.Y., 239
Garment Workers Union, 68, 257; *see also* International Ladies' Garment Workers Union (ILGWU)
General Electric Company, 228; "Boulwarism" in, 234–235
General Motors Corporation, 63, 71, 101, 223–234; cost-of-living increases from, 76–77, 234; Guaranteed Annual Wage proposal and, 225; Reuther and, 64 (*see also* Reuther, Walter P.); signed up by Lewis, 147
Georgetown University, 44
Gibbons, Harold J., 34, 40–41, 44; fraud charges against, 57
Glimco, Joey, 174
Goldberg, Arthur J., 87 n., 228, 233
Golden, Clinton, 86
Golden, Harry, 43
Goldfine, Bernard, 234
"goldfish bowl" law, proposed, 279, 281
Goldwater, Sen. Barry, 126 n., 257
Gompers, Henry, 124
Gompers, Samuel L., xv, 12, 14–15, 19, 103, 115–135, 144, 148, 223, 237, 260; background and early life, 120–121; battle with Socialists, 130–131; birth, 127; blueprint for AF of L by, 124–125; character and appearance, 117; defies injunction order in Bucks Stove case, 132; drinking exploits, 119–120; introduces idea of union contract, 129; involvement in politics, 131–132; makes Lewis lobbyist and organizer, 141; as night-life figure, 119; "pure and simple unionism" of, 116, 130, 261
government construction work, racial discrimination prohibited in, 216
Graff, Max H., 159
Great Atlantic & Pacific Tea Company, contract with Meat Cutters union, 198; "sweetheart" contracts and wage ceilings in, 195–199
Great Britain, unions and Labour party in, 249
Great Strike of 1877, 123
Green, William L., 10, 13, 16, 135, 145, 217, 242; death, 24

Lieberman, "Scarface Louie," 109
Lincoln Leaguers (trade union), 125
Little Steel, 84; organizing of, 83
London *Times,* 8
Long Island local, Operating Engineers Union, 183–184
Longshoremen's Union, *see* International Longshoremen's Association
Louis, Joe, 44
Lovestone, Jay, 245, 247–248; anti-Communist activities of for AFL-CIO, 237–241
Ludlow (Colo.) mine strike, 122
Lurye, William, 109

McCarty, Ted, 190
McClellan, Sen. John L., 8, 32, 156, 160, 269
McClellan Committee, 4, 33–34, 41, 46, 53–54, 57, 64, 71, 85, 92, 156–157, 162, 164–166, 168, 171, 174, 182, 184, 188, 191, 193–195, 202, 279–281; charges against Hoffa, 40; Hoffa's attempt to bribe, 44
McDonald, David J., 9, 15, 79–94, 152, 233; as "actor rising to a great role," 83; asks for dues increase plus personal salary hike, 88–89; conflict with Reuther, 86–87; denizen of café society, 85; high living expenses of, 278; "Horatio Alger" biography of, 83; opposition to in 1957 election, 80; panic at Rarick's vote for presidency, 93; use of union treasury in opposing Rarick "rebellion," 90; physical appearance and character, 81–82; in Pittsburgh society, 84; revolt against, 88; vice-president of AFL-CIO Executive Council, 80; *see also* United Steelworkers of America
McDonald, Rosemary (Mrs. David J.), 85
McFarland, Ed, xiii, 48–49
McFetridge, William L., 278
McGavin, Peter, 11
McGrath, John J., 188
McMahon, Eugenia, 21
McNiff, John, 203
Madden, Bernard C., 271
Madison Square Garden, 117
Magna Carta, Labor's 261
Maloney, William, 182–183, 187–188, 191
Management Engineering Department, ILGWU, 104
manners, lack of in labor unions, 17
Man of Steel, McDonald biography, 83
Maritime Union of America, National, 17
Marshall Plan, Communism and, 247
Marx, Karl, 102
Masters, Mates and Pilots Union, 271
Matheson, Min, xiv
mattress workers, "collective bargaining" frauds and, 162–163
Mazey, Emil, 70
Meany, Eugenia McMahon (Mrs. George), 21
Meany, George, 39, 56, 63, 86, 95, 126 n., 135, 151–152, 191, 204, 215, 219, 237, 241, 244–245, 248, 257, 279, 291; aid from Lovestone in combating Communism, 242; at Atlantic City Convention of 1957,

Meany George, (*cont.*)
3–12; attacks union self-rule, 26; becomes president of AF of L, 1952, 24; birth and early years, 21; bluntness of, 15–16; boss of 700-man staff, 19; calls for vote against Teamsters, 9; compared to "fullback," 18; current policy on Teamsters Union, 46; elected business agent of Plumbers Union, 22; emergence of as labor stateman, 20; expert knowledge of union history, 19; association with ex-tortionist Fay, 22–24; hobbies and pastimes, 20–21; as Labor's chief executive, 4; as lobbyist in New York State Federation of Labor, 24; as "loner" in labor movement, 16–17; as "Mr. Labor," 15; origin and backgrounds of, 13–27; power to control affiliated unions, 11; president of AF of L, 1952, 13; proposal against Fifth Amendment pleas, 98; relations with Reuther, 78; salary, 20; shifts power from internationals to Federation, 10; uncompromising fight against racketeers, 17; UN delegate, 1957, 237; unites AFL and CIO, 14
Meany, Mike, 21
Meat Cutters and Butcher Workmen of North America, Amalgamated, 195–197
Meli, Angelo, 167
membership, union, *see* union membership
Miami Beach, AFL-CIO Convention at, 82, 85; Teamsters meeting at, 9, 173, 178
Michigan Fair Grounds Coliseum, 43
middleman, role of in union corruption, 155, 157–158
Mikoyan, Anastas, 14
milk farmers, attempted organization of, 151
mine safety legislation, 140
Mine Workers Union, *see* United Mine Workers of America
minimum wage law, 200
Minneapolis Teamsters, "leapfrogging" tactics of, 38
Mitchell, Labor Secy. James, 251, 253
Modica, C. Don, 172
Mohammed Ben Youssef, King, 248–249
Mollenhoff, Clark, 34
Molotov, Vyacheslav, 239–240
Monitors, Teamsters Union and, 11 n., 52 ff., 55–56, 274 n.
monopoly, labor unions as form of, 132
monopoly rackets, 167–181
Moreland Act, New York State, 281
Moretti, Willie, 172
Movie Projectionists Union, 176
Mundt, Sen. Carl, 126 n.
murder, in garbage rackets, 170; in Operating Engineers Union, 189
Murder, Inc., 17, 105, 168
Murphy, Gov. Frank, 148
Murray, Philip, 16, 79, 82–83, 85–86, 91, 93, 135, 138, 147, 150, 217, 230, 233, 288; "corner office" of, 80–81; as kindly father and elder statesman of labor, 81

313

presidential election, U.S., labor's coming role in, 249–262
Presser, William, xiv
"productivity unemployment," 287
professional workers, organizing of, 27; *see also* white-collar workers
Prohibition era rackets, 167
Promised Land, The, 102
prostitution rackets, 180
"protection," destruction of union aims through sale of, 104–105, 107, 109–110
"provisional" officers, UMW, 142
Proxmire, Sen. William, 258
public opinion, rising tide of against union corruption, 4, 273
"public relations," garbage rackets and, 172; labor spies and, 161, 176
Public Review Board, Reuther's plan for, 76
public servant concept, of labor leader, 278–279
Puerto Rican workers, defrauding of, 199–201
Puerto Rico, Executive Council meeting at, 18
Pullman, George, 120
Pullman Company, labor spies of, 209
Pullman porters, unionizing of, 206 ff.; meager wages of, 1925, 210; *see also* Randolph, A. Philip
"pure and simple unionism," Gompers definition of, 116, 130, 261

questionnaire law, proposed, 280–281

racial discrimination, outlawing of by AFL-CIO, 206; Randolph's fight against, 211–212
racketeers and racketeering, 14, 97, 105, 155, 164, 278; in AF of L, 25; aid from Hoffa in, 39; clean-up of, 12; in garment industry, 107–108; labor bosses and, 167–181; manufacturers' collusion with, 199–200; Meany's uncompromising fight against, 16; *see also* corruption; gangsters; hoodlums
Rackets Bureau, New York County, 108, 168
radio and TV programs, labor union use of, 73, 90
railroad strike of 1877, 123
Railway and Steamship Clerks, Brotherhood of, 15–16, 191
Railway Labor Act, 144 n.
Randolph, A. Philip, xiv, 206 ff.
Randolph, Lucille (Mrs. A. Philip), 210
Randolph, Woodruff, 8
Rank, Joseph, 71
Rarick, Donald C., "rebellion" of against McDonald forces, 88–93
Raskin, Abe H., 93, 152
Reader's Digest, 177
recession, 1958, 26
Red-controlled unions, *see* Communism; Communist unions
Redding, John M., 258
reform, ineffectiveness of, 204

Republican party, Reuther's campaign against, 71–75; supports Right to Work proposals, 250–262
restaurant rackets, 174–175
Restaurant Workers Union, *see* Hotel and Restaurant Employees and Bartenders Union
Retail Clerks, International Association of, *see* International Association of Retail Clerks
Reuther, Linda, 66
Reuther, May (Mrs. Walter P.), 66
Reuther, Roy, 73
Reuther, Walter P., 7, 17, 19–20, 35, 39 n., 41, 63–78, 101, 233, 245, 257, 276, 283; appearance and attitudes, 68–69; assumes Murray's leadership of CIO, 86; attempted assassination of, 66, 175; bodyguards, 68; character and habits, 66; as chief vice-president of AFL-CIO, 78; concern with price controls, 75; "controversial" nature of, 69; goals and methods of, 75–78; guaranteed annual wage proposal, 225; as "idea man," 65; industry's distrust of, 77; Lewis' opinion of, 152; "march on Washington," 18; mixed feelings toward, in labor circles, 78; negotiations between Meany and, 25; negotiation strategy of, 223 ff.; political conflict with Hoffa in Detroit, 72; as politician, 71–75; relations with Meany, 78; Republican party and, 71–72; respect of top auto executives for, 77; salary as UAW head, 67; selling of personal viewpoint, 73; as top executive and "involver," 70–71; typical day described, 65–69
"Reuther plan," 75–76
Ricca, Paul (the Waiter), 167, 176, 178
Rice, Father Owen, 88
Riesel, Victor, 42, 99, 179
Right to Work proposals, 250–256
"ringers," use of in union elections, 268
Roberts, Curtis, 251
Rockefeller, John D., Jr., 122
Rockefeller, Nelson, 260, 283
Roosevelt, Eleanor, 77–78, 213
Roosevelt, Franklin D., 24, 65, 115 n., 136, 138, 143, 148–149, 212, 261, 277
Roosevelt, Theodore, 117
Rose, Alex, 8, 133 n.
Rosen, Nig (Harold Stromberg), 111
Ross, Michael, 237
Rothstein, Arnold, 180
Russia, *see* Soviet Union
Russian novels, Communism and, 241
Russian revolution, 240
Ryan, Joe, 23

Safeway Stores, garbage racketeers and, 170
St. Louis, Mo., Teamster violence in, 41
St. Louis Teamsters, 57
Salinger, Pierre, 163
San Juan, P.R., AFL-CIO meeting at, 67
satellite unions, racketeering and, 39, 179–180

315

Teamsters Union, (*cont.*)
57, 274 n.; as most powerful union in
U.S., 163; pay differentials in, 49; pay
for vacations in, 47; Philadelphia Local's
charges, 56–57; punishment of members,
48; resistance to change, 6; restaurant
rackets and, 174; rigged elections in, 53;
in Sears, Roebuck case, 162; supervision of
by Board of Monitors, 52 ff., 274 n.; suppression of members' rights in, 47–48;
swift retribution against dissidents, 50–51;
taxi local, Pittsburgh, 91; token clean-up
vetoed by Hoffa, 45–46; treasury looting
in, 51, 280; underworld contacts of, 177–
178; variety of trades encompassed by, 31;
Washington, D.C., headquarters, 41, 56;
see also Hoffa, James Riddle
television, use of in fight against Right to
Work proposals, 255
"Ten Commandments" of Labor, 278
"Ten Philosophers," as Gompers' mentors,
128
textile industry, segregation in, 218
Textile Workers Union of America, 219, 234,
258; decline in membership of, 1951–1959,
284
The Name Is Hoffa, 43
"Thirteen," Committee of, 54
Time, 140, 150
Tito (Broz), 239
Tobin, Dan, 7, 10, 16, 145
transfer machine, as "Detroit automation,"
285
treasury, union, *see* union treasury
trial machinery, unions', 271
Triangle Shirtwaist Company fire, 95
Triscaro, Babe, 167
Trotsky, Leon, 135
"troublemakers," denial of vote to, 268;
harassing and suppression of, 186 ff.;
splinter technique used on, 270
Truman, Harry S., 16, 22–23, 39, 151, 213,
251, 252
"trustee" device, abolition of self-rule
through, 273
typewriter, invention of, 121

UAW, *see* United Auto Workers
Un-American Activities Committee, 262
Underwood, Ray, efforts of to end miscon-
duct in Operating Engineers Union, 185–
194
underworld, labor bosses in, 167–181; *see
also* corruption; Hoffa, underworld connections of; gangsters; hoodlums; racketeers and racketeering
unemployment, 19, 118; automation and, 18,
26–27, 285 n.; extent of, 1959, 287
unemployment compensation, first employer-
contributed, 104
unemployment insurance, 225, 253; supple-
menting of by auto manufacturers, 76
union(s), absence of checks and balances in,
265; as "burglar's tool" for big-time looting, 266; corruption in, 155–167; defined,

union(s), (*cont.*)
xiv, 201; decline of in 1924, 134; government support of, 276; likened to voluntary
associations, 274, 278; manpower strength
of, 255–256; as most powerful single force,
249; negotiation tactics and strategy of,
223–236; political machine and, 65; political strength shown in defeating Right to
Work proposals, 250–256; as private government supported by public government,
277–278; rigged elections in, 266–268;
"stealing" of by ballot control, 265–274;
undemocratic nature of, 265 ff.
union autocracy, Lewis' pattern of, 142
union autonomy, 6, 10, 125, 272–273
union busting, 157–159; *see also* "protection"
Union Carbide Corporation, 284
union constitutions, as "contracts," 53; loop-
holes and booby traps in, 271–273
union contracts, frauds perpetrated through,
187–188; Gompers' introduction of, 129;
management-labor dilemma in, 129; secrecy
status of in Teamsters Union, 49; size and
coverage of, 239
union court, AFL-CIO demands for, 274–275
union funds, *see* union treasury
unionism, "anti-membership" type, 185 ff.;
oppression of, 1900's, 122; "pure and
simple" type, 116, 130, 261; rise of, 124 ff.
union leader(s), corruption of, 155–167; defined, xiv; power exercised by, 10; *see also*
labor "bosses"; labor leader
union members, poor voting records of, 250–
251
union membership, decline of, 284, 286; effect
of automation on, 12; segregation fight
and, 12; total U.S., xiii; *see also under individual unions*
union shop, attempted curbing of through
Right to Work bills, 250–256
union stealing, through ballot control, 265–
274
union treasury, looting of, 51, 173, 177, 187–
189, 266, 280; regulation of borrowing
from, 279
union welfare state, Dubinsky's, 103
union wrecking, Shefferman's role in, 156–
158
United Auto Workers (United Automobile,
Aircraft and Agricultural Implement
Workers of America), 7, 63, 164–166, 175,
211, 257; bargaining strategy of, 223–236;
campaign against Republican party, 73–74;
corporate structure of, 68; decline of membership in, 1955–1959, 64, 284; Detroit
headquarters of, 68; increased social
security pensions and, 76; membership of,
80 n.; political strength of, 72; radio and
TV programs for communicating with
members of, 73; Review Board, 274; strike
against Kohler of Kohler, 71; as "world's
most democratic union," 70; *see also*
Reuther, Walter P.
United Mine Workers of America, 91, 147,
150, 227, 277, 288; Communists in, 149;

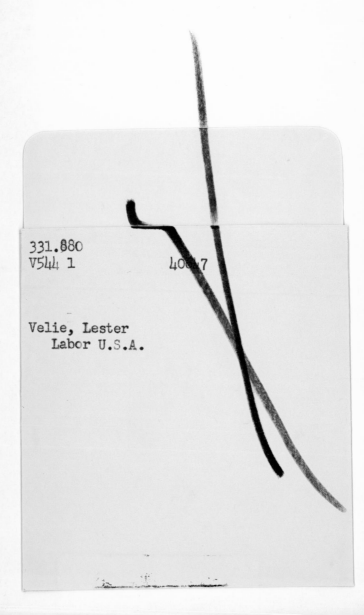